THE ESSENTIALS
OF INSTRUCTIONAL
DESIGN

THE ESSENTIALS OF INSTRUCTIONAL DESIGN

Connecting Fundamental Principles with Process and Practice

Abbie Brown
California State University, Fullerton

Timothy D. Green
California State University, Fullerton

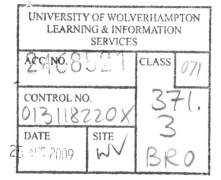

PEARSON

Merrill
Prentice Hall

Upper Saddle River, New Jersey
Columbus, Ohio

Library of Congress Cataloging in Publication Data

Brown, Abbie.
   The essentials of instructional design : connecting fundamental principles
with process and practice/Abbie Brown, Timothy D. Green.
     p. cm.
   Includes bibliographical references and index.
   ISBN 0-13-118220-X
  1. Instructional systems—Design.   I. Green, Timothy D.   II. Title.
   LB1028.38.B76 2006
   371.3—dc22

                            2005030175

Vice President and Executive Publisher:
Jeffery W. Johnston
Executive Editor: Debra A. Stollenwerk
Senior Editorial Assistant: Mary Morrill
Associate Editor: Ben M. Stephen
Production Coordination: Karen Ettinger,
The GTS Companies/York, PA Campus
Senior Production Editor: Linda Hillis Bayma

Design Coordinator: Diane C. Lorenzo
Photo Coordinator: Maria B. Vonada
Cover Designer: Terry Rohrbach
Cover Image: Corbis
Production Manager: Susan Hannahs
Director of Marketing: Ann Castel Davis
Marketing Manager: Darcy Betts Prybella
Marketing Coordinator: Brian Mounts

This book was set in Galliard by TechBooks/GTS York, PA Campus. It was printed and bound by
Courier Stoughton, Inc. The cover was printed by Courier Stoughton, Inc.

Photo Credits: Scott Cunningham/Merrill, pp. 44, 158; Ken Karp/PH College, p. 142; Frank LaBua/
PH College, p. 60; Anthony Magnacca/Merrill, pp. 104, 120, 176, 236; Mike Peters/Silver Burdett Ginn,
p. 2; Lynn Saville, p. 28; Barbara Schwartz/Merrill, p. 86; John Tuffin/Photolibrary.com, p. 204.

Pearson Prentice Hall™ is a trademark of Pearson Education, Inc.
Pearson® is a registered trademark of Pearson plc
Prentice Hall® is a registered trademark of Pearson Education, Inc.
Merrill® is a registered trademark of Pearson Education, Inc.

Pearson Education Ltd.
Pearson Education Singapore Pte. Ltd.
Pearson Education Canada, Ltd.
Pearson Education—Japan

Pearson Education Australia Pty. Limited
Pearson Education North Asia Ltd.
Pearson Educación de Mexico, S.A. de C.V.
Pearson Education Malaysia Pte. Ltd.

10 9 8 7 6 5 4
ISBN: 0-13-118220-X

Preface

Our intentions for this book are fourfold. We wrote it to provide a foundational overview of instructional design (ID) activities, to explain the principles of ID, to describe the processes used to implement these principles, and to offer examples of their practical application in a manner that transcends any single ID model or approach.

This book is for beginners. It introduces students who are new to the field to the essential elements of ID, providing an overview of the fundamental principles, processes, and practices that currently shape and define ID. As professionals who have served as K–12 teachers, corporate instructional media producers, and professors of ID, we have developed explanations of the principles and processes of ID that have proved successful in a number of undergraduate, postgraduate, and graduate ID courses for various institutions. We start by articulating a specific principle; then we describe, compare, and contrast the processes of applying the principle established by leaders in the field; and finally we offer practical examples of how to apply the principle on the basis of our personal ID experiences. To provide even more breadth to this text, we asked instructional designers from a number of professional settings to provide descriptions of how their organizations put the various ID processes into practice.

We base our discussion in this book on the following premise: Whenever a person develops instruction, he or she is attempting to change something. Instruction may change a person's attitude, the amount of information he or she has, or his or her skills. The principles, processes, and practices of ID facilitate these changes. Instruction is a type of intervention that is planned, executed, and evaluated to determine its effect. (We hasten to note that in many instances, an instructional intervention is *not* the answer. Sometimes, the solution that is needed is related to a human performance issue that instruction cannot address, such as the arrangement of a work or learning environment that inhibits an employee's or a learner's ability to accomplish a given task. Such a problem is a human performance technology, or HPT, issue. Although we introduce and describe HPT as an important activity corollary with ID, we do not deal directly or extensively with it.)

Regardless of the specific established model, the ID process generally has three phases: examination of the situation (needs, task, and learner analyses), creation of instruction (planning, creating, and implementing the intervention), and evaluation of the effect of the instruction. Once an individual understands these phases, he or she is ready to study and experiment with various methods of putting them into practice. In this book, we explain the components of each phase, referring to the most popular models and approaches and describing, comparing, and contrasting the strengths of each. We also include examples and recommendations for practical application.

Text Organization

Although the ID process can be said to have three major phases, we divided this book into four parts. We call the first part *Before You Begin Designing Instruction,* because it contains information that is necessary for every ID professional but is not part of the ID process itself. Part 1 comprises Chapter 1, which reviews the discipline of ID, and Chapters 2 and 3, in which we discuss what is known about thinking and learning. Chapter 4, on **project management,** is included at the request of many of our colleagues. This chapter deals with practical issues of producing instructional media. Although this task may not always be part of every instructional designer's job, it is often a part of an ID student's experience. Chapter 4 contains information about production management, communication, and conflict resolution that has proved helpful to students working on ID projects. Parts 2, 3, and 4 are the generally agreed-upon phases of ID and involve examining the situation, creating instruction, and evaluating the effect of the instruction.

Special Features

Throughout the text, special features highlight and provide examples of various concepts and ideas that are presented. These features also give students opportunities to extend their learning by interacting with the content in various ways. These special features are called *Professionals in Practice, ID Insight,* and *Connecting Process to Practice.*

- **Professionals in Practice:** In this feature we share our personal experiences as instructional designers and teachers, as well as the experiences of a number of other professional ID specialists. These reports from the field should help students better understand how such processes are applied in business and education settings.

- **ID Insight:** In this feature we examine issues and topics that are uppermost in the minds of many ID professionals. For example, principles of postmodern thought and its effect on ID processes are addressed. Another example is the inclusion of descriptions of the principles and processes of relatively new and different design approaches, such as *universal design for instruction* and *rapid prototyping*. Throughout the book, the reader will find many concepts and trends important to the ID community highlighted in these special sections.
- **Connecting Process to Practice:** This concluding section for each chapter includes questions and activities designed to give students the opportunity to think and act as ID professionals.

Our aim is to provide students with an introduction to the principles and processes of ID without placing undue emphasis on any single ID model. The practical examples and suggestions are included to help beginning instructional designers understand the issues that surround ID in practice. Furthermore, the descriptions of the processes and the practical examples are provided to help instructional designers apply them to their own projects.

Acknowledgments

We express our appreciation to our editor at Prentice Hall, Ben Stephen. Only through his insights, tireless efforts, and hours of telephone calls were we able to shape this book and see it through to completion. Thanks, Ben, for all your help.

Our gratitude also goes out to the individuals who contributed to the *Professionals in Practice* sections. We thank each of them for the time and energy they put into providing us with insights into how they practice the principles of ID:

- **Kara Andrew:** Instructional Designer, Distance Education, California State University, Fullerton.
- **Kursat Cagiltay:** Assistant Professor, Department of Computer Education and Instructional Technology, Middle East Technical University, Ankara, Turkey.
- **Lisa Hansen:** Lead Human Factors Specialist, The Home Depot, Atlanta, Georgia.

- **Erik Novak:** Distance Learning Course Developer, Interactive Intelligence, Inc., Indianapolis, Indiana.
- **Jody Peerless:** Sixth-grade teacher, Washington Middle School, La Habra, California.
- **Jona Titus:** Senior Training Specialist, Intel Corporation, Hillsboro, Oregon.

In addition, we extend our thanks to the following individuals who provided thoughtful feedback on the drafts of this book: Anthony K. Betrus, State University of New York, Potsdam; Barbara A. Bichelmeyer, Indiana University; Elizabeth Boling, Indiana University; Alison A. Carr-Chellman, Pennsylvania State University; Kim Foreman, San Francisco State University; Scott Fredrickson, University of Nebraska at Kearney; Dorothy Fuller, Black Hills State University; Kendall Hartley, University of Nevada, Las Vegas; Albert Ingram, Kent State University; Howard K. Kalman, Ithaca College; Emery "Trey" Martindale, East Carolina University; Mimi Recker, Utah State University; LeAnne K. Robinson, Western Washington University; Sharon E. Smaldino, Northern Illinois University; William Sugar, East Carolina University; and Jennifer Summerville, University of North Carolina at Wilmington. We understand how much time and energy providing such feedback requires, and we appreciate their efforts. The ideas and insights we received from these individuals were valuable in helping us shape the book.

Abbie Brown and Tim Green

Teacher Preparation Classroom

See a demo at
www.prenhall.com/teacherprep/demo

Your Class. Their Careers. Our Future. Will your students be prepared?

We invite you to explore our new, innovative and engaging website and all that it has to offer you, your course, and tomorrow's educators! Organized around the major courses pre-service teachers take, the Teacher Preparation site provides media, student/teacher artifacts, strategies, research articles, and other resources to equip your students with the quality tools needed to excel in their courses and prepare them for their first classroom.

This ultimate on-line education resource is available at no cost, when packaged with a Merrill text, and will provide you and your students access to:

Online Video Library. More than 150 video clips—each tied to a course topic and framed by learning goals and Praxis-type questions—capture real teachers and students working in real classrooms, as well as in-depth interviews with both students and educators.

Student and Teacher Artifacts. More than 200 student and teacher classroom artifacts—each tied to a course topic and framed by learning goals and application questions—provide a wealth of materials and experiences to help make your study to become a professional teacher more concrete and hands-on.

Research Articles. Over 500 articles from ASCD's renowned journal *Educational Leadership*. The site also includes *Research Navigator*, a searchable database of additional educational journals.

Teaching Strategies. Over 500 strategies and lesson plans for you to use when you become a practicing professional.

Licensure and Career Tools. Resources devoted to helping you pass your licensure exam; learn standards, law, and public policies; plan a teaching portfolio; and succeed in your first year of teaching.

How to ORDER *Teacher Prep* for you and your students:

For students to receive a *Teacher Prep* Access Code with this text, instructors **must** provide a special value pack ISBN number on their textbook order form. To receive this special ISBN, please email: **Merrill.marketing@pearsoned.com** and provide the following information:
- Name and Affiliation
- Author/Title/Edition of Merrill text

Upon ordering *Teacher Prep* for their students, instructors will be given a lifetime *Teacher Prep* Access Code.

Brief Contents

PART 1 **BEFORE YOU BEGIN DESIGNING INSTRUCTION   1**

1 **Defining Instructional Design   2**

2 **Understanding How People Think   28**

3 **Understanding How People Learn   44**

4 **Managing Instructional Media Production   60**

PART 2 **EXAMINING THE SITUATION: NEEDS, TASK, AND LEARNER ANALYSIS   85**

5 **Conducting Needs Analysis   86**

6 **Conducting Task Analysis   104**

7 **Analyzing the Learners   120**

PART 3 **CREATING INSTRUCTION: PLANNING, DESIGNING, AND IMPLEMENTING THE INTERVENTION   141**

8 **Developing Instructional Goals and Objectives   142**

9 **Organizing Instruction   158**

10 **Creating Learning Environments and Producing Instructional Activities   176**

PART 4 **EVALUATING LEARNER SUCCESS AND THE INSTRUCTIONAL DESIGN: DETERMINING THE EFFECT OF THE INTERVENTION   203**

11 **Evaluating Learner Achievement   204**

12 **Determining the Success of the Instructional Design Product and Process   236**

Index   261

Contents

PART 1 **BEFORE YOU BEGIN DESIGNING INSTRUCTION   1**

1 **Defining Instructional Design   2**
Key Terms   2
Guiding Questions   3
Chapter Overview   4
What Is Instructional Design?   5
  Models of Instructional Design/Development   9
  Professional Instructional Design Practice   13
  Traditional Approaches (Analyze, Develop,
  Evaluate)   14
  Nontraditional Approaches   16
Summary   24
Connecting Process to Practice   24
Recommended Readings   25
References   25

2 **Understanding How People Think   28**
Key Terms   28
Guiding Questions   29
Chapter Overview   30
Cognition and Basic Cognitive Functions   30
  Cognition   30
  Basic Cognitive Functions   31
Historical Perspectives on Thinking: A Brief History   32
Modern Views on Thinking: The Shift from Philosophy to
  Psychology   34
  Two Major Perspectives   35
  Two More Recent Perspectives   37
Instructional Designers' Views on Thinking   38
Summary   40
Connecting Process to Practice   40

Recommended Readings   41
References   41

3   **Understanding How People Learn   44**
Key Terms   44
Guiding Questions   45
Chapter Overview   46
What Is Learning?   46
Two Major, Divergent Approaches to How People Learn   47
Behaviorism   47
Cognitivism   50
A Third Approach: Constructivism   51
Use of All Three Approaches   52
Types of Learning   52
Cognitive Domain   53
Affective Domain   54
Psychomotor Domain   54
Summary   56
Connecting Process to Practice   57
Recommended Readings   57
References   57

4   **Managing Instructional Media Production   60**
Key Terms   60
Guiding Questions   61
Chapter Overview   62
The Production Process   62
Organization of a Production Team   63
Production Management   66
Production Calendar   67
Style Guides   71
Storyboards   71
Prototyping   74
Communication and Conflict Resolution   76
Product Evaluation   79
Usability Testing   80
A Final Thought   80
Summary   81
Connecting Process to Practice   82
Recommended Readings   82
References   83

PART 2   **EXAMINING THE SITUATION: NEEDS, TASK, AND LEARNER ANALYSIS   85**

5   **Conducting Needs Analysis   86**
Key Terms   86
Guiding Questions   87
Chapter Overview   88
Needs Analysis: An Overview   88
  Needs Analysis Questions   89
Popular Approaches to Needs Analysis   90
  Mager's Performance Analysis   90
  Morrison, Ross, and Kemp's Three Approaches   93
  Rossett's Five-Step Approach   95
  Smith and Ragan's Three Needs Assessment Models   97
Needs Analysis Procedure   98
  Determination of the Desired Change   98
  The Party Requesting the Desired Change   99
  Implementation Location for the Desired Change   99
  The Intervention   100
Evaluation of the Success of a Needs Analysis   100
Summary   101
Connecting Process to Practice   102
Recommended Readings   103
References   103

6   **Conducting Task Analysis   104**
Key Terms   104
Guiding Questions   105
Chapter Overview   106
What Is Task Analysis?   106
Popular Approaches to Task Analysis   107
  Jonassen, Hannum, and Tessmer's Approach   108
  Morrison, Ross, and Kemp's Three Techniques   108
  Dick, Carey, and Carey's Instructional Analysis   110
  Smith and Ragan's Analysis of the Learning Task   110
Task Analysis Procedure   111
  The Subject Matter Expert   112
  Task Analysis Document   112
  Influencing Factors   112
Evaluation of the Success of a Task Analysis   115
Summary   117

Connecting Process to Practice   118
Recommended Readings   118
References   119

7   Analyzing the Learners   120
Key Terms   120
Guiding Questions   121
Chapter Overview   122
Analysis of Learners   122
    Human Needs   123
    Captive Audience or Willing Volunteers?   124
Popular Approaches to Analyzing Learners   125
    Mager's Approach   125
    Heinich, Molenda, Russell, and Smaldino's Approach   127
    Dick, Carey, and Carey's Method   129
    Smith and Ragan's Approach   129
    Morrison, Ross, and Kemp's Approach   133
Learner Analysis Procedure   133
    Charting Learner Characteristics Data   133
    Creating a Fictitious Profile of the Typical Learner   134
    Comparing the Learner Ability Chart and the Learner Profile   134
Evaluation of the Success of a Learner Analysis   136
Summary   137
Connecting Process to Practice   137
Recommended Readings   138
References   138

PART 3   **CREATING INSTRUCTION: PLANNING, DESIGNING, AND
IMPLEMENTING THE INTERVENTION   141**

8   Developing Instructional Goals and Objectives   142
Key Terms   142
Guiding Questions   143
Chapter Overview   144
Instructional Goals and Objectives   144
    The Difference Between Goals and Objectives   144
Popular Approaches to Setting Goals and Objectives   146
    Mager's Approach   146
    Dick, Carey, and Carey's Approaches   146
    "ABCD" Approach   146
    Morrison, Ross, and Kemp's Approach   147

Goal Setting   147
Translation of Goals into Objectives   149
Evaluation of the Success of Instructional Goal Setting and
    Objective Specification   153
Summary   154
Connecting Process to Practice   155
Recommended Readings   156
References   156

9 **Organizing Instruction   158**
Key Terms   158
Guiding Questions   159
Chapter Overview   160
Scope and Sequence of Instruction   160
    Levels of Organization: Macro, Micro, Vertical, and
        Horizontal   162
    Organizational Structures: Content and Media   162
Events of Instruction   162
Continuum of Learning Experiences   164
Instructional Delivery   167
    Methods of Instructional Delivery   167
    Two Categories of Instructional Delivery   169
Instructional Activities in Noneducational Situations   170
    Job Aids   171
Effective Instruction   171
Summary   172
Connecting Process to Practice   173
Recommended Readings   174
References   174

10 **Creating Learning Environments and Producing
    Instructional Activities   176**
Key Terms   176
Guiding Questions   177
Chapter Overview   178
Development of Instruction   178
    Teaching Pitfall   178
Learning Environments   180
    Four Perspectives on the Design of Learning Environments   180
    Directed and Open-Ended Learning Environments   181
Research Support for Instructional Practices   186

Activities Based on Proven Effective Practices 189
Identifying Similarities and Differences 189
Summarizing and Note Taking 192
Reinforcing Effort and Providing Recognition 193
Homework and Practice 194
Nonlinguistic Representations 194
Cooperative Learning 196
Setting Objectives and Providing Feedback 196
Generating and Testing Hypotheses 197
Questions, Cues, and Advance Organizers 198
Summary 198
Connecting Process to Practice 199
Recommended Readings 200
References 200

PART 4 **EVALUATING LEARNER SUCCESS AND THE INSTRUCTIONAL DESIGN: DETERMINING THE EFFECT OF THE INTERVENTION 203**

11 **Evaluating Learner Achievement 204**
Key Terms 204
Guiding Questions 206
Chapter Overview 206
Evaluation, Assessment, and Measurement 206
Purpose of Evaluation 207
Goal of Learner Evaluation 208
Development of Learner Evaluations 210
Validity and Reliability 210
Criterion Referenced and Norm Referenced: Simplified 211
The Starting Point: Instructional Objectives 212
Implementation of Learner Evaluations 229
Preinstruction 229
During Instruction 230
Postinstruction 230
Determination of the Success of Learner Evaluations 231
Instructional Designer's Role 231
Summary 232
Connecting Process to Practice 233
Recommended Readings 234
References 235

12 **Determining the Success of the Instructional Design Product and Process   236**
Key Terms   236
Guiding Questions   237
Chapter Overview   238
Formative and Summative Evaluation   238
   Formative Evaluation   238
   Summative Evaluation   248
Group Processing: Evaluating the Instructional Design Team   255
Summary   256
Connecting Process to Practice   257
Recommended Readings   258
References   258

Index   261

Note: Every effort has been made to provide accurate and current Internet information in this book. However, the Internet and information posted on it are constantly changing, so it is inevitable that some of the Internet addresses listed in this textbook will change.

PART 1

BEFORE YOU BEGIN DESIGNING INSTRUCTION

1 Defining Instructional Design
2 Understanding How People Think
3 Understanding How People Learn
4 Managing Instructional Media Production

Chapters 1 through 4 provide background information you will find useful as you begin your study of instructional design. Chapter 1 is an overview of the history, traditions, and current state of the instructional design discipline. In Chapters 2 and 3, we describe how people think and learn. Chapter 2 provides an introduction to and a review of cognition and the basic cognitive functions. Chapter 3 covers the most popular descriptions of what learning is and how it occurs. In Chapter 4, we introduce the concept of project management, including information on producing media, managing media-production teams, communicating, and resolving conflicts.

DEFINING INSTRUCTIONAL DESIGN

Key Terms

ADDIE process *(page 11)*
Behavioristic *(page 16)*
Educational psychology *(page 5)*

General systems theory *(page 4)*
Positivistic *(page 19)*

Postmodernism *(page 17)*
Rapid prototyping *(page 21)*

As an instructional designer, I am a member of a professional discipline with its own history, culture, and common language. This fact may not be uppermost in my mind each day, but my understanding of the discipline helps me put my job in perspective. Knowing the history and culture of instructional design gives me an appreciation of how my professional activities fit in with the rest of my organization and my clients.

—Jona Titus,
Senior Training Specialist,
Intel Corporation,
Hillsboro, OR

Guiding Questions

- What is an instructional designer?
- How did the discipline of instructional design develop?
- What is an instructional design/development model?
- How has general systems theory affected instructional design?
- How does the historical and philosophical "postmodern" approach affect instructional design?

Chapter Overview

Taking a logical and structured approach to the process of developing, delivering, and evaluating instruction and instructional materials has been popular among scholars and practitioners for nearly a century. Several models have been developed to help explain the processes of instruction as well as the process of designing and developing materials for instruction. This chapter provides an overview of instructional design from its beginnings in the late 19th century, through its blossoming in conjunction with the development of **general systems theory,** to its continuing development in the postmodern era. In this chapter, we also describe the essential processes of instructional design as they are articulated through traditional instructional design models, and we examine the potential of nontraditional models, describing rapid prototyping in particular as an innovative instructional design approach.

A Historian's View of Instructional Design

No particular event or date marks the beginning of a modern science and technology of instruction. Yet it is clear that at the beginning of the twentieth century there occurred a series of related events that together might be interpreted as the beginning of a science of instruction.

William James (1842–1910), for example, in his book, *Talks to Teachers on Psychology,* makes one of the first distinctions between the art and the science of teaching, calling for a scientific approach to instruction. Similarly, also in 1901, John Dewey (1859–1952) interpreted a method of empirical science in educational terms, viewing the classroom as an experimental laboratory. In 1902, Edward Thorndike (1874–1949) offered the first course in educational measurements at Columbia University and became the first to apply the methods of quantitative research to instructional problems. G. Stanley Hall (1846–1924) published his *Adolescence* (1904), a landmark in the scientific study of the child. The French psychologist Alfred Binet (1857–1911) and Theodore Simon, his collaborator, published *A Method of Measuring the Intelligence of Young Children* (1905). Moreover, a true science of behavior, and especially of learning theory, began to emerge, no longer based primarily on metaphysical or philosophical speculation. This new science and learning theory would eventually be applied to a technology of instruction.

—Paul Saettler (1990, p. 53)

What Is Instructional Design?

The purpose of any design activity is to devise optimal means to achieve desired ends.

—Charles Reigeluth (1983, p. 4)

People have been instructing each other since the first humans walked the Earth. Teaching an infant how to speak, showing an apprentice how to forge an ax head, guiding a daughter's hands as she attempts to make a clay pot—humans have been learning from each other for a long time.

The ritual dance around the fire at the front of the cave depicting the hunt and kill of a large animal may be one of humankind's earliest forms of designed instruction. The hunters of the group had to find ways to teach other potential hunters the process of stalking and bringing down a large animal. Creating a dramatic display that described the procedures for the hunt in a ritualized fashion captured the group's attention and provided them with a stylized presentation of how hunting works. This type of instructional design, based on inspiration and creativity, remained prevalent for millennia. However, the *science* of instructional design is relatively new.

Throughout history, a number of individuals gave careful thought to the design of instruction. For example, the scholar John Amos Comenius (1592–1670) was among the first to plan for the use of visual aids in teaching. Comenius's *Orbis Sensualium Pictus (The Visible World Pictured)* was the first illustrated textbook designed for children's use in an instructional setting (Heinich, Molenda, Russell, & Smaldino, 1996). However, until the late 1800s, no organization had gathered these individuals' work together, offered like-minded persons a forum for discussion on the topic, or sought to continue its development: Educational science did not exist.

No organization had evolved to study how people learn or how to study methods of delivering instruction. Although scattered attempts had been made to improve instruction throughout history, no specific discipline had emerged to guide these efforts. Education-oriented organizations protected and directed the curriculum and content of the instruction; however, little attention was paid to how instruction might be made more effective. The psychology of education—how the learner learned—was a school of thought in search of an organizing body. With the formation of the American Psychological Association in 1892, the discipline of **educational psychology** began.

In the late 1800s and early 1900s, education was still the province of persons with religious backgrounds and training (Berliner, 1993). (Keep in mind that teachers were originally clergy members and that prior to World War I, one of the main purposes of education in the United States was to ensure that people could read passages from the Bible.) Convincing individuals who believed education to be a moral and philosophical endeavor that scientific methods might be used to improve educational processes was not easy. With the establishment of the discipline of educational psychology, though, educators interested in improving instructional practice through scientific means found both a home organization and like-minded persons with whom to commune.

With the formation of the land-grant universities in the late 1800s (each state was entitled by the federal government to form its own university within the borders of the state) and the subsequent need to determine what constituted the "college readiness" of an individual, educational psychologists were called on to develop valid and reliable tests and measures of academic achievement. As an example, the Scholastic Achievement Test, or SAT (now known as the *Scholastic Aptitude Test*), was first offered in 1901 and is to some extent an indicator of a trend toward scientifically testing learners to determine the next, appropriate course of action in their education.

At the beginning of the 20th century, John Dewey (1900), one of the world's most influential educators, called for a "linking science" between what is known about how people learn and the practice of delivering instruction. At the time, this idea was considered radical.

By 1915, the application of scientific methods to the solution of educational problems had won out among the leaders in American education, which set the stage for the development of Dewey's linking science. Scholars such as Snellbecker (1974) suggested that Dewey's linking science is the discipline of instructional design. Educators began to develop an experimental view of instruction. Along with testing students to determine what they knew, adherents to the newly organized discipline of educational psychology devised tests to discover whether the instruction worked. In the traditional approach, educators had focused completely on the information that should be included in the lesson; instructional design mandated that educators consider how the information should be organized and presented on the basis of what they know about the learners and their abilities.

As the century progressed and more scholars focused their attention on the science of designing instruction, educational psychology blossomed into university departments and international organizations that reported and discussed research in the field. The discipline of instructional design descended directly from educational psychology. Although some scholars argue that it is not a separate field but rather a subactivity within educational psychology, instructional design can point to its own university departments and international organizations as indicators that it is now a distinct discipline.

As a "linking science," instructional design is a discipline in which practitioners constantly look to the findings of other disciplines (e.g., cognitive psychology, communication) to study and improve methods of developing, delivering, and evaluating instruction and instructional practices. According to Smith and Ragan (1999), instructional design is "the systematic and reflective process of translating principles of learning and instruction into plans for instructional materials, activities, information resources, and evaluation" (p. 2).

The Applied Research Laboratory at Pennsylvania State University is attributed with developing a four-part definition of instructional design (University of Michigan, 1996):[1]

> *Instructional Design as a Process:* Instructional Design is the systematic development of instructional specifications using learning and instructional theory to ensure the quality of instruction. It is the entire process of analysis of learning needs and goals and the development of a delivery system to meet those needs. It includes development of instructional materials and activities; and tryout and evaluation of all instruction and learner activities.
>
> *Instructional Design as a Discipline:* Instructional Design is that branch of knowledge concerned with research and theory about instructional strategies and the process for developing and implementing those strategies.
>
> *Instructional Design as a Science:* Instructional design is the science of creating detailed specifications for the development, implementation, evaluation, and maintenance of situations that facilitate the learning of both large and small units of subject matter at all levels of complexity.
>
> *Instructional Design as Reality:* Instructional design can start at any point in the design process. Often a glimmer of an idea is developed to give the core of an instruction situation. By the time the entire process is done the designer looks back and she or he checks to see that all parts of the "science" have been taken into account. Then the entire process is written up as if it occurred in a systematic fashion.

[1] From "Definitions of Instructional Design." Adapted from "Training and Instructional Design," Applied Research Laboratory, Penn State University. In *Education 626: Educational Software Design and Authoring.* Course web site, University of Michigan, 1996 [Available online: http://www.umich.edu/~edu626/define.html]. Copyright 1996 by the University of Michigan and Carl Berger, Instructor. Reprinted with permission.

An instructional designer's job is to create something that enables a person or a group of people to learn about a particular topic, develop or improve a set of skills, or encourage the learner to conduct further study. The "something" created can take many forms: a lecture, a multimedia presentation, the curriculum for a year's study, a piece of computer software, an in-person demonstration, a test-preparation booklet. The list is almost endless. Everything an instructional designer creates, however, has something in common with all other instructional designs: The designer has identified a need for instruction and decided on a method for delivering it. Most instructional designs (the best ones, we would argue, and those that follow the precepts of the discipline as it is defined by its governing organizations) also include a strategy for evaluating not only whether the instruction produced and delivered achieved the desired effect, but also how the design might be improved.

An important premise of instructional design is to make use of the available research on how people think and how people learn, the technologies available for communication (information technologies), and analysis methods. An instructional design is practical application of this knowledge to create a situation in which learning is most likely to occur effectively.

As scholars and practitioners have examined the process of developing, delivering, and evaluating instruction, they have devised a number of models to explain the process; these models are intended to help instructional designers perform their job better. You should be aware of the more popular models and be cognizant of special cases that are a topic of discussion within the instructional design community. Perhaps even more important, you should understand the "big picture" of designing instruction for a particular situation in terms that go beyond the application of any one instructional design model or adherence to any one instructional design theory. To become a well-rounded instructional designer, you must be able to take a broad view of the ideas and practices that define the field.

Probably the most popular approach to designing instruction is to follow some variation of what is essentially a three-step process:

1. Analyze the situation to determine what instruction is necessary and the steps that need to be taken to deliver the instruction.
2. Produce and implement the instructional design.
3. Evaluate the results of implementing the instructional design.

One of the most popular descriptions of this process is ADDIE, an acronym that divides the three steps into five actions: analyze, design, develop, implement, and evaluate. ADDIE is not a specific instructional design/

development model but an illustration of the conceptual components of many instructional design/development models (see the section titled "A Special Case: ADDIE" later in this chapter).

As practitioners of a "linking science," instructional designers have become adept at examining and making use of ideas developed in many specializations. Students of instructional design learn from other disciplines, sometimes borrowing development models created for activities similar to designing instruction (e.g., software development, which shares the purpose of creating something of use and usable to people). One tradition within the discipline of instructional design is taking a systematic approach and following accepted protocols for development. However, at this point in time (in what many people refer to as the *postmodern* world), the instructional designer may take an eclectic approach as well, borrowing ideas and strategies from various unconventional sources.

Models of Instructional Design/Development

Models by definition are a reflection of reality: temporary stand-ins for something more specific and "real." Models are helpful for explaining concepts that may be difficult to describe. Nevertheless, any model is just a shadow or reflection of the *real* thing. A model may describe commonalities among a number of similar items; a model may illustrate a process; a model may be a representation of something:

- A *model* home in a new housing development will not be exactly like every home, but the model gives the potential buyer a good idea of what is available for sale.
- Participation in *model* congress and *model* United Nations (UN) activities gives students an opportunity to better understand how the real organizations work, even though these activities are not the same as participating in the actual UN or congressional meetings.
- Hobbyists build *model* trains, automobiles, and airplanes. These models are usually significantly smaller and do not operate in exactly the same way as their full-size counterparts.

In a professional setting, good models can be helpful tools. They offer guidelines and can ensure a level of quality and uniformity by providing a means of comparison. Well-considered models of instructional design and development can perform this task, helping to explain in general the instructional design process in a way that can be applied to a number of specific situations.

Several well-established and respected models for instructional design/development provide guidelines and procedures that can be applied to a wide variety of specific situations. Using these models to design and develop instruction can help significantly reduce training and education costs (Nixon & Lee, 2001).

We selected, and next describe, two of the most famous models of instructional design/development with which every instructional designer should become familiar: Dick and Carey's systems approach model and Kemp, Morrison, and Ross's plan. Additional instructional design/development models can be found on the Internet at sites like David Maier's (2003) *Instructional Technology Global Resource Network*. These models are intended to guide the instructional designer through the ADDIE process—analysis, design, development, implementation, and evaluation—which is discussed after the two models.

The Systems Approach (Dick and Carey's) Model for Designing Instruction. Dick and Carey's systems approach model (Figure 1.1) is a classic

FIGURE 1.1

Dick and Carey's Systems Approach Model for Designing Instruction

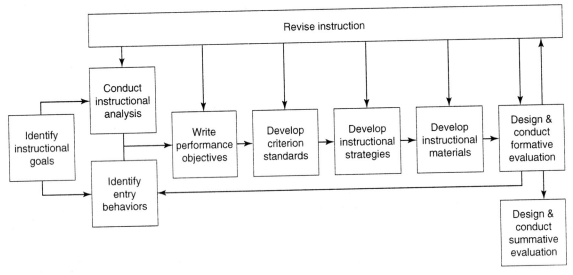

Source: Adapted from *The Systematic Design of Instruction* (5th ed., p. 2), by W. Dick, L. Carey, and J. O. Carey, 2001, Published by Allyn and Bacon, Boston, MA. Copyright © 2005 by Pearson Education. Adapted by permission of the publisher.

example of performing an instructional design task systematically. When this model was developed, taking into consideration components of the instructional context like the learners and the environment in which the instruction was to be offered was a significant departure from the more traditional approach of presenting information through some combination of lecture, textbook reading, review, and testing. With the traditional approach, the burden is placed squarely on the learners to do the best they can with the content, and little thought is given to adjusting or improving the instruction. Dick and Carey's model was designed to emphasize the importance of examining and refining the instruction and provides guidance for making improvements (Dick, Carey, & Carey, 2001).

Kemp, Morrison, and Ross's Instructional Design Plan. The Kemp, Morrison, and Ross plan (Figure 1.2) is expressed as nine elements:

1. Identify instructional problems and specify goals for designing instruction.
2. Examine learner characteristics that will influence your instructional decisions.
3. Identify subject content, and analyze task components related to stated goals and purposes.
4. Specify the instructional objectives.
5. Sequence content within each instructional unit for logical learning.
6. Design instructional strategies so that each learner can master the objectives.
7. Plan the instructional message and develop the instruction.
8. Develop evaluation instruments to assess the objectives.
9. Select resources to support instruction and learning activities. (Morrison, Ross, & Kemp, 2004, pp. 7–8)[2]

One interesting aspect of this design plan is that it is not illustrated as a specific sequence. According to Morrison et al. (2004), each of the nine elements of development is presented in an oval without lines or arrows pointing the way because each element may be addressed at any time during instruction development.

A Special Case: ADDIE. One of the most commonly used descriptions of instructional design/development is the **ADDIE process** (Figure 1.3). ADDIE is an acronym for analyze, design, develop, implement, and evaluate. Although many practitioners use ADDIE as a prescriptive model for

[2]Reprinted from Morrison, Ross, and Kemp, *Designing Effective Instruction*, 4th ed. 2004. Reprinted with permission by John Wiley & Sons.

FIGURE 1.2

Kemp, Morrison, and Ross's Instructional Design Plan

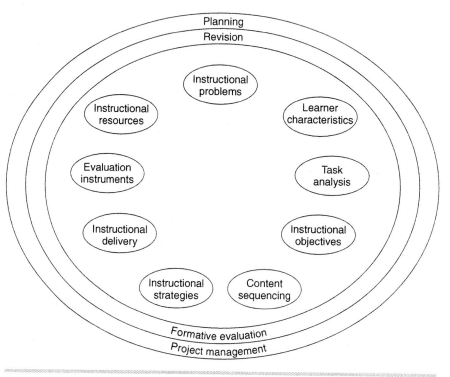

Source: Adapted from *Designing Effective Instruction* (4th ed., p. 1), by G. R. Morrison, S. M. Ross, and J. E. Kemp, 2004, New York: Wiley. Copyright 2004 by John Wiley & Sons. Adapted with permission.

developing instruction, it is actually a means of describing the essential components of *any* instructional design model (Molenda, 2003).

Scholars generally agree that ADDIE is an illustration of the essential steps of the instructional design/development process (Molenda, 2003; Reiser & Dempsey, 2002). ADDIE is particularly useful as a framework for comparing and contrasting more formally and completely developed instructional design/development models.

Caveat. The two models and ADDIE are intended to guide individuals through the process of creating and evaluating instruction. Each model articulates the steps involved in creating an instructional intervention

FIGURE 1.3

The ADDIE Process

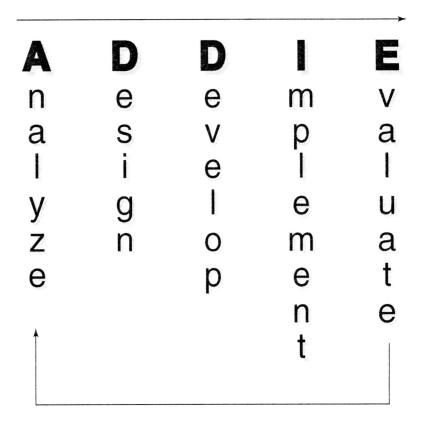

differently, and these models are only a few of many instructional design models scholars have created through the years. Often, an instructional designer uses a particular model because it is popular within his or her professional setting. However, you should bear in mind that these are *models* of instructional design/development; no single model should be considered the only correct way to design instruction.

Professional Instructional Design Practice

Deciding how to design and develop instruction often depends on the organizational setting in which the instructional design professional finds him- or herself. Organizations that have established traditions of delivering instruction may demand that certain forms be followed. For example, universities in North America and Europe traditionally require that for each course offered, a syllabus be created beforehand and students receive evaluation in the form of letter grades (an evaluation strategy developed at Cambridge University in the early 1800s). University courses traditionally require weekly 3-hour meetings (or semiweekly 1.5-hour meetings). These requirements necessarily affect the way college professors design their instruction.

K–12 environments are under similar constraints. Designers who create instruction for K–12 school settings (including teachers, textbook writers, educational software manufacturers, etc.) must work within the constraints of a system that has a specific time frame (in the United States, typically 182 days of school, with approximately 7 hours of instruction each day beginning with the first grade), an assigned curriculum (established by state and local authorities), and evaluation procedures that include awarding letter grades and promoting students to higher grade levels.

Nonacademic organizations have their own traditions and requirements for instructional design. For example, the U.S. military has a tradition of using specific theories and development models to guide instructional design activity. During the 20th century, the U.S. military offered instructional designers numerous opportunities to contribute to the knowledge base of the discipline: Military actions that required amassing troops from a civilian population also required the troops to receive training for their new roles. In peacetime, military personnel must receive training on a variety of highly technical, demanding, and dangerous tasks for which public school and college has not prepared them. These models continue to be used as protocols, allowing designers to develop instruction efficiently and (it is hoped) effectively.

Traditional Approaches (Analyze, Develop, Evaluate)

What are generally considered traditional approaches to instructional design are in fact based on relatively recent developments in the theory of how people think about the way the world works. In the 1950s, the basic concepts and principles of a "general theory of systems" were established by scholars (notably Ashby, Bertalanffy, Boulding, Fagen, Gerard, Rappaport, and Weiner) who were, at the time, pioneers of a new method of thinking about how people and things operate (Banathy, 1996; Banathy & Jenlink, 2004). One critical argument was Bertalanffy's observation that modern science was becoming increasingly specialized and that people therefore perceived science not as an integrated realm, but rather as a series of small specializations that operated according to their own premises,

ID INSIGHT

General Systems Theory and the Search for a Unified Field Theory

Currently in the scientific discipline of physics, some theories seem to successfully explain how the universe works at the submicroscopic level (electromagnetic forces), and other theories seem to successfully explain how the universe works on a larger level (gravitational forces). However, the two sets of theories cannot be combined into one logical theory that explains how the universe works on every level. The *unified field theory* is what physicists hope will explain the fundamental interactions of the physical universe, both electromagnetic and gravitational. Work on the general systems theory (GST) is in some ways the social scientists' version of a unified field theory; the GST is what they hope will explain, in general, how systems work, regardless of the specific setting.

The quest for a unified field theory can also be used as an example of how little is known about the world. In physics, various theories are used for practical purposes to explain and predict phenomena, but physicists are still working to discover "the truth" about how the physical world works. Like physicists, educators use a variety of theories to explain and predict how learning and instruction work. However, no educational theory is universally accepted, and no one knows "the absolute truth" about instruction and learning environments.

techniques, and structures. The goal of general systems theory (GST) is to explain the common elements of the theoretical constructions of the various scientific disciplines.

The academic community was deeply influenced by systems theory ideas. This influence continues to this day; most people take for granted the concept that much of what occurs in the world is influenced by, and in turn influences, actions and events that may not seem at first related to one another. A more modern and extreme example is *chaos theory*, which was popularized by the idea that a butterfly's wings beating in the Amazon has an effect on the amount of rainfall Newfoundland receives in a year (Gleick, 1987).

In examining a systems approach to designing instruction, Hoban (1977) wrote,

> In any system, everything is related to everything else, sooner or later and in one way or another. This means that every essential element, factor, or component, and some seemingly inconsequential ones, can seriously affect the final product, outcome, or output of the system. What media people do or don't do not only affects other people in the system but the quality of the output of the entire system. This follows from general systems theory. (p. 71)

Systems theory caused educators to examine how the various factors that influence learning interact to create a complete instructional experience. How the learner thinks, what the learner knows prior to the instructional event, what motivates the learner, how the teacher teaches, what the consequences of evaluation are, and many other factors became objects of consideration. This once-innovative approach to instruction has become the modern standard.

Nontraditional Approaches

A systems approach to instructional design is the modern approach. The word *modern* in this case refers to the period in history called the *modern age* (the age of approaching problems logically and scientifically, solving these problems systematically by using new and innovative technologies). One school of thought argues that the current era is a "post-modern" age (Hlynka, 1995, 2004). It is *post*modern because scholars can identify and describe the reasons for "modern" approaches. Whether experts agree or disagree with the approaches and the reasoning behind them, once they are identified and described, they are relegated to a specific time period; the current generation is outside that time period—hence the term *postmodern*.

The discipline of instructional design blossomed at a time when systems thinking was a dominating force in the scientific and academic community. For this reason, it is often referred to as *instructional systems design* or *instructional systems technology*. Instructional systems design is used primarily to teach adult learners and is based on a "mastery" approach (a student may move on to the next task only after he or she has mastered the previous task). This approach is **behavioristic** in that it works only for instruction that is immediately measurable (the ability to perform a task) and requires that the instruction follow from a specific behavioral objective (e.g., "At the end of the instruction, the student will be able to take apart and put together a carburetor"):

> The ISD [instructional systems design] model begins at the curriculum level with analysis of content, definition of overall objectives, delineation of

sequences and subsequences of the curriculum. It proceeds with the selection of instructional methods and media, designing individual lessons to enhance learner mastery of the objectives, developing delivery systems for the individual lessons, and ends with evaluation of the lessons and the entire instructional system. Evaluation in ISD emphasizes measurement of observable target behaviors. (Alessi & Trollip, 2001, p. 18)

Instructional systems design has been criticized for generating models that are too complex to use effectively and for focusing too much on strictly observable (behavioral) outcomes without addressing the more subtle aspects of learning such as reflection, retention, and motivation (Alessi & Trollip, 2001). Teaching, having shifted from placing all responsibility on the learner without regard for the design of the instruction, had shifted to a point where the learner was becoming an overlooked portion of the instructional design process.

In the 1980s and 1990s, instructional design theorists began to develop models that included approaches that diverged from the strictly behavioral. Cognitive and constructive approaches became topics of discussion and research (Alessi & Trollip, 2001; Reigeluth, 1999).

Eclecticism and Postmodern Approaches. We have offered a general definition for the term *postmodern:* after the historical period referred to as *modern.* The guiding principles of postmodern thought, however, are far more difficult to define. **Postmodernism** is concurrently a historical epoch, an intellectual movement, and a general social condition (Hlynka, 2004; Solomon, 2000).

A postmodern approach to instructional design recognizes that the instructional designer must take four societal factors into account:

1. Society is past the point where only a limited number of authorities are available to a classroom student. The modern classroom had two authoritative sources: the teacher and the textbook. This situation no longer exists because students have access to many other sources, including the Internet, television, and in some cases friends and family who are more educated than the teacher is (Hlynka, 1995).

2. No longer can there be an agreed-upon, single type of "well-educated" individual. Determining a curriculum and including all "important" artistic and scientific works that would be appropriate for all individuals is impossible.

PROFESSIONALS IN PRACTICE

Where do the roots of my instructional design (ID) philosophy come from? The first one comes from my undergraduate study of mathematics. I believe many concepts of mathematics are helpful for instructional technologists. I am particularly under the influence of the concepts of chaos theory while working on any ID project. Unfortunately, I am not the inventor of this idea. This connection between chaos theory and ID was already realized by other researchers in our field (e.g., Jonassen, 1990; You, 1993). Why is chaos theory important for me and why is it a part of my ID approach? Here is a quick summary.

Several researchers agree that the traditional systems approach to problem solving has a reductionist nature and it tends to solve a problem by fragmentation, one stage at a time (Finegan, 1994; Jonassen, 1990; You, 1993). This approach may work for some small-scale and well-defined situations. However, the systems associated with human activity are complex and not well defined. According to Jonassen (1990), "Simple systems behave in simple ways, and complex systems behave in complex and less predictive ways. The behavior of a system cannot be examined accurately by analyzing its components" (p. 34).

As an alternative to a linear, reductionist, and deterministic approach, chaos, or the dynamical systems approach, is proposed. In a complex system, "the components are related and interlock with one another such that a change in one component invariably affects another part of the system, or eventually even the entire system" (Murnare, cited in Chieuw, 1991, p. 25). Gordon and Greenspan explained chaos as the study of disorder, and it appears in nonlinear systems (as cited in King, 1991). Since chaos deals with nonlinear and disorderly systems, many disciplines, including technological, social, and economic, are appropriate for applying its principles. As stated by Highsmith (2000), "From physics to biology to chemistry to evolution, complex adaptive systems theory began to help explain occurrences in the real world that the linear approximations of the old science could not" (p. 10). According to King (1991), for many different disciplines, chaos gives new data, suggests innovative approaches to old ideas, and reaffirms certain approaches. Before proceeding further, in order not to cause a misunderstanding, I should state that nonlinear systems are not completely disorderly systems. As Chieuw (1991) said, such systems have an interconnected nature, and a subtle order is always present.

Actually, instructional systems design (ISD) is inherently a complex process, which some instructional designers have already noted. For example, Appelman (2000) stated that in real life, when experts implement the ISD process, they realize that the linear approach does not work. He said, "It appears to be almost a random pattern of attention being focused on different steps of the process out of order" (p. 137). So, it is not wrong to say that ISD is a chaos-based system.

—Kursat Cagiltay,
Associate Professor, Department of Computer Education and
Instructional Technology, Middle East Technical University,
Ankara, Turkey

3. The currently popular cognitive paradigm—constructivism—does not recognize or advocate a traditional, linear educational sequence. With information available from a variety of sources outside the classroom, learners will inevitably deviate from a linear instructional model by observing and reacting to other examples, nonexamples, and divergent examples of the concepts they study in school.

4. No single, objective truth exists. Truth is a construct based on an individual's personal interpretation or on the consensus of a group of people for their purposes. The truth, also known as "the right answer," may change, depending on the context and the individuals involved.

Postmodernism may also be referred to as *postpositivism* because the "modern" approach was **positivistic.** In a positivistic worldview, any problem has only one correct answer; postpositivism suggests that any one problem may have a number of correct answers, depending on the worldview of the person attempting to derive the answer.

According to Solomon (2000), a postmodern philosophy of instructional design has the following tenets at its core:

- The philosophical "core" of post-modern instructional technology is a belief in pluralism, which can be described as respect for difference and resistance to single explanations.

- Knowledge, truth and reality are constructed by people and groups of people.
- Criticism is an appropriate method for inquiry in instructional technology.
- Systems are interpreted as highly complex entities with adaptive qualities. (p. 423)

According to the postmodern approach, completely isolating the learner, or the instructional event, may not be possible. Furthermore, isolating the process of instructional development to apply a traditional instructional design/development model in the way it was originally intended may not be possible.

Postmodernism in instructional design does not necessarily reject the more traditional systems approach. To some extent, postmodern thought suggests only that the system may be far more complex than anyone had originally thought.

Postmodernism coincides with the proliferation of computing tools that allow individuals greater freedom in creating sophisticated printed work and interactive software. Before the proliferation of desktop publishing and multimedia authoring programs, creating high-quality instructional media was the province of specialists. The ubiquity and popularity of programs like Microsoft's PowerPoint® attest to the fact that everyone now considers him- or herself competent to create and deliver media that are adequate for professional presentation and distribution. Prior to the mid-1980s, an individual had to rely on a trained specialist with access to esoteric tools to create materials such as handouts, brochures, slide presentations, videos, and interactive software.

Instructional designers became aware of the limitations of a systems approach around the same time they gained control of tools that would allow them to design and create instructional media without having to rely entirely on people who specialized in the development and production portion of the instructional design/development process. Access to these new computing tools meant the process of creating mock-ups, prototypes, and finished products became less costly and time consuming. One concern about all this newfound flexibility in creating instructional media is that it can lead to slipshod development:

Experienced designers and typographers were appalled that so many people (including some of their longtime clients) could be hoodwinked into thinking that the results of "dumping text" into page layout templates and "copying and pasting" clip-art were synonymous with expert design. Although professionals tacitly knew that quality design and illustration were not just a "click" away, very few of them could characterize their expertise in ways that nondesigners could appreciate. (Schriver, 1997, p. 43)

This awareness that a person might not have to follow a systems model to the letter and that an individual has the power to create the necessary media with his or her laptop computer leads instructional designers to experiment more with nontraditional approaches. It can easily lead them to take an eclectic approach, picking and choosing the better aspects of any number of design procedures and recommended practices.

An eclectic approach allows the designer to choose specific elements from a variety of sources. This approach can be viewed both as "taking the best there is to offer" and as "taking things out of context." You can easily see why this approach might make scholars of instructional design uncomfortable: If not carefully considered, articulated, and evaluated, the "linking science" that so many people worked to create might be seen as changing to a less rigorous, less "scientifically sound" activity.

However, just as some well-established, dedicated educators were dismayed at the advent of a science of instructional design at the end of the 19th century, some well-established, dedicated instructional designers are dismayed at the advent of a change in the science of instructional design at the beginning of the 21st century. A heightened awareness of the greater complexity of systems, and the new, increasingly ubiquitous, computer-based media-production tools have created a situation in which instructional designers must adapt their views and practices.

Rapid Prototyping: An Example of a Postmodernist Approach. Rapid prototyping is a different approach to the design and development of instruction. It represents a relatively recent "paradigm shift" in instructional design because it does not strictly follow the traditional systems process of design and development. Part of the conversation among instructional designers for more than a decade, rapid prototyping is a development approach used in a variety of professions and has been found particularly useful in engineering-oriented activities (e.g., automobiles are designed by creating a series of testable prototypes). The essential idea behind rapid prototyping is to arrive at a final product through the creation of a number of prototypes. Each prototype is evaluated by some combination of experts and end users; each successive prototype is more like the final product: That is, the "fidelity" of the prototypes increases with each new one until a working product is achieved.

For example, a typical set of prototypes developed in the process of creating a working piece of instructional software might include the following succession:

1. Rough pencil sketches
2. Refined pencil sketches
3. Computer-generated printouts (a "paper mock-up")
4. A computer-based prototype with little or no interactive programming
5. A computer-based prototype programmed with appropriate interactions and navigation
6. The final product

A rapid prototyping approach requires that the design environment allow for the relatively quick and easy creation of instructional materials (Tripp & Bichelmeyer, 1990). The current availability of computing tools that facilitate the creation of instructional media (including word-processing, image-editing, and software-authoring software) greatly increases the attractiveness of the rapid prototyping approach.

As Rathbun, Saito, and Goodrum (1997) pointed out, "The intermediate prototypes become an important means of getting feedback; the design and development process become intertwined" (p. 291). This method is different from traditional instructional design approaches, in which the design process and the development process are separate.

In traditional instructional design models, once the design has been prepared, no critical feedback about the design is offered during the development process. When instructional design is accomplished by a large group of specialists, separating the design and the development has a certain utility: "Make the product according to the specifications that an expert has provided: Send the finished product to experts for evaluation." One underlying assumption of this approach is that an expert in a specific area oversees each stage of the instructional design process. The traditional process focuses on creating an effective end product without much regard for the efficiency of the process, which is time consuming and costly (Nixon & Lee, 2001; Tripp & Bichelmeyer, 1990).

Rapid prototyping is one example of a new way of viewing the instructional design process. The traditional approach to instructional design is based on the underlying assumption of the objectivity of science and the scientific method. With rapid prototyping, the scientific method is not rejected, but a more constructive (as opposed to objective) approach to the

ID INSIGHT

Theatrical Production: An Artistic Form of Rapid Prototyping

A time-honored approach to preparing a theatrical presentation is the process of rehearsal and criticism. The play begins as an idea that a writer puts down on paper. The successive "prototypes" include a *read-through*, in which the actors speak their lines to each other without any staging or costumes or lighting; a *walk-through*, a performance with actors in their street clothes; a *dress rehearsal*, with sets, costumes, and lighting (but no audience); and a *preview,* with sets, costumes, lighting, and an invited audience who is aware that the play is a work in progress. At each point in this process, the actors and designers receive feedback from the director as well from the other actors and designers (and, in the last stage, the preview audience). This incremental feedback is used to improve and refine each new performance until *opening night,* when the play is considered a completed artwork. Even after the work is considered complete, the director, cast, and crew continue to monitor performances to evaluate their success and determine what (minor) changes might be necessary.

problem can be taken by incorporating more opportunities for everyone involved in an instructional design project (the clients, the designers, the producers, the learners) to participate in evaluation, problem solving, and revision. Rapid prototyping is a popular way of thinking about and approaching instructional design problems, but it is not a perfect solution. We end this section with an admonition from Tripp and Bichelmeyer (1990):

> The main disadvantage of prototyping can be summed up in one complaint that is easy to imagine: it has a tendency to encourage informal design methods which may introduce more problems than they eliminate . . . Prototyping can lead to a design-by-repair philosophy, which is only an excuse for lack of discipline . . . Prototyping may lead to premature commitment to a design if it is not remembered that a design is only a hypothesis. (p. 42)

This warning should serve as a reminder that a "Let's try it and see what happens" approach is no substitute for careful planning and evaluation.

SUMMARY

Instructional design is the "linking science" that applies logic and scientific methods to the problems involved in designing and developing instruction. It evolved from the discipline of educational psychology, which came into being at the turn of the 20th century. Instructional design became particularly popular with the articulation and acceptance of a general systems theory around the 1950s. One problem instructional designers face is the long association of instructional design with strictly behavioristic approaches to teaching. Instructional design scholars have produced models of instructional design/development that describe the process of analysis, design, development, implementation, and evaluation.

Recent approaches to the instructional design process include breaking from the tradition of systems models in favor of more eclectic approaches that combine the five processes of instructional design instead of formally separating them. Two critical factors that foster this type of approach are a "postmodern" approach to solving a problem and new, and relatively easy-to-use, computer-based multimedia production tools. A particularly popular postmodern approach to instructional design is rapid prototyping, in which the product is taken through a series of mock-ups that can be evaluated and refined; each new mock-up is closer to how the final product will look and operate. One potential pitfall of rapid prototyping is an informality that may produce an undisciplined approach to the instructional design problem. For any instructional design problem, careful planning and evaluation are always recommended.

CONNECTING PROCESS TO PRACTICE

1. How would you describe the field of instructional design to a friend who is not an instructional designer?
2. As a novice instructional designer, which aspects of developing instruction do you consider to be inherently artistic? Which aspects of developing instruction do you consider inherently scientific?
3. Which model of instructional design/development would you most likely follow? Why do you suppose that model is particularly appealing to you?

4. Do you consider your view of the world to be positivistic or postpositivistic? How might your feelings about positivism affect your approach to instructional design?
5. Would you consider rapid prototyping to be an eclectic approach to instructional design? Why or why not?

RECOMMENDED READINGS

Gagne, R. M. (1985). *The conditions of learning and theory of instruction.* New York: Holt, Rinehart & Winston.

Maier, D. (2003). Model library. In *Instructional technology global resource network.* Retrieved September 17, 2003, from *http://www.ittheory.com/models.htm*

Reigeluth, C. M. (1983). *Instructional design theories and models: An overview of their current status.* Hillsdale, NJ: Erlbaum.

Reigeluth, C. M. (1999). *Instructional-design theories and models: A new paradigm of instructional theory* (Vol. II). Mahwah, NJ: Erlbaum.

The Theory Into Practice database. *http://tip.psychology.org/index.html*

REFERENCES

Alessi, S. M., & Trollip, S. R. (2001). *Multimedia for learning: Methods and development* (3rd ed.). Boston: Allyn & Bacon.

Appelman, R. (2000). An iterative development model: A genesis from pedagogical needs. *International Journal of Engineering Education and Lifelong Learning, 10*(1–4), 136–141.

Banathy, B. (1996). Systems inquiry and its application in education. In D. Jonassen (Ed.), *Handbook of research for educational communications and technology* (pp. 74–92). New York: Macmillan.

Banathy, B. H., & Jenlink, P. M. (2004). Systems inquiry and its application in education. In D. Jonassen (Ed.), *Handbook of research for educational communications and technology* (2nd ed., pp. 37–57). Mahwah, NJ: Erlbaum.

Berliner, D. C. (1993). The 100-year journey of educational psychology: From interest, to disdain, to respect for practice. In T. K. Fagan & G. R. VandenBos (Eds.), *Exploring applied psychology: Origins and critical analyses* (pp. 37–78). Washington, DC: American Psychological Association.

Chieuw, J. (1991). *An alternative approach to educational planning based on a conceptual framework of the educational system as dynamic: A theoretical study.* Unpublished doctoral dissertation, Florida State University, Tallahassee.

Dewey, J. (1900). Psychology and social practice. *The Psychological Review, 7,* 105–124.

Dick, W., Carey, L., & Carey, J. O. (2001). *The systematic design of instruction* (5th ed.). New York: Addison-Wesley/Longman.

Finegan, A. (1994). Soft systems methodology: An alternative approach to knowledge elicitation in complex and poorly defined systems. *Complexity International, 1.* Retrieved from *http://journal-ci.csse.monash.edu.au/ci/vol01/finega01/html/*

Gleick, J. (1987). *Chaos: Making a new science.* New York: Viking Press.

Heinich, R., Molenda, M., Russell, J. D., & Smaldino, S. E. (1996). *Instructional media and technologies for learning* (5th ed.). Upper Saddle River, NJ: Merrill/Prentice Hall.

Highsmith, J. A. (2000). *Adaptive software development: A collaborative approach to managing complex systems.* New York: Dorset House.

Hlynka, D. (1995). Six postmodernisms in search of an author. In G. J. Anglin (Ed.), *Instructional technology: Past, present, and future* (pp. 113–118). Englewood, CO: Libraries Unlimited.

Hlynka, D. (2004). Postmodernism in educational technology: Update: 1996–Present. In D. Jonassen (Ed.), *Handbook of research for educational communications and technology* (2nd ed., pp. 243–246). Mahwah, NJ: Erlbaum.

Hoban, C. F., Jr. (1977). A systems approach to audiovisual communications. In L. W. Cochran (Ed.), *Okoboji: A 20 year review of leadership, 1955–1974* (pp. 67–72). Dubuque, IA: Kendall/Hunt. (Reprinted in *Classic writings on instructional technology,* Vol. I, pp. 57–90, by D. P. Ely & T. Plomp, Eds., 1996, Englewood, CO: Libraries Unlimited.)

Jonassen, D. H. (1990). Thinking technology: Chaos in instructional design. *Educational Technology, 30*(2), 32–34.

King, J. W. (1991). *Chaos, communication and educational technology.* Paper presented at the annual meeting of the Association for Educational Communications and Technology, Orlando, FL.

Maier, D. (2003). Model library. In *Instructional technology global resource network.* Retrieved September 17, 2003, from *http://www.ittheory.com/models.htm*

Molenda, M. (2003). In search of the elusive ADDIE model. *Performance Improvement, 42*(5), 34–35.

Morrison, G. R., Ross, S. M., & Kemp, J. E. (2004). *Designing effective instruction* (4th ed.). New York: Wiley.

Nixon, E. K., & Lee, D. (2001). Rapid prototyping in the instructional design process. *Performance Improvement Quarterly, 14*(3), 95–116.

Rathbun, G. A., Saito, R. S., & Goodrum, D. A. (1997). Reconceiving ISD: Three perspectives on rapid prototyping as a paradigm shift. In *Proceedings of Selected Research and Development Presentations at the 1997 National Convention of the Association for Educational Communications and Technology* (pp. 291–296). Washington, DC: Association for Educational Communications and Technology.

Reigeluth, C. M. (Ed.). (1983). *Instructional design theories and models: An overview of their current status.* Hillsdale, NJ: Erlbaum.

Reigeluth, C. M. (Ed.). (1999). *Instructional-design theories and models: A new paradigm of instructional theory* (Vol. II). Mahwah, NJ: Erlbaum.

Reiser, R., & Dempsey, J. (2002). *Trends and issues in instructional design and technology.* Upper Saddle River, NJ: Merrill/Prentice Hall.

Saettler, P. (1990). *The evolution of American educational technology.* Englewood, CO: Libraries Unlimited.

Schriver, K. A. (1997). *Dynamics in document design.* New York: Wiley.

Smith, P. L., & Ragan, T. J. (1999). *Instructional design* (2nd ed.). New York: Wiley.

Snellbecker, G. (1974). *Learning theory, instructional theory, and psychoeducational design.* New York: McGraw-Hill.

Solomon, D. L. (2000). Toward a post-modern agenda in instructional technology. In *Annual Proceedings of Selected Research and Development Papers Presented at the National Convention of the Association for Educational Communications and Technology* (pp. 415–428). Washington, DC: Association for Educational Communications and Technology.

Tripp, S. D., & Bichelmeyer, B. (1990). Rapid prototyping: An alternative instructional design strategy. *Educational Technology Research and Development, 38*(1), 31–44.

University of Michigan. (1996). Definitions of instructional design. In *Education 626: Educational software design and authoring.* Retrieved September 12, 2003, from *http://www.umich.edu/~ed626/define.html*

You, Y. (1993). What can we learn from chaos theory? An alternative approach to instructional systems design. *Educational Technology Research and Design, 41*(3), 17–32.

Chapter 2

UNDERSTANDING HOW PEOPLE THINK

Key Terms

Behaviorism *(page 36)*

Cognition *(page 30)*

Cognitive abilities
(page 32)

Cognitivism *(page 36)*

Constructivism *(page 37)*

Eclecticism *(page 39)*

Epistemology *(page 34)*

Executive abilities
(page 32)

Memory *(page 31)*

Mental power *(page 31)*

Metacognition *(page 32)*

Metaphysics *(page 34)*

Pragmatism *(page 39)*

Scholasticism *(page 33)*

I don't directly consider the thinking process and how that plays into the overall design of the courses I develop. When I say *consider*, I mean that there is no formal process that I go through. I believe it just happens because I understand the basics of the thinking process and have been creating online instruction for several years now. If you were to look at the courses I've designed, I believe they would reflect that the thinking process has been considered.

—Kara Andrew,
Instructional Designer,
Distance Education,
California State University, Fullerton

Guiding Questions

- Why must instructional designers understand how people think?
- How have historical and current perspectives on thinking and the thinking process in instructional design been influenced by philosophy and educational psychology?
- What viewpoint do instructional designers typically have with regard to thinking and the thinking process?

Chapter Overview

No words are oftener on our lips than thinking *and* thought. *So profuse and varied, indeed, is our use of these words that it is not easy to define just what we mean by them.*

—*John Dewey (1910, p. 1)*

Take a moment to reflect on your definition of *thinking.* If you struggled to produce what you believe is a clear definition, you are not alone. The words that Dewey (1910) wrote in *How We Think* still ring true. Thinking is often used in a variety of contexts to indicate extremely different concepts; therefore, understanding what is meant by *thinking* at any given time can be difficult. Despite the challenges inherent in understanding thinking and the thinking process, having knowledge about how people process, store, and retrieve information—in other words, *think*—is crucial for instructional designers if they are to help develop instructional interventions that are efficient, effective, and meaningful for their clients.

This chapter provides you with a framework for understanding how people think, which will ultimately help you in understanding how people learn because thinking and learning are closely interconnected. Our intention for this chapter is to simplify, if possible, how thinking has been conceptualized historically and in more modern times. Two major topics provide a focus. The first is how instructional designers typically look at thinking and the thinking process. The second is how thinking is viewed from various historical and contemporary perspectives.

Cognition and Basic Cognitive Functions

Cognition

Before we begin a discussion on how instructional designers typically view thinking and the thinking process, you must understand an important concept: cognition. How people go about the process of thinking is often referred to as *cognition.* **Cognition** is the mental process of knowing, including aspects such as awareness, perception, reasoning, and judgment. In essence, cognition includes all the mental input and output of the brain. It encompasses the spectrum from engaging in basic activities like using language and math functions during a trip to the hardware store, to making complex decisions such as selecting between two job offers, to writing a creative story, to being able to understand another person's perspective.

Cognition and *thinking* are interchangeable terms. This statement may not resonate well with some people; however, this book is not the place for a debate over the intricacies of cognition and how the term *thinking* may or may not be synonymous. Such a debate should take place in other arenas like a course on learning and cognition. Rather, as an instructional designer, you must realize that *cognition* and *thinking* can be and are used, in essence, to refer to the same thing.

Basic Cognitive Functions

Numerous technical terms are used in relation to cognition. Making sense of them is not easy. Hundreds of terms are used for specific components of cognition; and many have the same or similar meanings. What makes dealing with these components of cognition especially difficult is that they can mean different things in different settings. Some of the differences may reflect important scientific or theoretical nuances, but many are simply jargon specific to a particular discipline or profession.

The point to remember is that cognition and the components of cognition are important to understand because, as mentioned previously, understanding how people think helps you to understand how they learn. Understanding how people learn will help you as an instructional designer assist your clients in developing effective and efficient instructional interventions. Although you do not have to be a cognitive scientist to have an adequate understanding of how people think, you should understand a few basic concepts.

Memory. **Memory** is much more than just a passive storage system of knowledge. Memory is a set of active processes that encode information. Memory places information into "packages" or "packets," which makes information easier to remember and allows it to be associated with related items already in memory. Memory also involves storing information. Part of this process is the constant rearranging of what has been stored in order for new knowledge to be integrated with what has already been stored. In addition, memory allows information to be located and retrieved as it is needed.

Mental Power. **Mental power** is the basic energy that supports mental activity. This term refers to how much mental work can be performed during a specific period. Power can be used to sustain something simple, such as using a television remote control, or something more complex, such as operating a computer. In either case, the central issue focuses on having enough power on hand to complete the task. In the cognitive domain, *power* refers to arousal level, concentration span, channel capacity, and mental stamina.

Specific Cognitive Abilities. Specific **cognitive abilities** are an individual's stored supply of knowledge and skills. This supply includes abilities such as reading, writing, comprehension, motor, and visuospatial skills.

Executive Abilities. Executive abilities encompass a large category of cognitive functions. Executive abilities include such higher order thinking skills as being able (a) to anticipate future needs and plan accordingly, (b) to set priorities, and (c) to self-correct and regulate actions. In essence, these capacities allow an individual to use his or her mental power and specific **cognitive abilities** to meet social, professional, and psychological needs.

Metacognition. Metacognition is the ability to control your cognitive processes. It is often referred to as the practice of "thinking about thinking." In using metacognition, an individual takes an introspective look at the thought process through which he or she has gone. Metacognition allows the person to critically consider how he or she arrived at certain ideas, concepts, and thoughts. It is a reflective process that helps improve an individual's control over his or her thinking process and learning (Bleiberg, 2001; Flavell, 1979; Ormrod, 2004; Sternberg, 1986; Woolfolk, 2004).

Historical Perspectives on Thinking: A Brief History

Historically, thinking was consigned to the realm of philosophy. Possibly the earliest theory about how the mind works was offered in the fourth and fifth centuries B.C. by Greek philosophers like Empedocles, Democritus, and Epicurus. These philosophers believed that the mind perceived images given off by objects. The perceived images were then copied as sense impressions and stored in memory. "Knowledge then becomes a matter of knowing these mental copies, and the earliest copy theories suggested that the mind knew directly what the sensory nerves brought to it" (Herrnstein & Boring, 1965, as cited in Driscoll, 2000, p. 13).

A different perspective, suggested by Plato (and much later by Kant), generally known as *idealism*, stated that the mind does not directly comprehend reality or copy it. According to this theory, reason is considered the primary source for understanding and knowledge. The major proposition behind this perspective is that all data coming from the senses are interpreted by the mind according to the innate tendencies of the mind (Collinson, 2002; Driscoll, 2000).

Philosophers followed this theme (with numerous slight variations) until the influence of the Church shifted philosophical thought around the ninth century. This influence led to what was called **scholasticism,** a philosophical perspective based on a mixture of Aristotelian and Church writings and thought. Scholastic philosophy was built around a highly organized system of truths, which were distinct from Church doctrines but not in opposition to them. Scholastic philosophers, such as Thomas Aquinas, believed that human intellect was incapable of acquiring knowledge of intelligible things without illumination from God. Individual interaction and participation with the Word of God was necessary if knowledge was to be gained. Thinking was directly related to what God provided to individuals through His inspiration (or "illumination"; Nichols, 2003).

Another shift in the view on thinking began with the dawn of the Renaissance and continued into the 17th and 18th centuries. A movement began that shifted attention away from the belief that truth was divinely inspired by God and that the individual was incapable of discerning what is real or what is truth. Philosophers like Descartes and Locke believed that what they saw with their eyes and experienced with their senses was true. Rather than assuming God played the key role in the universe, humans began to be the standard for judging what was real and what truth was.

ID INSIGHT

Influence of Scholasticism on Instructional Design

According to Saettler (1990), in *The Evolution of American Educational Technology,* "Scholasticism, an intellectual movement that flourished in Europe during the twelfth and thirteenth centuries, was a vitally productive and effective method of instruction" (p. 27). Scholasticism was derived from *doctor scholasticus*, a medieval term that referred to teachers in monastic or cathedral schools. These teachers, such as Pierre Abelard and Thomas Aquinas, developed instructional methods that were used to "examine ideas in a systematic and rational manner" (p. 28).

ID INSIGHT

Metaphysics and Epistemology

Two terms you will come in contact with in relationship to thinking and learning are *metaphysics* and *epistemology*. Understanding these terms is important because the perspectives you hold with regard to them will influence how you approach instructional design. Although you may have never consciously thought about or explored metaphysics or epistemology, you most likely have your own perspectives on both.

Metaphysics: Metaphysics is a branch of philosophy that examines the nature of reality, including the relationship between mind and matter, substance and attribute, and fact and value.

Epistemology: The branch of philosophy in which the nature of knowledge, its assumptions and foundations, and its breadth and validity are studied is **epistemology** (Blackburn, 1996).

Human intellect was deemed capable of discriminating between truth and error. Certain defined methods for discovering truth and evaluating evidence came to be considered reliable and sufficient for discovering truth. Thinking focused more on observation, experience, rational thought, and the scientific method rather than solely on God and tradition (Almog, 2002; Locke, 1996; Sorell, 2001).

Modern Views on Thinking: The Shift from Philosophy to Psychology

While philosophy continues to play a role in how thinking and the thinking process is conceptualized, the emergence of psychology (especially educational psychology) in the mid- to late 19th century had and continues to have the most significant influence on how instructional designers view thinking. Educational psychology, which originated as a separate branch of psychology in 1892 (Berliner, 1993), has provided a concentrated look at thinking and learning through a more scientific perspective—based on research and a focus specifically on how thinking and learning are interconnected.

Two Major Perspectives

Two major perspectives, with several variations, emerged from psychology and have dominated the way instructional designers view how people think, and, in turn, how people learn. Provided in this section are brief explanations of these two distinct perspectives—behaviorist and cognitivist—with mention of key individuals who have influenced the development of these perspectives.

As an instructional designer, you must keep in mind that neither perspective is inherently better than the other. Each perspective offers important contributions that will help you understand how individuals think, and as discussed in Chapter 3, how people learn. Although most instructional designers feel more comfortable with one perspective than the other, they use principles and practices from both as they design and develop instructional interventions.

ID INSIGHT

Positivism and Interpretivism

Two contrasting philosophical perspectives that are important for you to understand are *positivism* and *interpretivism*. These two perspectives are often seen as a dichotomy for describing individual approaches to how knowledge is generated and verified. This brief discussion is included to provide an additional explanation for how some individuals come to an understanding of how people think and learn.

Positivists presume only two sources of knowledge exist: logical reasoning and empirical experience. Logical knowledge includes mathematics, which is reducible to formal logic. Empirical knowledge includes such areas as physics, biology, and psychology. Experience is the only judge of scientific theories (and therefore knowledge). However, positivists observe that scientific knowledge does not exclusively come from the experience: Scientific theories are genuine hypotheses that go beyond the experience (Blackburn, 1996).

Interpretivism is based on the view that knowledge is a matter of perspective. To understand the world, an individual must interpret it. Schwandt (1998) wrote, "What we take to be objective knowledge and the truth is the result of perspective. Knowledge and truth are created, not discovered by the mind" (p. 167).

Behaviorism. The behaviorist perspective, known as **behaviorism,** dominated psychology for the first half of the 20th century (Brandt & Perkins, 2000). Behaviorism includes a group of theories that share several beliefs— "the generalizability of learning principles across species, the importance of focusing on observable events, and the 'blank slate' nature of organisms" (Ormrod, 2004, p. 48). According to behaviorists, mental processes are invisible and thus cannot be studied scientifically. What can be observed is outward behavior; therefore, rather than speculating on internal causes for why things take place, researchers should focus on how organisms respond to different stimuli (Brandt & Perkins, 2000; Ormrod, 2004; Woolfolk, 2004). From a behaviorist perspective, the human mind is malleable, capable of being shaped and formed into producing desired responses and behaviors if specific conditions and circumstances are accounted for and controlled.

The early foundational work of behaviorism was carried out by individuals such as Pavlov (1849–1936), Thorndike (1874–1949), Watson (1878–1958), and Guthrie (1886–1959). Their research was most notably conducted with animals—typically rats, pigeons, cats, and, in the case of Pavlov, dogs. An example is Pavlov's experiments related to salivation in dogs. He observed that a dog's behavior could be conditioned so that if a dog was provided with a specific stimulus (e.g., a ringing bell), a particular behavior (e.g., salivation) would result. Pavlov conditioned a dog to associate a ringing bell with eating, which he did by repeatedly ringing the bell and then immediately feeding the dog some meat. After following this process repeatedly, Pavlov eventually rang the bell but did not give the dog meat; nevertheless, the dog salivated in response to hearing the bell. Thus, the dog was *conditioned* to associate the bell with food (Pavlov, 1927). This phenomenon became known as the *classical conditioning model.*

B. F. Skinner (1904–1990), unquestionably the best known behaviorist, built on this early body of research by developing what is called *operant conditioning.* By observing pigeons and rats, Skinner observed that the frequency of a behavior was more likely to increase if it was followed immediately by a reinforcer (i.e., a reward; Skinner, 1978).

Cognitivism. In the years after World War II, psychologists began to move away from behaviorism toward a different perspective of the mind and how people think. This perspective was called **cognitivism.** According to cognitivist theory, internal mental processes are considered important and capable of being identified and studied (Brandt & Perkins, 2000; Ormrod, 2004). From a cognitivist perspective, the human mind is considered highly complex. Cognitivists typically use the metaphor of a computer to describe the mind. Like a computer, the mind processes information through a series of procedures that work together as a complete system.

Several individuals have had tremendous influence on the cognitive perspective. The foundations of cognitivism were built on the work of Vygotsky (1896–1934), Dewey (1859–1952), Piaget (1896–1980), and Bruner (1915–   ).

Two More Recent Perspectives

Although behavorist and cognitivist perspectives have dominated the way in which thinking has been perceived, two more recent perspectives have influenced instructional designers' views on how people think. These perspectives are constructivism and postmodernism.

Constructivism. **Constructivism**, a variant of cognitivism, is centered around the principle that an individual constructs his or her understanding of the world in which he or she lives by reflecting on personal experiences. An individual generates *mental models*, which he or she uses to make sense of experiences. Brandt and Perkins (2000) wrote,

> Both a philosophical and psychological stance, constructivism argues that the human mind does not simply take in the world but makes it up in an active way. The creative role of the mind is obvious in contexts such as scientific inquiry and artistic endeavor, but constructivists believe that the constructive process also figures prominently even in such seemingly routine mental operations as perception and memory. (p. 167)

The work of Gardner (1943–   ), Sternberg (1949–   ), and Jonassen (1947–   ) has had a tremendous influence on the development of constructivism.

Postmodernism. In the late 20th century and into the early 21st century, an approach called *postmodernism* has provided a different perspective on how humans think:[1]

> Postmodernism is largely a reaction to the assumed certainty of scientific, or objective, efforts to explain reality. In essence, it stems from a recognition that

[1]From Glossary for *Faith & Reason* Web site, by Public Broadcasting System, 1998, http://www.pbs.org/faithandreason/gengloss/postm-body.html. Copyright 1998 by the Public Broadcasting System. Reprinted with permission.

reality is not simply mirrored in human understanding of it, but rather, is constructed as the mind tries to understand its own particular and personal reality.

In addition,[2]

In the postmodern understanding, interpretation is everything; reality only comes into being through our interpretations of what the world means to us individually. Postmodernism relies on concrete experience over abstract principles, knowing always that the outcome of one's own experience will necessarily be fallible and relative, rather than certain and universal.

As mentioned, postmodern philosophers question (and often reject) the idealized view of truth and of knowing inherited from past philosophical traditions. To the postmodernist, thinking is a dynamic, ever-changing function that depends on an individual's interpretation of the world in which the individual lives (Butler, 2003).

Instructional Designers' Views on Thinking

An individual's perspective on thinking depends largely on a combination of the person's education, training, philosophical beliefs, and profession. The perspectives of instructional designers are no different. An instructional designer's perspective on thinking, and in turn learning, is highly influenced by his or her training and the nature of his or her profession.

Instructional designers tend to look at thinking from a pragmatic viewpoint—that is, what is important to know about thinking and the studies done on thinking that will help them develop efficient and effective instructional interventions. Thus, instructional designers are considered to be *eclectic*—they borrow from different perspectives and use what works for a given situation to produce the desired results. Instructional designers also usually take a systems theory approach to thinking (and learning) by exploring it from several perspectives rather than focusing narrowly on one aspect of what thinking is or is not. They realize that thinking is a complex process that includes various interconnected elements and therefore cannot be encapsulated in one neat and tidy description or theory. This view has been shaped by centuries of thought and study that philosophers and psychologists conducted on thinking and how the mind works.

[2]From Glossary for *Faith & Reason* Web site, by Public Broadcasting System, 1998, http://www.pbs.org/faithandreason/gengloss/postm-body.html. Copyright 1998 by the Public Broadcasting System. Reprinted with permission.

ID INSIGHT

Pragmatism and Eclecticism

Pragmatism is based on the principles of usefulness and practicality of ideas. With pragmatism, if something works for an individual, it is valid; if it does not, it should be discarded (Berliner, 1993). Pragmatism, as an American philosophical movement, originated with C. S. Peirce and was moved forward by William James. James, in a lecture given in 1904, spoke about Peirce and pragmatism:

> The term is derived from the same Greek word *pragma,* meaning action, from which our words "practice" and "practical" come. It was first introduced into philosophy by Mr. Charles Peirce in 1878. In an article entitled *How to Make Our Ideas Clear,* in the *Popular Science Monthly* for January of that year Mr. Peirce, after pointing out that our beliefs are really rules for action, said that, to develop a thought's meaning, we need only determine what conduct it is fitted to produce: that conduct is for us its sole significance. And the tangible fact at the root of all our thought-distinctions, however subtle, is that there is no one of them so fine as to consist in anything but a possible difference of practice. To attain perfect clearness in our thoughts of an object, then, we need only consider what conceivable effects of a practical kind the object may involve—what sensations we are to expect from it, and what reactions we must prepare. Our conception of these effects, whether immediate or remote, is then for us the whole of our conception of the object, so far as that conception has positive significance at all. (James, 1995, p. 17)

Eclecticism can be defined as a philosophical perspective that follows a variety of approaches rather than a single belief or doctrine. Eclecticism is based on the approach of a group of ancient philosophers who developed their own system of philosophy by selecting from existing philosophical beliefs and doctrines that suited their particular needs (Fieser & Dowden, 2004).

SUMMARY

Attempts to understand and describe the human mind and how it works can be noted throughout history. Consideration of the topic began in ancient times with the writings of the Greek and Roman philosophers and has continued into modern times with the research conducted in psychology, cognitive science, and neuroscience. As understanding of the human mind and how it works continues to grow, instructional designers need to be able to continue to resolve how this information can be used to positively affect their work. Successful instructional designers know that understanding different and often divergent perspectives on how people think will provide insights into how people learn. This understanding is extremely important because understanding how people learn is a key element in designing successful instructional interventions.

As you begin to read Chapter 3, you will notice that the line between thinking and learning is subtle and often blurred. However, differences do exist. In Chapter 3, we build on the ideas and concepts regarding the human mind and how people think that were presented in this chapter as we undertake the topic of how people learn.

CONNECTING PROCESS TO PRACTICE

1. Why must instructional designers understand different perspectives on how people think?
2. An instructional designer colleague is discussing metacognition with you. He asks you why you think metacognition is an important process for instructional designers and how it could be used. What do you say to your colleague?
3. You are having a discussion with a client. Your client says she recently read an article about behaviorism and cognitivism, but she is not certain whether she clearly understands each perspective on human thinking. She asks you if you could help her clear up any misconceptions she might have by describing the two perspectives. How would you describe them to her?
4. You have been asked to give a brief talk about how perspectives on how humans think have changed with time. What major topics would you discuss?

5. What might a simple training session to teach someone how to properly change a flat tire consist of if you took a behaviorist approach to designing the training? If you took a cognitivist approach or a constructivist approach?

RECOMMENDED READINGS

Aquinas, T. (1998). *A summary of philosophy.* Indianapolis, IN: Hackett.

Bigge, M. L., & Shermis, S. S. (2004). *Learning theories for teachers.* Boston: Allyn & Bacon.

Brown, J. S., Collins, A., & Duguid, S. (1989). Situated cognition and the culture of learning. *Educational Researcher, 18*(1), 32–42.

Bruner, J. (1992). *Acts of meaning.* Cambridge, MA: Harvard University Press.

Dewey, J. (1997). *Experience and education.* New York: Free Press.

Heshusias, L., & Ballard, K. (1996). *From positivism to interpretivism and beyond: Tales of transformation in educational and social research (the mind–body connection).* New York: Teachers College Press.

James, W. (1955). *Principles of psychology.* Toronto, Ontario, Canada: Dover.

James, W. (2002). *The meaning of truth.* Toronto, Ontario, Canada: Dover.

Kant, I. A. (1999). *Critique of pure reason.* Cambridge, England: Cambridge University Press.

REFERENCES

Almog, J. (2002). *What am I? Descartes and the mind–body problem.* London: Oxford University Press.

Berliner, D. C. (1993). The 100-year journey of educational psychology: From interest, to disdain, to respect for practice. In T. K. Fagan & G. R. VandenBos (Eds.), *Exploring applied psychology: Origins and critical analyses* (pp. 37–78). Washington, DC: American Psychological Association.

Blackburn, S. (1996). *The Oxford dictionary of philosophy.* London: Oxford University Press.

Bleiberg, J. (2001). *The road to rehabilitation: Part 3. Guideposts to recognition: Cognition, memory & brain injury.* McLean, VA: Brain Injury Association of America. Retrieved October 15, 2004, from http://www.biausa.org/word.files.to.pdf/good.pdfs/roadToRehab3.pdf

Brandt, R. S., & Perkins, D. N. (2000). The evolving science of learning. In R. S. Brandt (Ed.), *Education in a new era* (pp. 159–183). Alexandria, VA: Association for Supervision and Curriculum Development.

Butler, C. (2003). *Postmodernism: A very short introduction.* London: Oxford University Press.

Collinson, D. (2002). *Fifty major philosophers: A reference guide.* Oxford: Taylor & Francis.

Dewey, J. (1910). *How we think.* Boston: Heath.

Driscoll, M. P. (2000). *Psychology of learning for instruction* (2nd ed.). Boston: Allyn & Bacon.

Fieser, J., & Dowden, B. (Eds.). (2004). *The Internet encyclopedia of philosophy.* Retrieved October 31, 2003, from http://www.utm.edu/research/iep/

Flavell, J. H. (1979). Metacognition and cognitive monitoring: A new area of cognitive-developmental inquiry. *American Psychologist, 34,* 906–911.

Herrnstein, R. J., & Boring, E. G. (Eds.). (1965). *A source book in the history of psychology.* Cambridge, MA: Harvard University Press.

James, W. (1995). *Pragmatism.* Toronto, Ontario, Canada: Dover.

Locke, J., & Kenneth, W. (Eds.). (1996). *Essay concerning human understanding.* Indianapolis, IN: Hackett. (Original work published 1690)

Nichols, A. (2003). *Discovering Aquinas: An introduction to his life, work, and influence.* Grand Rapids, MI: Eerdmans.

Ormrod, J. E. (2004). *Human learning* (4th ed.). Upper Saddle River, NJ: Merrill/Prentice Hall.

Pavlov, I. (1927). *Conditioned reflexes* (G. V. Anrep, Trans.). London: Oxford University Press.

Public Broadcasting System. (1998). Glossary for *Faith & reason* Web site. Retrieved October 27, 2003, from http://www.pbs.org/faithandreason/gengloss/postm-body.html

Saettler, P. (1990). *The evolution of American educational technology.* Englewood, CO: Libraries Unlimited.

Schwandt, T. (1998). Constructivist, interpretivist approaches to human inquiry. In N. Denzin & Y. Lincoln (Eds.), *The landscape of qualitative research: Theories and issues* (pp. 221–259). Thousand Oaks, CA: Sage.

Skinner, B. F. (1978). *About behaviorism.* New York: Random House Trade Books.

Sorell, T. (2001). *Descartes: A very short introduction.* London: Oxford University Press.

Sternberg, R. J. (1986). *Intelligence applied.* New York: Harcourt Brace Jovanovich.

Woolfolk, A. (2004). *Educational psychology.* Boston: Allyn & Bacon.

Chapter 3

UNDERSTANDING HOW PEOPLE LEARN

Key Terms

Classical conditioning
model *(page 48)*
Learning *(page 46)*

Learning objective
(page 56)

Operant conditioning
model *(page 48)*

The various ways in which learning takes place is very much a consideration that impacts the instruction I help create. I believe that every course has its own unique elements that must be considered in relationship to how people learn. Most of the courses I am a part of designing are online and instructor led, and they have both asynchronous and synchronous aspects. I have to consciously consider and talk to the instructor about issues related to these aspects to determine if they are going to help students be successful and meet the course goals. Overall, I believe it is my job as an instructional designer to mesh the course design with principles of how people learn.

—Kara Andrew,
Instructional Designer,
Distance Education,
California State University, Fullerton

Guiding Questions

- What is learning?
- Why must instructional designers understand how people learn?
- What are two of the most common theories on how people learn that instructional designers use in their work?
- What are the different types of learning?

Chapter Overview

In Chapter 1, we discussed that an instructional designer's job is to help create something that enables a person or a group of people to learn about a particular topic, develop or improve a set of skills, or encourage the learner to conduct further study. For any of these to occur, the instructional designer must possess a variety of skills and have a solid understanding of different concepts, ideas, and theories. How people learn falls within the domain of information that you as an instructional designer should be able to understand, discuss, and put into practice. However, understanding how people learn is no easy task. **Learning** is a complex process, and, much like thinking, it can be described from various perspectives. These perspectives on learning have been derived from psychological theory, which was developed throughout the 20th century and continues to evolve in the 21st century.

In this chapter, we look at two major psychological perspectives on learning—behaviorism and cognitivism—and describe how each conceptualizes the learning process. This discussion will provide you with a framework for understanding the complexities of how people learn. The organization of this chapter centers on three major topics: defining learning, describing behaviorism and cognitivism as theories of learning, and discussing different types of learning.

What Is Learning?

As is the case with thinking, learning can be conceptualized in various ways. Two good, straightforward, general definitions come from Jeanne Ormrod (2004) in *Human Learning:*

1. Learning is a relatively permanent change in behavior as a result of experience.
2. Learning is a relatively permanent change in mental representations or associations as a result of experience. (p. 3)

She explained that these definitions have commonalities: Both describe learning as including a relatively permanent change. The changes that occur from learning will last for some time, but they may or may not last forever. Likewise, some changes may be readily observable, such as when a child learns to hold a pencil and write letters, whereas other changes may be more subtle, such as when an individual gains a better appreciation for classical music (Ormrod, 2004). In addition, the changes that occur may be deliberate or unintentional, correct or incorrect, and conscious or unconscious (Hill, 2002).

Another commonality the definitions share is associating the change that occurs with experience. Learning occurs "as a result of one or more events in the learner's life" (Ormrod, 2004, p. 3). In other words, as an individual interacts with his or her environment, a change takes place.

However, not all changes can be attributed to learning. Driscoll (2000) wrote,

> Some behavior changes, such as the acquisition of fine motor control, can be attributed to maturation and are therefore not considered learned. Other behavior changes, such as searching for food when hungry or becoming garrulous when drunk, are obviously explained on the basis of temporary states. These also do not imply learning. (p. 9)

Ormrod (2004) concurred: "Other changes, such as those caused by maturational changes in the body, organic damage, or temporary body states (e.g., fatigue, drugs), are not attributable to experiences and so do not reflect learning" (p. 3).

Despite their commonalities, the two definitions differ—most notably in terms of what changes when learning occurs. The first definition refers to a change in *behavior*, whereas the second refers to change in *mental representations* or *associations*. This difference reflects the divergent viewpoints of two psychological perspectives: behaviorism and cognitivism.

Two Major, Divergent Approaches to How People Learn

Unquestionably, scholars have more than two perspectives on how humans learn. Arguably, however, two of the most popular perspectives that have had the greatest impact on instructional design are behaviorism and cognitivism. Throughout much of the first half of the 20th century, behaviorism dominated how instructional designers approached their work; not until after World War II did cognitivism begin to supplant behaviorism by providing an alternative viewpoint. Both perspectives, along with their various branches, continue to influence instructional design activities in the 21st century. In this section, we provide a brief overview of each perspective.

Behaviorism

From a behaviorist perspective, *learning* is defined as a change in behavior— as a result of experience—that can be measured (Burton, Moore, & Magliaro,

2004; Driscoll, 2000; Ormrod, 2004). Woolfolk (2004) wrote, "Behaviorism attempts to explain learning by focusing on external events as the cause of changes in observable behaviors" (p. 198). Brandt and Perkins (2000) added,

> [Behaviorists believe] organisms learn through classical and operant conditioning. Complex behaviors are built up through "shaping," starting with parts of or rough approximations of the target behavior and providing reinforcement in ways that gradually shape the pattern of behavior in the intended direction. Much learning in natural circumstances occurs because the environment shapes behavior in this way. Not only direct rewards like food but also indirect "tokens" of reward shape behavior through learned associations." (pp. 161–162)

Classical and operant conditioning models provide explanations for how learning specifically takes place within the behaviorist perspective. The **classical conditioning model** (developed by Pavlov) describes a type of associative learning. Classical conditioning occurs when two stimuli are presented at approximately the same time. One of the stimuli is an *unconditioned* stimulus (i.e., it has been shown to elicit an unconditioned response). The other stimulus (a neutral stimulus), through its association with the unconditioned stimulus, begins to bring on a response as well—it becomes a conditioned stimulus that brings about a conditioned response. Table 3.1 shows an example of classical conditioning based on Pavlov's experiment with dogs (see Chapter 2 for a discussion of this experiment).

Skinner developed the **operant conditioning model.** He believed two types of learning existed: classical conditioning and operant conditioning. *Operant conditioning* results when a response is followed by a reinforcing stimulus. The response produced is voluntary. The individual (or other

TABLE 3.1

Classical Conditioning Analysis: Pavlov's Experiment on Dogs

Step	Stimulus	Response
1	Neutral (bell)	None
2	Neutral (bell) plus Unconditioned (meat)	Unconditioned (dog salivates)
3	Conditioned (bell)	Conditioned (dog salivates)

FIGURE 3.1

Differences Between Classical and Operant Conditioning

UCS = unconditioned stimulus; CS = conditioned stimulus; CR = conditioned response.

	Classical Conditioning	Operant Conditioning
Occurs when	Two stimuli (UCS and CS) are paired.	A response (R) is followed by a reinforcing stimulus (S_{Rf}).
Nature of response	Involuntary: elicited by a stimulus	Voluntary: emitted by the organism
Association required	CS $\longrightarrow$ CR	R $\longrightarrow$ S_{Rf}

Source: From *Human Learning* (p. 55), by J. E. Ormrod, 2004, Upper Saddle River, NJ: Merrill/Prentice Hall. Copyright 2004 by Merrill/Prentice Hall. Reprinted with permission.

organism) producing the response has complete control over whether the response occurs. According to Ormrod (2004), "Skinner's term operant reflects the fact that the organism voluntarily *operates* on, and thereby has some effect on, the environment" (p. 54). Figure 3.1 provides a comparison of operant and classical conditioning.

Ormrod (2004) wrote that, despite the variants of behaviorism, historically behaviorists have shared certain basic assumptions:

- Principles of learning should apply equally to different behaviors and to different species of animals;
- Learning processes can be studied most objectively when the focus of study is on stimuli and responses;
- Internal processes are largely excluded from scientific study;
- Learning involves a behavior change;
- Organisms are born as blank slates;
- Learning is largely the result of environmental events; and
- The most useful theories tend to be parsimonious ones. (pp. 30–31)

Role of the Learner. Skinner (1968) stated that a learner "does not passively absorb knowledge from the world around him but must play an active role" (p. 5). Therefore, learners learn by doing, experiencing, and engaging in repeated trial and error. Burton et al. (2004) wrote, "The emphasis is on the active responding of the learner—the learner must be engaged in the behavior in order to learn and to validate that learning has occurred" (p. 9).

Cognitivism

From a cognitivist perspective, learning is a change in mental representations and associations brought about by experiences. Greeno, Collins, and Resnick (1996) wrote that cognitivists view learning as "transforming significant understanding we already have, rather than simple acquisitions written on blank slates" (p. 18). This perspective follows the standard cognitivist view of learning in which the main assumption is that mental processes exist and can be studied scientifically. Brandt and Perkins (2000) noted that early research on cognitivism "focused primarily on information processing, especially pattern recognition, memory, and problem solving. The mind was considered a rule-governed computational device. A scientist's task was to identify the specific rules by which the mind manipulates symbols to arrive at results" (p. 165). This view reflects a common metaphor many cognitivists use: The mind works in the same way as a computer. Therefore, learning takes place by applying set-in-place algorithms. Brandt and Perkins went on to write, "Over time, cognitive scientists gradually expanded their attention to include a remarkable array of human activities: the formation of judgments, decision making, creativity, critical thinking, and even the emotions" (p. 165).

Role of the Learner. Cognitivists believe that learners are not passively influenced by environmental events but are instead active participants in their cognition (Ashcraft, 2002). As individuals engage in the learning

ID INSIGHT

What Is Learned?

The behavioral and cognitive perspectives differ in their underlying assumptions about what is learned. From the cognitive perspective, knowledge is learned. The increase in knowledge makes changes in behavior possible. According to the behavioral perspective, the new behaviors themselves are learned (Shuell, 1986).

process, they "actively choose, practice, pay attention, ignore, reflect, and make many other decisions as they pursue goals" (Woolfolk, 2004, p. 236).

A Third Approach: Constructivism

In addition to the two major approaches to how people learn, a relatively new approach, called *constructivism*, has emerged since the 1970s and has had a tremendous impact on learning. Constructivism has its roots in both psychology and philosophy. A variant of cognitivism, constructivism has grown out of the work of individuals such as Vygotsky, Piaget, Dewey, and Bruner, and in more recent times it has been influenced by researchers such as Duffy, Cunningham, and Jonassen. Constructivism goes beyond the traditional view of cognitivism that "people represent information in their minds as single or aggregated sets of symbols, and that cognitive activity consists of operating on these symbols by applying to them learned plans, or algorithms" (Winn, 2004, p. 79). Marzano (2000b) wrote, "Constructivism refers to the general principle that learners use their prior knowledge to construct a personally meaningful understanding of new content that is the focus of learning" (p. 81). Brooks and Brooks (1993) described the underlying principle of constructivism in more detail:

> Each of us makes sense of our world by synthesizing new experiences into what we have previously come to understand. Often, we encounter an object, an idea, a relationship, or a phenomenon that doesn't quite make sense to us. When confronted with such initially discrepant data or perceptions, we either interpret what we see to conform to our present set of rules for explaining and ordering our work, or we generate a new set of rules that better accounts for what we perceive to be occurring. Either way, our perceptions and rules are constantly engaged in a grand dance that shapes our understandings. (p. 4)

Driscoll (2000) added that constructivism "rests on the assumption that knowledge is constructed by learners as they attempt to make sense of their experiences. Learners, therefore, are not empty vessels waiting to be filled, but rather active organisms seeking meaning" (p. 376). Driscoll summarized the conditions necessary for learning in a constructivist environment:

- Embed learning in complex, realistic, and relevant environments;
- Provide for social negotiation as an integral part of learning;

- Support multiple perspectives and the use of multiple modes of representation;
- Encourage ownership in learning; and
- Nurture self-awareness of the knowledge construction process. (pp. 382–383)

Use of All Three Approaches

All three approaches provide useful perspectives on how people learn. Strictly following only one approach is generally not advisable when you are carrying out instructional design activities because every instructional context is different and brings with it different variables that need to be accounted for (e.g., the context, the learners, and the type of learning that needs to occur). No single approach can completely account for all these variables. For successful instructional design to occur, instructional designers must be able to borrow from the different approaches to develop instructional interventions that take into consideration all these variables.

Types of Learning

As mentioned, one of the variables that are part of every instructional context is the type of learning that needs to take place. Instructional designers must be able to identify different types of learning in order to design efficient and effective instructional interventions. Probably the most well-known and well-used distinction made among types of learning involves learning domains. Three commonly used learning domains refer to specific types of learning: cognitive, affective, and psychomotor. The major idea behind the learning domains is that learning can be organized and measured along a continuum from low-level to higher level knowledge, attitudes, or skills.

Benjamin Bloom (1913–1999) and colleagues are typically credited with developing, in the mid-20th century, the original idea and the work behind the three learning domains (Eisner, 2000). The result of Bloom's work originated out of his efforts to improve university examinations (Eisner 2000; Ormrod, 2004). The result of this work was three taxonomies of educational objectives corresponding to three learning domains. In more recent years, other researchers (e.g., Anderson & Krathwohl, 2001; Cangelosi, 1990;

Marzano, 2000a) have published revisions to Bloom's original work. Despite such revisions, the major premise behind Bloom's original work remains intact.

The learning domains are especially useful if you consider them when you are developing learning objectives for instruction. Learning objectives are descriptions of what an individual should know or be able to do once he or she has completed an instructional intervention. Besides being used to develop learning objectives, the domains can be helpful when you plan assessments (these ideas are covered in more detail in Chapters 8 and 11).

Cognitive Domain

The cognitive domain is typically referred to as *Bloom's taxonomy of the cognitive domain*. This taxonomy includes six levels: knowledge, comprehension, application, analysis, synthesis, and evaluation (Bloom, Engelhart, Frost, Hill, & Krathwohl, 1956; Table 3.2). These levels are commonly considered a *hierarchy*—each level building on those below. This conception is not entirely accurate for every subject or discipline (Seddon, 1978), and some subjects or disciplines—like mathematics—do not fit this structure extremely well (Gronlund, 2000). At the bottom level of the domain (knowledge), individuals are able to remember basic information without necessarily

TABLE 3.2

Bloom, Engelhart, Frost, Hill, and Krathwohl's (1956) Cognitive Domain

Term	Definition
Evaluation	Ability to judge the value or worth of material for a given purpose
Synthesis	Ability to create something new from various parts
Analysis	Ability to break down material into its various components in order to understand the organizational structure of the material
Application	Ability to apply learned material in new and concrete contexts
Comprehension	Understanding of new material
Knowledge	Remembering previously learned material

TABLE 3.3

Krathwohl, Bloom, and Masia's (1964) Affective Domain

Term	Definition
Characterizing value	Acting openly and consistently with a new value; internalizing a new value
Organizing	Integrating a new value into a general set of values; giving the value some ranking among an individual's general priorities
Valuing	Exhibiting some explicit involvement or commitment; showing interest or motivation
Responding	Actively participating; exhibiting a new behavior as a result of experience
Receiving	Paying attention to something in the environment

understanding, using, or manipulating it. With evaluation, the highest level, individuals are capable of making judgments about complex ideas, materials, and processes as they are applied in various contexts.

Affective Domain

The affective domain deals with emotional responses. The levels in this domain range from least committed to most committed (Krathwohl, Bloom, & Masia, 1964). They are receiving, responding, valuing, organizing, and characterizing value (Table 3.3). At the basic level of this domain (receiving), an individual is able to pay attention to a certain idea (e.g., listening to music at a concert) but does not show any concerted interest. With characterizing value, the highest level, an individual can adopt a new idea or value and act consistently with it (e.g., openly demonstrate an appreciation for classical music).

Psychomotor Domain

The psychomotor domain involves physical abilities and skills. Several taxonomies (Cangelosi, 1990; Harrow, 1972; Simpson, 1972) depict this domain; they typically describe levels that move from basic physical actions to

TABLE 3.4

Simpson's (1972) Psychomotor Domain

Term	Definition
Perception	Ability to recognize sensory cues to guide physical activity
Set	Willingness to act; ability to show knowledge and awareness of the behaviors needed to perform a skill
Guided response	Ability to perform a complex skill: beginning stage
Mechanism	Ability to perform a complex skill: intermediate stage
Complex overt response	Ability to perform a complex skill correctly and without hesitation: advanced stage
Adaptation	Ability to modify and adjust a skill in a new context
Origination	Ability to create something original or to modify an existing skill with a new skill

more skilled and creative movements. Simpson (1972) outlined a domain with seven levels: perception, set, guided response, mechanism, complex overt response, adaptation, and origination (Table 3.4). Cangelosi (1990) stated that one useful way to look at the psychomotor domain is as either voluntary muscle capabilities (e.g., flexibility, agility, or speed) or the ability to perform a specific skill (e.g., tie shoes).

ID INSIGHT

Learning Domains in Action: A Few More Words on Learning Objectives

Although how the learning domains can be used is covered in more detail in Chapter 7, including an example in this chapter seems

(continued)

appropriate. As mentioned, the domains are typically used to describe learning objectives. One approach to developing learning objectives that instructional designers often use was created by Robert Mager. According to Mager (1962), a **learning objective** is simply "a description of a pattern of behavior (performance) we want the learner to be able to demonstrate" (p. x). Mager recommended using three components when you are writing learning objectives:

1. *Action.* Identify the action the learner will be taking when he or she has achieved the objective.
2. *Condition.* Describe the relevant conditions under which the learner will be acting.
3. *Criterion.* Specify how well the learner must perform the action.

An example of a learning objective using Mager's three recommended criteria is as follows:

Given the proper tools [condition], the learner will be able to change a flat tire [action] in 30 minutes or less [criterion].

SUMMARY

Successful instructional designers have a solid understanding of how people learn. They are able to understand the basics of various psychological perspectives that describe different approaches to how people learn. This ability allows them to use this knowledge as they help create instructional interventions that meet their clients' goals.

As described in this chapter, behaviorism and cognitivism (and their various branches) are two major psychological perspectives that have dominated how learning has been viewed throughout the 20th century and into the 21st century. These two divergent perspectives provide unique approaches to how learning takes place. According to behaviorists, learning is due to a change in behavior as a result of experience, whereas cognitivists stresses that learning is a change in mental representations and associations resulting from experience (Ormrod, 2004). Neither approach should be used exclusively.

CONNECTING PROCESS TO PRACTICE

1. You have been asked to write a brief outline of the differences between behaviorism and cognitivism. Create a one-page outline that highlights the major differences.

2. Write a short briefing for the general public that compares and contrasts the behaviorist and cognitivist perspectives on learning.

3. Your client mentions to you that he has been hearing a great deal about constructivism, but he is not sure exactly what it is. What do you tell him?

4. How would you differentiate among the types of learning? Discuss how you would describe these differences to your client.

5. Take a look at instruction you have participated in recently. What approach do you believe was taken in the development of the instruction? What examples can you provide that indicate the approach taken?

RECOMMENDED READINGS

Byrnes, J. P. (2001). *Cognitive development and learning in instructional contexts.* Boston: Allyn & Bacon.

Gagne, E. D., Yekovich, C. W., & Yekovich, F. R. (1985). *The cognitive psychology of school learning* (2nd ed.). New York: Harper Collins.

Gagne, R. M. (1985). *The conditions of learning and theory of instruction* (4th ed.). New York: Holt, Rinehart & Winston.

Gustafsson, J.-E., & Undheim, J. O. (1996). Individual differences in cognitive functioning. In D. Berliner & R. Calfee (Eds.), *Handbook of educational psychology* (pp. 186–242). New York: Macmillan.

REFERENCES

Anderson, L. M., & Krathwohl, D. R. (Eds.). (2001). *A taxonomy for learning, teaching, and assessing: A revision of Bloom's taxonomy of educational objectives.* New York: Longman.

Ashcraft, M. H. (2002). *Cognition* (3rd ed.). Upper Saddle River, NJ: Prentice Hall.

Bloom, B. S., Engelhart, M. D., Frost, E. J., Hill, W. H., & Krathwohl, D. R. (1956). *Taxonomy of educational objectives. Handbook I: Cognitive domain*. New York: McKay.

Brandt, R. S., & Perkins, D. N. (2000). The evolving science of learning. In R. S. Brandt (Ed.), *Education in a new era* (pp. 159–183). Alexandria, VA: Association for Supervision and Curriculum Development.

Brooks, J. G., & Brooks, M. G. (1993). *In search of understanding: The case for constructivist classrooms*. Alexandria, VA: Association for Supervision and Curriculum Development.

Burton, J. K., Moore, D. M., & Magliaro, S. G. (2004). Behaviorism and instructional technology. In D. Jonassen (Ed.), *Handbook of research on educational communications and technology* (pp. 3–36). Mahwah, NJ: Erlbaum.

Cangelosi, J. (1990). *Designing tests for student achievement*. New York: Longman.

Driscoll, M. P. (2000). *Psychology of learning for instruction* (2nd ed.). Boston: Allyn & Bacon.

Eisner, E. W. (2000). Benjamin Bloom: 1913–99. *Prospects, 30*(3). Retrieved from http://www.ibe.unesco.org/International/Publications/Thinkers/thinhome.htm

Greeno, J. G., Collins, A. M., & Resnick, L. B. (1996). Cognition and learning. In D. Berliner & R. Calfee (Eds.), *Handbook of educational psychology* (pp. 15–46). New York: Macmillan.

Gronlund, N. E. (2000). *How to write and use instructional objectives* (6th ed.). Upper Saddle River, NJ: Merrill/Prentice Hall.

Harrow, A. J. (1972). *A taxonomy of the psychomotor domain: A guide for developing behavior objectives*. New York: McKay.

Hill, W. F. (2002). *Learning: A survey of psychological interpretations* (7th ed.). Boston: Allyn & Bacon.

Krathwohl, D. R., Bloom, B. S., & Masia, B. B. (1964). *Taxonomy of educational objectives. Handbook II: Affective domain*. New York: McKay.

Mager, R. (1962). *Preparing instructional objectives*. Palo Alto, CA: Fearon.

Marzano, R. J. (2000a). *Designing a new taxonomy of educational objectives*. Thousand Oaks, CA: Corwin Press.

Marzano, R. J. (2000b). The 20th century advances in instruction. In R. S. Brandt (Ed.), *Education in a new era* (pp. 67–95). Alexandria, VA: Association for Supervision and Curriculum Development.

Ormrod, J. E. (2004). *Human learning* (4th ed.). Upper Saddle River, NJ: Merrill/Prentice Hall.

Seddon, G. M. (1978). The properties of Bloom's taxonomy of educational objectives for the cognitive domain. *Review of Educational Research, 48,* 303–323.

Shuell, T. J. (1986). Cognitive conceptions of learning. *Review of Educational Research, 56,* 411–436.

Simpson, E. (1972). *The classification of educational objectives in the psychomotor domain: The psychomotor domain* (Vol. 3). Washington, DC: Gryphon House.

Skinner, B. F. (1968). *The technology of teaching.* New York: Appleton-Century-Crofts.

Winn, W. (2004). Cognitive perspectives in psychology. In D. Jonassen (Ed.), *Handbook of research on educational communications and technology* (pp. 79–112). Mahwah, NJ: Erlbaum.

Woolfolk, A. (2004). *Educational psychology* (9th ed.). Boston: Allyn & Bacon.

Chapter 4

MANAGING INSTRUCTIONAL MEDIA PRODUCTION

Key Terms

Client *(page 66)*

CPM charts *(page 70)*

Drop-dead dates
(page 68)

Expert review *(page 79)*

Gantt charts *(page 70)*

Milestones *(page 68)*

Navigation layout
(page 74)

Peer review *(page 79)*

PERT charts *(page 70)*

Postproduction *(page 62)*

Preproduction *(page 62)*

Production calendar
(page 67)

Prototyping *(page 74)*

Storyboards *(page 68)*

Style guides *(page 71)*

My organization's structure for instructional design [ID] project management is identifying people who specialize in specific pieces of instructional design. For example, we have key people who specialize in training package development, media production, and project management. We each have several roles. In addition to our usual roles, we have instructional design roles that include package developers, media-production specialists, and video-production specialists. For all ID projects, we do have an established process. We all use a set of forms and attend a TRG (training review group). A TRG is a "high-level" examination of a training product to identify gaps or weaknesses before it is released to the customer. The TRG also serves as a method to ensure that the necessary elements are included, such as evaluation measures, a tracking component, and identification of long-term ownership.

For each TRG, the following steps are taken:

1. The product developer follows the process map, completing appropriate forms.
2. The developer selects four to five peers for the review group. (It is helpful if members have some experience or previous knowledge of the topic, the audience, or a similar product.)
3. The completed forms, and any other helpful documents, are given to the group.
4. A review meeting is scheduled, usually for 1 hour.
5. Reviews are held at two strategic points in the process. The outcome of each review is a decision either to continue or to revise before proceeding. Reviewers may be the same for both TRGs or different, depending on the product.

—Jona Titus, Senior Training Specialist,
Intel Corporation, Hillsboro, OR

Guiding Questions

- What are the phases of the production process?
- What are the production team members' roles and responsibilities?
- How does the instructional designer manage a production project?
- What are recommended methods of minimizing and resolving conflict among production team members?
- How does the instructional designer evaluate an instructional media product?

Chapter Overview

Instructional media production is the process of bringing to life the instructional designer's plans and specifications. Once an instructional designer or design team conducts the necessary analyses, develops the goals and objectives, specifies the activities, and determines the appropriate evaluation procedures, some person or group must create the media that will provide the instruction or instructional support. These media can take many forms. They can be print based (e.g., worksheets, textbooks), audiovisual (e.g., films, videos, slide presentations, sound recordings), interactive (e.g., software), or any combination of the three.

In some work environments, the instructional designer is separate from the production team; however, just as often he or she is an active participant in the production process. Often the instructional designer for an organization is also in charge of the team that produces and delivers the instruction. Depending on the setting, the instructional designer may also take on a number of media-production roles.

Regardless of whether you as an instructional designer have specific production responsibilities, you should have some idea of how media are produced in order to have appropriate expectations about the production team's capabilities and the quality of the finished instructional products. Therefore, as a novice instructional designer, you should become familiar with instructional media–production processes.

In this chapter, we focus on the practical aspects of managing and working with a production team. Topics in this chapter include the specific functions of media-production team members, methods of organizing a project, methods of managing the group and communicating, and methods of evaluating the finished product.

The Production Process

Any media-production project consists of essentially three phases: preproduction, production, and postproduction. **Preproduction** is the planning phase, production involves design and development, and **postproduction** includes distribution, integration, and product archival.

In the preproduction phase of a media project, a clear description of what the product will be when it is finished is developed. Also, all the resources necessary to realize the project are determined and a time frame for completing the various production tasks is worked out. With instructional media, instructional designers provide the description of what the product will be through needs, task, learner, and goal analyses and the specification of activities and evaluation strategies. The production team must then determine what resources are available to realize the vision of the instructional design (this process is sometimes called *planning and costing*) and how best to deploy these resources during a specified period.

In the production phase, the final project design is developed and all the necessary components for its completion are created and integrated. Depending on the type of media being produced, these components may include the creation of specific graphic elements, typeset text, sound tracks, video footage, or computer software.

In the postproduction phase, the finished product is made ready for distribution to the individuals who will use it. Often during postproduction the product is also archived so that future production teams have access to the product and its components.

Although each phase of the production process can be viewed separately, no hard-and-fast rules exist for defining the components of each phase. Individual production teams will have their own ideas about what constitutes preproduction, production, and postproduction. However, most media producers will agree that preproduction is the time when the team looks at what needs to be accomplished and decides how to make it happen, production is when plans are put into action and the final product is completed, and postproduction is when the product is formatted for distribution.

Organization of a Production Team

A production team takes the raw material resources available and uses them to create a finished product. Good production teams comprise people with a variety of skills and talents. Teams may be large and highly specialized, or small, with each member assuming a broad range of responsibilities. Regardless of the number of individuals involved, any production team has three essential components: managers, directors, and artists.

Managers are the organizers of the production. They take responsibility for accomplishing tasks within the constraints of the resources available. *Directors* are the guiding force that suggests how the resources available will be used to create the finished product. Directors establish the artistic guidelines and style for the product. *Artists* are the human component of the resources available. They are the individuals who apply their creative skills to the product (during production, actors, who by definition fall within the artist category, are referred to separately as *talent*).

PROFESSIONALS IN PRACTICE

Our three-person online learning team works independently from the other developers. Since the team is small, we are usually each managing a project at any given moment, in addition to working as media-production specialists (we call them *multimedia developers*) for other projects, depending on what skill is needed. We have a loose protocol for online learning:

1. Goal analysis
2. Task analysis
3. Rapid prototyping (storyboarding)
4. SME [subject matter expert] review of storyboards
5. Revision
6. Multimedia development
7. SME review of multimedia product
8. User testing (usually someone from another department)
9. Revision
10. Release

—Erik Novak,
Distance Learning Course Developer,
Interactive Intelligence, Inc.,
Indianapolis, IN

The roles and responsibilities of the members of any production team depend on the type of product being created. For example, a team responsible for producing computer-based multimedia might include the following:

Production Manager: The person responsible for the organization and timing of the production. The production manager ensures that everyone knows what he or she should be doing and when specific tasks need to be accomplished. The production manager may also be called on to resolve conflict within the team.

Subject Matter Expert (SME): An individual who is a specialist in and an authority on the content area of the product (e.g., an astronomer helping with a product that teaches the basics of stellar cartography).

Writer: The team member responsible for generating text, scripts, and documentation.

Art Director: The person responsible for the "look and feel" of the product. He or she specifies such things as color schemes, artwork, and typefaces. The art director oversees the efforts of the graphic artists.

Graphic Artist: An individual responsible for creating the graphic elements specified by the art director.

Sound Designer: The member responsible for designing and producing audio elements.

Video Director: The person responsible for gathering and creating video elements.

Video Editor: The individual responsible for preparing video elements specified by the video director.

Interface Designer: The team member responsible for specifying the human–computer interactions of the product. The interface designer oversees the programmers' efforts.

Programmer: The person responsible for making a working version of the software.

Talent: The actors whose bodies, faces, and voices interpret the writer's scripts.

In many cases, a production team member takes on multiple roles. The production manager might take on direction or artistic responsibilities; the interface designer might also be the artistic director as well as the programmer. Any combination of roles is possible. However, for a production to run smoothly, the team must agree on who has final responsibility (and authority) for management, for each aspect of direction, and for the production of each necessary element.

PROFESSIONALS IN PRACTICE

Our team comprises a director, a consultant, two instructional designers, a web developer, a media-production specialist, and a graphic artist. The projects themselves are typically managed by the instructional designer who is working on the course, but they are all handled differently.

—*Kara Andrew,*
Instructional Designer,
Distance Education, California State University, Fullerton

Clients and Priorities

As part of a production team, you have a responsibility to your team-mates. In some ways, you are one another's clients because your team is counting on you for a certain facet of production. Depending on how you define the word *client* in the context of creating instruction, you may also consider the target audience (the learners) as clients for your work. By the same token, you may consider the instructor or organization that plans to implement your design as a client. If you are working on a production project as part of a course you are taking, you may want to identify the person who will evaluate the project for a grade as a client.

Once you have a list of the clients involved, you may want to arrange the list in order of priority. Such a list can help when design and implementation decisions must be made.

Perhaps the most important role in any production project is that of the **client.** The client is typically the person for whom the project is being created. Anyone with whom the producer or production team has entered into an agreement to create a specific product is a client. In a large business organization, the instructional media–production unit may view other units (i.e., customer service or human resources) as clients. In a school setting, faculty members or departments may be considered the instructional media specialist's clients. If you are participating in a course on instructional design, the course instructor might be considered the client for any instructional media projects assigned to you. No matter who the client is specifically, in general he or she is the person who has requested the product, and the client's satisfaction is in large part a measure of the success of the project.

Production Management

Production management includes the establishment and execution of the tasks and procedures that facilitate the completion of a project within a set of specified parameters. The parameters include a time frame and a given set of available resources (including access to tools, skills of production team

ID INSIGHT

The Media-Production Triangle

The media-production triangle represents the interplay among time, money, and quality. The ideal is always to produce a high-quality product quickly and inexpensively. However, one adage among experienced media producers is that at any one time you can choose only two of three options: fast, cheap, or good. That is, you are always faced with three less-than-ideal choices. A product can be created quickly and well, but it will not be cheap; it can be created inexpensively and well, but it will take time; or it can be created quickly and inexpensively, but it will not be good.

members, and money). Management also includes maintaining communication among the participants and stakeholders of a project. Establishing and maintaining communication reduces the risk of misunderstandings and increases the potential for successfully completing a project. The goal of any good production manager is to complete a project that is of the highest quality "on time and under budget." This task is not easy. Careful planning, organization, and supervision are necessary to keep a production project on task.

Production Calendar

Given a finite amount of time to complete a production project, the production team may be able to create a high-quality product without planning what will be accomplished at various points between the beginning and the end of the project—but doing so is *highly unlikely*.

One of the critically important aspects of production management is time management. Even a production "team" comprising a single individual benefits from developing early on a time line that anticipates the completion of various tasks. When a production is the responsibility of more than one person, a time line is also helpful as a means of communication among team members; anyone may refer to it to see what and when specific tasks need to be completed. Most production teams establish a **production calendar** during preproduction. The production calendar establishes when specific tasks are to be completed and often includes notes on who is specifically responsible for completing each task. Figure 4.1 is an example of 1 month from the

FIGURE 4.1

Sample Production Calendar
Shown is 1 month from a production calendar for a graduate-level instructional media–production project.

▓ Progress Meeting	■ Production Plan	▓ Storyboards	■ Development	▓ ALPHA	▓ BETA	▓ Final Product

Sunday	Monday	Tuesday	Wednesday	Thursday	Friday	Saturday
1	2	3	4	5	6	7 Production
8 Production Calendar	9 ...	10 ... • Meeting after EDEL 515 –	11 ...	12 ...	13 ...	14
15 Storyboards	16	17 • Meeting after EDEL 515 –	18	19	20 • Meeting with • Production	21
22 Storyboards	23	24 • Meeting after EDEL 515 –	25	26 ...	27 ... • Meeting Paul and • Storyboards	28
29 Development	1	2 • Meeting after EDEL 515 –	3	4	5 • Meeting with Abbie Location	6

Source: Designed and produced by Paul Hunt and Tony Macias. Reprinted with permission.

production calendar created for a student project in an advanced instructional media–production course.

The production calendar comprises a combination of milestones and drop-dead dates. **Milestones** are the dates when important activities are to be accomplished; these activities include finalization of the style guidelines, completion of **storyboards** or prototypes, production team meetings, and meetings with the client. **Drop-dead dates** are when specific tasks must be completed (or abandoned if they are not complete); such tasks include completion of filming, final artwork, and programming, and submission of the completed product to the client (Table 4.1).

Many production plans include a list of critically important dates, along with a description of who is responsible for approving design elements prior to production. The person responsible for approving an element

TABLE 4.1

Typical Production Milestone (boldface) and Drop-dead Tasks for a Multimedia Project

Production Stage	Task
Preproduction	Review project parameters. Determine budget and resources (cost and plan). Establish team assignments. **Create production calendar.**
Production	Complete text components. Establish style manual or guide for product elements. Complete initial prototype (a "rough draft" that outlines the final form of the product). Get client feedback and approval for initial prototype. Complete graphic elements. Produce video elements. Produce audio elements. Complete alpha version (a functional prototype). Get client feedback and approval for alpha version. Complete beta version (a functional prototype ready to be tested with end users). **Submit finished product to client.**
Postproduction	Distribute or deploy product. Archive product and project elements. **Review production process with team (what worked, what needs improvement).**

needs to be informed that once he or she signs off on a design, that element is going into production as is (this warning may also be given to the instructional designer, the SME, and any other production team member who is responsible for creating preproduction or production specifications). Having everyone agree to these "milestone" dates in advance is highly recommended.

Establishing milestone dates goes hand in hand with determining *dependencies*. In any production situation, some activities will depend completely on completing other activities. For example, a video production with live actors in period costumes cannot be shot until the costumes have been obtained or created and fit to each actor. Shooting the video depends on completion of the costumes by the shooting date. You must determine which production activities depend on each other before you can prepare a reasonable production calendar.

Often, the first item placed on a production calendar is the deadline date for the finished product, because this date is usually the one date agreed on before even preproduction begins. A common, and highly recommended, practice is to begin with the finished-project deadline date and work backward to establish the other deadlines and milestones that compose the entire production cycle.

When a Simple Calendar Is Not Sufficient: Gantt, PERT, and CPM Charts. For small projects in which a single piece of instructional media is produced, a simple production calendar is usually more than sufficient. For large or complex projects, or when the same production team handles multiple projects simultaneously, more specialized methods of keeping track of time and resources may be necessary. Three of the most popular project management charting techniques are Gantt, PERT, and CPM.

Gantt charts, named for project management expert Henry Laurence Gantt (1861–1919), are used to show the scheduled and actual progress of various elements of a project. On the vertical axis is a list of all the tasks to be performed. The horizontal axis lists the estimated task duration, the skill level necessary to complete the task, and the individual assigned to the task.

PERT charts and **CPM charts** visually display task, dependency, and duration information. PERT (program evaluation and review technique) and CPM (critical path method) charts begin with a horizontal line that indicates the first task in the project, the duration of the task, and the number of people assigned to complete it. Successive horizontal lines drawn below the first supply the same information for each successive task, illustrating where tasks may overlap on the time line.

When you are managing large, complex production projects or multiple projects that use the same team members, Gantt, PERT, or CPM charts can prove to be valuable tools. Microsoft Project software is considered the industry standard for producing and maintaining these management tools, providing a vast array of options and simplifying a number of repetitive setup tasks. However, we caution against using such specialized software for smaller projects because the time required to master the software alone may prove counterproductive.

Style Guides

Creating and agreeing on a few **style guides** that all members use as they contribute to the project is highly recommended. Style guides help to unify the project, providing standards for the visual look, feel, and functionality of the product. We recommend starting by deciding what style you will use for documentation. A team member may take on the role of documentation editor. The editor makes all the final decisions on how the documentation looks.

Depending on the project and the roles assigned to team members, you may want to establish technical guidelines as well—for example, "The colors used in all graphics are to be reduced to a Web-safe palette," "The operating platform for the finished product is Windows 2000," or "All sound files are to be 16-bit stereo." Doing so may seem overly prescriptive, but agreeing and adhering to a set of technical guidelines in the preproduction phase can save everyone a great deal of trouble during production.

As the project progresses, a style manual should be created for all media that will be incorporated into the final product. A style manual often contains specific details about the following:

- *Fonts* (typefaces) *and font sizes* (including specific guidelines for headings, the body text, captions, etc.).
- *Color scheme* (the background color, font colors, palettes, etc.).
- *Graphics* (the type of graphic: cartoon, iconographic, photorealistic, etc.). In the case of computer-based instructional media, graphics may (and probably should) also include specifications for the pixel depth and resolution of images.
- *Sound* (bit depth, stereo or mono, MIDI [musical instrument digital interface] or analog recording, etc.).

Storyboards

Virtually all film, video, and animation projects are, in the earliest stages of production, translated from a script to a *storyboard*. The storyboard visually depicts the script. Traditionally, a storyboard is a big board on which rough sketches are posted that visually "tell the story." The entire project can then be seen as a series of pictures, which allows everyone working on the project to share a single vision of what the product should look like in its final form (Figure 4.2).

FIGURE 4.2

Examples of Storyboards

Shown are excerpts of the storyboards for a graduate-level instructional media–production project.

STORYBOARD

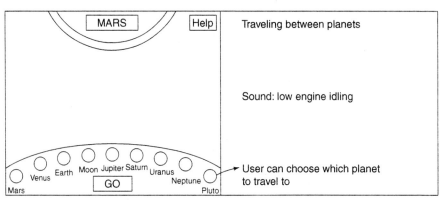

Travel animation

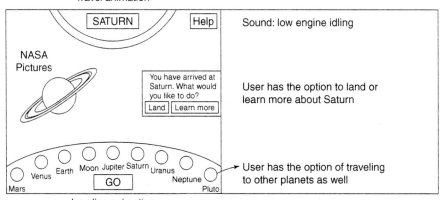

Landing animation

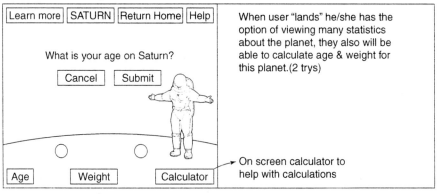

STORYBOARD

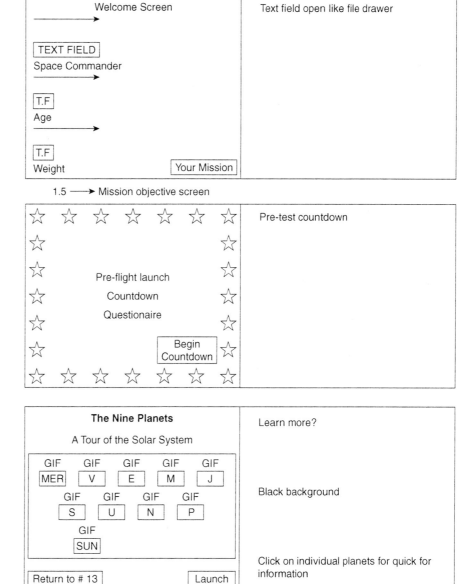

Source: Designed and produced by Paul Hunt and Tony Macias. Reprinted with permission.

Some wonderful examples of storyboards are available as "extras" on the DVD versions of films and animated features. The DVD of Disney–Pixar's animated feature *Monsters, Inc.* (Carrigan, 2002) includes a brief feature that shows the process of taking an idea from script to storyboard to finished animation. The DVD of *The Beatles' Yellow Submarine* (King Features & Dunning, 1968) allows you to watch the finished animation and the original storyboard simultaneously on a split screen.

Computer-based multimedia projects are often translated into a storyboard early in the production process as well. The storyboard of a multimedia project gives a screen-by-screen view of how the finished product should look. Multimedia storyboards are often accompanied by a **navigation layout.** A navigation layout is a visual display of the possible choices that can be taken in navigating the multimedia presentation; this layout is most often accomplished by creating a flowchart depicting each screen and showing how each screen connects to the other screens (Figure 4.3).

Prototyping

Prototyping is a common production method (used for automobiles, architecture, animation, and software development), and myriad examples of successful applications of this method can be found. *Rapid prototyping* is a production strategy that requires starting with a sketchy idea that evolves through multiple prototypes to arrive at a finished piece. Rapid prototyping requires the evaluation and revision of each prototype as part of the production process (rapid prototyping as an instructional design strategy is described in Chapter 1). Each successive prototype is meant to increase in *fidelity* (accuracy in its presentation of the product everyone has in mind) until a final product is achieved.

Alessi and Trollip (2001) suggested, "All intermediate components of the project should be tested, evaluated, and, if necessary, revised before they are incorporated into the final program" (p. 410). Thus, for multimedia projects, each media element should be treated as a discrete product that should be developed through a series of prototypes until it is considered ready to be incorporated into the larger production project.

A production team may want to decide how many prototypes to develop as part of the production plan and whether creating and testing prototypes of specific media elements will be necessary. Keep in mind that storyboards should be considered early prototypes and treated as such.

FIGURE 4.3

Example of a Navigation Layout

This navigation plan is for a graduate-level instructional media-production project—creating instructional software on the solar system—developed for elementary students.

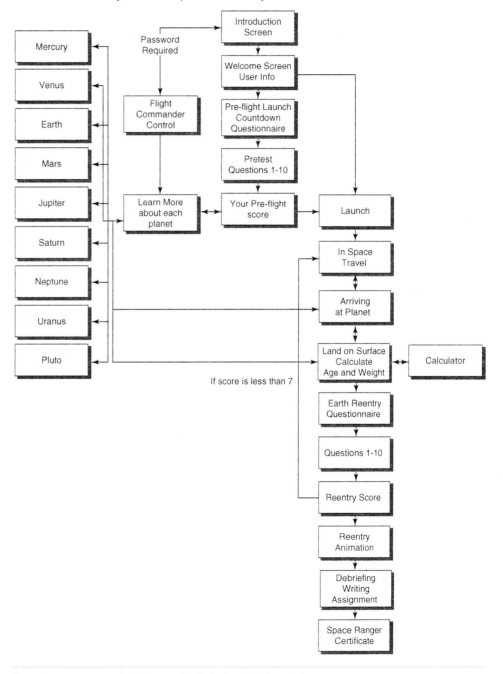

Source: Designed and produced by Paul Hunt and Tony Macias. Reprinted with permission.

PROFESSIONALS IN PRACTICE

When I create instructional software, I make a list of the functions that are specified for the product that I have never before attempted. I then make a small mock-up piece of software that employs only that function to test whether it will meet the design specifications. I think of this as a mini prototype for one portion of the finished product. For example, I was once asked to author a program in Macromedia Director that would allow students taking a test to save their answers onto a floppy disk: something I had never attempted. The final product had to be cross-platform, so this function had to work equally well in Macintosh and Windows environments. I began by creating this function alone (one platform at a time) and testing it to be sure it was stable. Incorporating the function into the final product was then largely a matter of cutting and pasting.

—Abbie Brown

Communication and Conflict Resolution

One of the most important steps any team can take to keep production moving in a positive direction is to establish reliable channels of communication and healthy communication habits. All team members should know what is expected of them. Everyone should also have a reliable means of voicing and dealing with problems as they arise. Likewise, keeping good and reliable channels of communication open with the client is critically important to the success of a project. Four key communication strategies that can help are respect, regular consultation, specificity, and paper trail maintenance (Brown, Green, & Zatz, 2001):

Respect: Individuals must realize that each team member brings to the project a set of unique skills and talents as well as a unique perspective. The health of any project depends on each team member's recognizing the value of each other team member's contributions by listening to everyone and accepting critical comments in the spirit in which they are intended.

Regular Consultation: Regular meetings, telephone conversations, and correspondence are an important part of the production process. Such consultation allows team members and the client to share ideas, provide clarifications, and ensure that the product is being designed to match the shared vision.

Specificity: Everyone involved in the production process should strive to be as specific as possible. For example, the term *a clever animation* does not adequately describe how a finished animation should look (one person's "clever" is another's "trite"). Specific examples should be clarified and shown as often as possible.

Paper Trail Maintenance: During preproduction and in the early stages of production, everyone should share layouts, sketches, and storyboards as much as possible to establish a shared vision of the finished product. During the later stages of production, "sign-off" dates should be established. These dates are when the production manager, team members, or the client must sign an authorization that the product component is acceptable for incorporation into the final product. Sign-off dates are established for the alpha and beta prototypes when the client authorizes each prototype.

The importance of good communication among team members cannot be overstated. Teams take a while to form into effective working groups, and much of why teams operate effectively is still a mystery. However, *effective* teams always have effective communication strategies in place.

ID INSIGHT

Watch Out for Cowboys

One classic problem many instructional design teams face is sometimes referred to as *cowboy* (or *hero* or *superhero*) *syndrome*. A *cowboy* is someone who is usually highly competent but does not work well with others. The cowboy tends to make statements such as "I'll take care of that—no one else on the team needs to worry about it." The cowboy does not take direction well and does not share what he or she is doing until it is completed, often at the last minute, when little or no time is available for changes. Many times, cowboys are people who have previously been rewarded for their expertise and their ability to work independently. This syndrome is common among specialists who often have no one else around who understands what they do. You should recognize cowboys' good intentions; they have probably spent a good deal of their professional lives "riding in to save the day." However, a team that is functioning well has no room for cowboys or superheroes. The old saw, "There is no *I* in *team,*" is true. The trick is to develop the proper balance between independently dealing with tasks and collaborating with team members.

ID INSIGHT

Tips for Successful Teamwork

In the introduction to the chapter "Collaborative Problem Solving" in the text *Instructional Design Theories and Models: A New Paradigm of Instructional Theory,* Vol. II, Laurie Miller Nelson (1999) wrote,

> Often in our daily lives we find ourselves working in small groups, whether it be in the context of a work project, a civic group, a classroom, or a family. Group problem solving is one of the most common and natural situations in which we accomplish the work of society. (p. 244)

Working in teams is commonplace, and most instructional designers operate as members of various teams during any given week. We are members of departments, faculties, work groups, classes, and so forth, and we take on specific roles within these groups to accomplish tasks important to us as individuals and to the group as a whole.

Teamwork has its benefits and its drawbacks. As you begin to form teams and plan for completing a production project, you may want to consider the following three points:

1. *Teamwork requires communication.* Make sure your team knows how to communicate effectively (e.g., specific days or times of day when everyone should have checked his or her e-mail; weekly meetings or telephone conferences).

2. *Teams should comprise people with explicit roles.* Members of the team should take specific responsibilities, including project manager (the person who coordinates everyone's efforts), subject matter expert (the person who decides the content of the instruction), and media producer. Other roles teams may want to assign include editor (the person responsible for making all the documentation flow together), artistic director (the person who designates the "look and feel" of the instructional media), and assessment director (the person who develops and implements the assessment protocols).

3. *Teamwork requires consensus.* Team members must discuss and agree on the elements critical to successful project completion. All team members must agree on team communication

> protocols and assigned roles (therefore, all team members should have input into the decision processes). The team should devise a roster of each team member's specific roles, as well as a time line that indicates when each team member's production obligations are to be met.

Product Evaluation

Describing the production of instructional software, Alessi and Trollip (2001) wrote,

> Although there is much research in learning and instruction to guide us in developing instruction, the best guarantee that a program will be effective is to try it out, revise it, try it again, and so on until you get it right. (p. 408)

In "trying it out," the critically important evaluative activity involves close attention to the reactions and responses of the clients and the end users. The question to constantly consider is this: "Is the product meeting the specified instructional goals and objectives?"

We recommend ongoing, iterative evaluation of the product as it develops. In the earliest stages of preproduction and production, product ideas and rough sketches can be evaluated through expert review. An **expert review** is just that: soliciting input from a person or persons with a great deal of experience with the type of instructional media under development. Because of his or her experience, an expert can gain a sense of the production team's vision from extremely rough drafts (a cocktail napkin with a few sketches and an oral description are often sufficient to give an expert an idea of the finished product).

In the middle and later stages of development, the product can be evaluated through **peer review.** Other producers and instructional designers may be asked to review the product in its storyboard or alpha prototype form to get an "informed outsider's" opinion of the product (often a fresh pair of eyes can see potential problems the design team cannot).

At the later stages of development, potential end users may effectively review the product. As the product takes on its final shape, persons who will use the product can test it and offer advice or criticism. Such product review is often accomplished through *usability testing.*

ID INSIGHT

Mission Creep

Media-production specialists often say that no multimedia project is ever completed; it is merely abandoned. One problem faced by a team that successfully creates a prototype product is that once the fact that the product will work becomes evident, the individuals contributing to the project will want to add components and make improvements. One possible result of this natural desire to add to a successful product is that the product never reaches completion. At some point, someone must declare the product completed.

Usability Testing

A concept originally borrowed from engineering that has gained popularity among software developers, multimedia producers, and instructional designers is *usability testing*. Usability testing consists of evaluating the product by observing it in action with potential end users. Typically, in a usability test, evaluators observe one or more users interacting with the product under controlled conditions. The users interact with the product for a specified amount of time, having been asked to complete a set of tasks determined in advance by the evaluation team. The tasks are based on the goals and objectives the product is designed to meet. Results of a usability test inform the production team of the problems inherent in the design (e.g., the graphic for a button is not well understood, or the instructions are worded in a confusing manner) and suggest, through observation of end users in action, ways to effectively eliminate such problems.

A Final Thought

All aspects of production management and evaluation should serve the project, not the converse. Think of the calendar, priority list, prototypes, and evaluation strategies as support pieces that aid in creating a high-quality piece of instructional media. If at some point any of these support pieces creates more problems than it solves, you may need to reevaluate it and create a modified or new support piece to replace the one that is not offering support. Think of each production planning item as a small contract; if honoring that contract becomes impossible, you may need to renegotiate it. Using the contract metaphor is deliberate on our part. Contracts are generated to protect the interests of all parties; one person who has trouble with a contract is still bound by it if the other parties insist on honoring it.

SUMMARY

Depending on the work setting, an instructional designer may either submit plans and specifications to an instructional media–production team or be an integral part of that team. In either case, the instructional designer must have some idea of how instructional media are produced in order to have appropriate expectations about the finished product.

Any production project has three phases: preproduction, production, and postproduction. In preproduction, a production team is formed that consists of managers, directors, and artists. Managers are responsible for project organization, timing, and the deployment of resources. Directors are responsible for the "look and feel" of the product. Artists create the elements necessary for project completion. A project is usually instigated at the request of a client, and the client's satisfaction with the project is in large part a measure of its success.

Production projects typically begin with the creation of a production calendar that includes milestones and deadline dates critical to project success. Style guides are then created and agreed on to unify the product. Finally, the project is produced through a series of prototypes, often beginning with a script, progressing to a storyboard, then to alpha and beta prototypes in preparation for a final-release product.

Although conflict is almost inevitable among any team, maintaining good communication among team members can facilitate problem resolution. Four strategies that contribute to good communication include respecting each team member's input, regularly consultating with team members, carefully using specific terms to describe aspects of the production, and maintaining a complete "paper trail."

The instructional media product is best evaluated through an ongoing, iterative process. This process includes expert review, peer review, and usability testing (observation of the product in action).

One important point to keep in mind is that all aspects of production management and evaluation should contribute to the success of the project. If any supporting activity creates more problems than it solves, the existing activity may need to be modified or a new one created to replace it.

CONNECTING PROCESS TO PRACTICE

1. You are assigned the task of producing a booklet that contains information about your organization's options for health insurance. What are the critically important preproduction, production, and postproduction activities for this project?

2. You are the manager of a large video-production project. The client is a philanthropist who would like to create something that inspires young people to choose biochemistry as a career path. The client has specific ideas about what she would like a specific video segment to look like, but the video-production team is not sure it can match her vision and stay within the budget. What do you do?

3. You are part of a five-person instructional media–production team that works for a large university. Each team member is an experienced instructional designer and has extensive media-production skills. The team has been assigned a project that requires development of instructional software for a chemistry professor (the project is being paid for by a grant the professor received). What are the roles and responsibilities each team member will need to be assigned? What roles or responsibilities would the chemistry professor assume?

4. You are part of a team developing computer-based interactive instruction that supports reading skill development for second-grade students. The team has 3 months to complete the project. What activities would you build into the production calendar to ensure the finished product is both effective instruction and well received by the students?

5. You are the manager of an instructional multimedia project. The member of your production team responsible for completing the graphics for the project is not ready on the day all graphics are to be turned over to the software author. What do you do?

RECOMMENDED READINGS

Alessi, S. M., & Trollip, S. R. (2001). *Multimedia for learning: Methods and development* (3rd ed.). Boston: Allyn & Bacon.

Chapters 12 through 15 address the design and development of instructional multimedia.

Dumas, J. S., & Redish, J. C. (1999). *A practical guide to usability testing* (Rev. Ed.). Portland, OR: Intellect.

Elin, L. (2001). *Designing and developing multimedia: A practical guide for the producer, director, and writer.* Boston: Allyn & Bacon.

Kuniavsky, M. (2003). *Observing the user experience: A practitioner's guide to user research.* San Francisco: Morgan Kaufman.

REFERENCES

Alessi, S. M., & Trollip, S. R. (2001). *Multimedia for learning: Methods and development* (3rd ed.). Boston: Allyn & Bacon.

Brown, A., Green, T., & Zatz, D. (2001). Developing and designing multimedia production projects: A set of guidelines. *EDUCAUSE Quarterly, 2*(4), 26–29.

Carrigan, D. (Director). (2002). *Monsters, Inc.* [DVD]. United States: Disney–Pixar.

King Features (Producer) & Dunning, G. (Director). (1968). *The Beatles' Yellow Submarine* [Motion picture]. Great Britain: Apple Films.

Nelson, L. M. (1999). Collaborative problem solving. In C. Reigeluth (Ed.), *Instructional design theories and models: A new paradigm of instructional theory* (Vol. II, pp. 244–267). Mahwah, NJ: Erlbaum.

PART 2

EXAMINING THE SITUATION

Needs, Task, and Learner Analysis

5 Conducting Needs Analysis

6 Conducting Task Analysis

7 Analyzing the Learners

According to the principles of instructional design, before you can begin to create an instructional intervention for any group of learners, you need to thoroughly analyze the situation to determine the best course of action. In Chapters 5, 6, and 7, we describe the instructional design processes that help answer the question "What type of intervention is needed?"

In Chapter 5, we introduce the principles, processes, and practices of *needs analysis*, which helps determine what kind of change the instruction should help implement. Chapter 6 provides an introduction to *task analysis*, which is a way of understanding the content or tasks that will form the basis for the instruction being developed. Chapter 7 covers *learner analysis*, a method for getting to know the people for whom the instruction is being developed.

These analysis activities are essential elements of instructional design. They help the instructional designer to decide on the goals and objectives of the instructional event and to select and organize the best possible activities for instruction.

Chapter **5**

CONDUCTING NEEDS ANALYSIS

Key Terms

Goal analysis *(page 94)*   Needs assessment   Performance analysis
Needs analysis *(page 89)*   *(page 89)*   *(page 90)*

I work for a software company that creates telephony software. All instructional design, whether for classroom or distance learning, starts with a formal needs analysis built around one central question: "Is this a concept the student needs?" From there, we drill down more: "What tasks need to be performed?" "What tasks are not being performed correctly?" "What is the gap between required performance and actual performance?" "Is there a single behavior or class of behaviors that will indicate the presence of the required performance, about which there is general agreement?"

The method and instrument we use most frequently is the SME [subject matter expert] interview and/or questionnaire. The primary challenge we face as instructional designers in a technology company is that our learning content is driven by the technology, not necessarily the learners. It's a classic "If we build it, they will come" situation. Our largest challenge is creating learner-centered content for a highly technical system.

—Erik Novak,
Distance Learning Course Developer,
Interactive Intelligence, Inc.,
Indianapolis, IN

Guiding Questions

- What is a needs analysis?
- Why is conducting a needs analysis important?
- What do instructional design experts recommend about conducting a needs analysis?
- What steps should an instructional designer follow to conduct a successful needs analysis?
- What is the final outcome of a needs analysis?
- How can an instructional designer evaluate the effectiveness of a needs analysis?

Chapter Overview

Instruction is designed for a purpose: to help produce a desired change. The change could be one of many, such as an improvement in employees' attitudes toward a particular job task, an increase in high school students' knowledge about history, or an upgrade of the skill level of consumers using a new word processor. Therefore, an early step, if not the first, in the instructional design process is to identify the change that is requested and the variables surrounding this change. These variables include who wants the change to occur and in what environment it should occur. The process for determining these factors is called a *needs analysis*. The information gathered during a needs analysis will help the instructional designer to be clear about what instruction needs to be developed or whether instruction is even necessary to help bring about the desired change.

In all phases of the instructional design process, various perspectives are held about how these phases can be approached and carried out. In this chapter, we explore instructional design experts' different perspectives on needs analysis. In addition, we discuss how to conduct a thorough needs analysis to help ensure that data are collected that will accurately inform the instructional designer how to proceed through the instructional design process. Finally, several methods for evaluating the success of a needs analysis are described.

Needs Analysis: An Overview

As mentioned in the previous section, instructional design is carried out for a purpose: to bring about a particular change. Typically, the change is an improvement in performance of some kind. Attitudes, knowledge, and skills are all areas in which improvement could be needed. Therefore, improving performance can take on different forms, such as increasing a student's knowledge in a particular content area, increasing a factory worker's productivity, or increasing consumer ease in using a new product.

The instructional designer's job is usually to help determine exactly what change needs to occur on the basis of what is going on in the environment. In some cases, however, the instructional designer may be told up front what change is needed. In such instances, the wise instructional designer confirms this need by getting other perspectives on the situation. In either scenario, the instructional designer is being asked to solve a problem by identifying it and devising a solution to help solve it.

Instructional designers use a **needs analysis** process to locate the source of a problem. To do this, they must gather specific information through various means such as interviews, observation, and reviews of available artifacts. The gathered information is then used to determine how to carry out the rest of the instructional design process.

Needs Analysis Questions

In typical needs analysis, information is sought that will help answer the following questions:

- What is the change being requested (including who is being asked to change and what is currently taking place)?
- Who is requesting this change?
- Where will this change need to take place?

ID INSIGHT

Is a Needs Analysis Always Necessary?

According to Morrison, Ross, and Kemp (2004), "The instructional design process begins with the identification of a problem or need" (p. 31).[1] Rossett (1995) similarly stated, "The important role that **needs assessment** plays is to give us information, at the beginning of the effort, about what is needed to improve performance" (p. 184). Conducting a needs analysis early in the instructional design process helps an instructional designer get to the core of the problem. If little or nothing is known about the problem, a full-scale needs analysis is necessary. In some situations, however, an instructional designer does not carry out a full-scale needs analysis because he or she is brought into the instructional design process at a stage at which the client has already clearly determined what the problem is and possibly even identified why it may be occurring. If this is the case, the instructional designer does not need to conduct a formal needs analysis because information that would be gained from doing so most likely exists and conducting an analysis would be a waste of resources. This situation does not mean that the instructional designer will not require additional information. It indicates only that a formal needs analysis is unnecessary.

[1]Reprinted from Morrison, Ross, and Kemp, *Designing Effective Instruction*, 4th ed. 2004. Reprinted with permission by John Wiley & Sons.

- Is instruction the most appropriate means for bringing about the desired change?

As mentioned, the instructional designer's job is to find answers to these questions so that he or she can design, develop, and implement an elegant solution—one that is both efficient and effective in providing the appropriate change.

Popular Approaches to Needs Analysis

An instructional designer can use various approaches to carry out a needs analysis. In this section, we discuss several approaches that respected instructional design scholars have developed. These approaches are worth examining as you begin to develop your own understanding of and approach to the needs analysis process. As you read the different approaches, be sure to note that varying terminology is used to refer to the needs analysis process. Despite such variance in terminology, the outcome of the approaches is the same.

Mager's Performance Analysis

Robert F. Mager is an author of instructional design texts that have been popular for decades. His approach to needs analysis is a good place to start. Mager (1997) described a process for determining "the proper course of action in those instances where people aren't doing what they should be doing" (p. 24).[2] He called this process **performance analysis.** Performance analysis allows an instructional designer to determine what individuals are currently doing and what they should be doing. If a difference exists, the instructional designer must determine why. The reason for a difference could be that an individual does not know how to do something; if so, instruction is necessary. If the individual already knows how to do something and is not doing it, a remedy other than instruction is needed.

Mager (1997) recommended taking the following 12 steps during a performance analysis (Figure 5.1):

1. Describe the person or people whose performance is being questioned.
2. Describe as specifically as possible what it is they are doing that causes someone to say there is a problem.
3. Describe specifically what it is they should be doing.
4. Determine the "cost" of the discrepancy by estimating what it is costing in such things as aggravation, frustration, turnover, scrap, insurance

FIGURE 5.1

Performance Analysis Flowchart

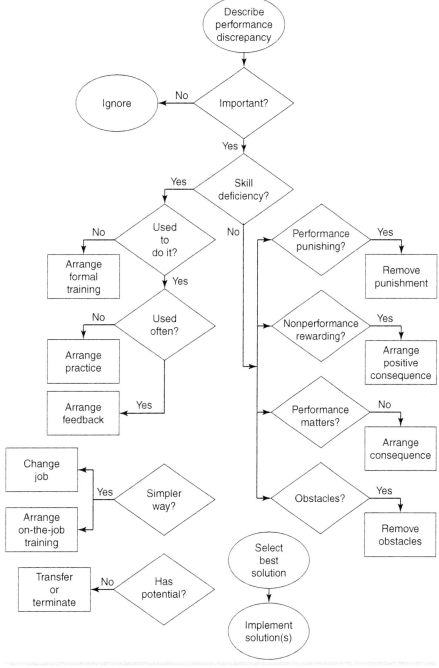

Adapted from Mager, R. F. (1997). Making instruction work, or skillbloomers (2nd ed.). Atlanta, GA: Center for Effective Performance.

rates, time lost, money lost, equipment damage, customers lost or good-will damage, accidents, and so on.

5. If the estimated cost of the discrepancy is small, stop. In other words, if it's only a problem because you say it is, and it isn't having any impact on the rest of the world, stop.

6. If the cost is great enough to warrant going on, determine whether the target people know how to do what is expected of them. Answer the question "Could they do it if their very lives depended on it?"

7. If they could, then they already know how. Now determine why they aren't doing what they already know how to do. This is done by determining the consequences and obstacles of performing.

   i. What happens to the performers if they do it right?

   ii. What happens to them if they do it wrong?

   iii. What are the obstacles to performing as desired?

8. If they couldn't do it, answer these questions:

   i. Can the task be simplified to the point where they could do it?

   ii. Did they ever know how to do it? (If so, they only need practice.)

   iii. Is the skill used often? (If they do it often and still don't do it right, they need feedback. If they don't do it often, and they used to know how, they need a job aid, such as a checklist or a piece of sheet music.) [Job aids are described in Chapter 9.]

   iv. Do they have the potential to learn to do it? (If not, they should be transferred or terminated.)

9. The answer to these questions leads to the drafting of potential solutions. These solutions must address the problems exposed during the analysis. For example, if it is discovered that people aren't performing because they don't have the authority to perform as desired, then one part of the solution must propose a way to remove that obstacle.

10. Once potential remedies are drafted, determine how much it will cost to implement each remedy.

11. Compare the cost of the solutions to the cost of the problem.

12. Select one or more solutions that are (a) less expensive than the problem itself and (b) practical to apply. (pp. 25–26)[3]

Mager (1997) indicated that a performance analysis should generally take only a few minutes to complete. However, when information needed to answer the questions must be located, more time will be necessary.

Morrison, Ross, and Kemp's Three Approaches

Morrison and colleagues (2004) approached needs analysis in a more technical manner through the use of a method they called a *needs assessment*. They treated the process almost as if it were a study. A needs assessment serves four functions:

1. It identifies the needs relevant to a particular job or task, that is, what problems are affecting performance.
2. It identifies critical needs. Critical needs include those that have a significant financial impact, affect safety, or disrupt the work or educational environment.
3. It sets priorities for selecting an intervention.
4. It provides baseline data to assess the effectiveness of the instruction. (p. 32)[4]

When conducting a needs assessment, the instructional designer must complete the following four phases:

- *Phase I: Planning*
  In the planning phase, the instructional designer begins by defining the audience and the type of data that needs to be collected about the audience. Once these two elements are established, a decision must be made about the segment of the audience from which the data will be collected. The final step in the planning phase is to establish how the data will be collected. Interviews, questionnaires, focus-group meetings, and reviews of artifacts (e.g., "paper trails") are all data-collection techniques that can be used. This phase is complete when the data-collection instruments (e.g., questionnaires) have been designed.

- *Phase II: Collecting Data*
  In phase II, consideration is given to the sample size and how the data-collection instruments will be distributed and collected. An appropriate representation of the audience must be selected. The ideal situation would be to include every individual from the target audience. However, doing so is virtually impossible because of the logistics and costs that would be involved. Therefore, a representative sample of the audience is used. (Statistical principles and formulas are available to help

[4]Reprinted from Morrison, Ross, and Kemp, *Designing Effective Instruction*, 4th ed. 2004. Reprinted with permission by John Wiley & Sons.

instructional designers determine the optimal sample size; however, these topics are beyond the scope of this book and are usually covered in an advanced statistics course.)

- *Phase III: Analyzing the Data*
  Morrison et al. (2004) indicated that the output of the data analysis is an identification of needs (which can be classified as six types: normative, comparative, felt, expressed, anticipated, and critical incident) and prioritization of them. These researchers stated that needs can be prioritized "on the basis of economic value (e.g., cost value to the company), impact (number of people affected), a ranking scale, frequency of identification, or timeliness" (p. 38).[5] Morrison et al. suggested using the *Delphi method* to prioritize needs. This method is a structured process for collecting and analyzing knowledge gathered from a group of experts through the use of a series of questionnaires intermixed with controlled opinion feedback.

- *Phase IV: Compiling a Final Report*
  Preparing a final report on the findings is the concluding phase. Four sections should be included in a final report: a summary of the purpose; a summary of the process, including how it was carried out and who was involved; a summary of the results in both quantitative (e.g., charts, graphs) and qualitative (e.g., a brief narrative) formats, if appropriate; and recommendations based on the data. The recommendations should be appropriate to the identified problem. As mentioned, the recommendations may or may not be instruction (Morrison et al., 2004, pp. 36–39).[6]

In addition to delineating the needs assessment method, Morrison et al. (2004) described two other needs analysis methods: **goal analysis** and performance assessment (which is similar to Mager's performance analysis). They wrote, "Goal analysis takes less time than a needs assessment and its focus is typically much narrower. The goal analysis starts with a problem someone has identified, and then it focuses on a solution" (p. 43).[7] This situation is typical of what instructional designers are generally involved in (instructional goals and goal analysis are covered in detail in Chapter 8).

In a goal analysis, the instructional designer is not being asked to identify the problem (as is the case with a needs assessment). Rather, the instructional designer is asked to focus primarily on determining an appropriate intervention. Instruction may not always be the appropriate intervention for an existing problem. According to Morrison et al. (2004), "Problems that on the

---

[5-7]Reprinted from Morrison, Ross, and Kemp, *Designing Effective Instruction*, 4th ed. 2004. Reprinted with permission by John Wiley & Sons.

surface seem to require an instructional intervention can often be solved with a change in policy, coaching, or the environment" (p. 31).[8]

Before the instructional goals can be developed, the need or problem to be addressed must be identified through the use of needs assessment and analysis processes. According to Morrison et al. (2004),

> After the problem is identified, the designer attempts to identify the causes of the problem, and then identifies an array of solutions that could be implemented to solve the problem. Seldom is instruction the single answer to the problem. Usually a combination of changes is required to solve the problem effectively. (p. 18)

Rossett's Five-Step Approach

Allison Rossett (1995) wrote that instructional designers engage in needs analysis when they are responding to a request for assistance. A needs assessment allows an instructional designer to gather information that will allow him or her to make "data-driven and responsive recommendations" (p. 184) about how to solve a problem, which is typically the need to improve some type of performance. She stated that the needs assessment drives the entire instructional design process by eventually shaping the decisions made about design, development, implementation, and evaluation. She wrote that when a needs analysis is conducted, it allows an instructional designer to gather information about the following five factors:

1. *Optimal performance:* What does an individual who is performing at an optimal level know or do that allows him or her to perform at this level? Instructional designers must consult a variety of sources, such as experts, documentation, standards, practices, texts, and tests, to answer this question.

2. *Actual performance:* How is an individual currently performing? What is happening to cause a particular event to take place? Why is a change being requested? An instructional designer can use employee performance records, observation, and interviews to help gather data to provide answers to these questions.

3. *Feelings:* Instructional designers want to know how individuals feel about the topic, about training on the topic, about the topic as a priority, and about their confidence surrounding the topic.

4. *Causes:* Rossett identified four reasons individuals may not be performing as they should: (a) They lack the skill or knowledge, (b) the

[8]Reprinted from Morrison, Ross, and Kemp, *Designing Effective Instruction,* 4th ed. 2004. Reprinted with permission by John Wiley & Sons.

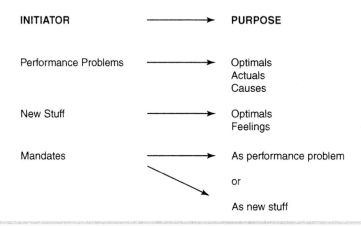

FIGURE 5.2

Initiators and Purposes

INITIATOR		PURPOSE
	⟶	
Performance Problems	⟶	Optimals Actuals Causes
New Stuff	⟶	Optimals Feelings
Mandates	⟶	As performance problem or As new stuff

Scource: Adapted from "Needs Assessment," by A. Rossett, in *Instructional Technology: Past, Present, and Future* (2nd ed., p. 190), edited by G. Anglin, 1995, Englewood, CO: Libraries Unlimited. Copyright 1995 by Libraries Unlimited. Adapted with permission of Greenwood Publishing Group, Inc., Westport, CT.

environment is an obstacle, (c) no, few, or improper incentives exist, and (d) the employees are unmotivated.

5. *Solutions:* What solutions are possible?

Rossett (1995) outlined a five-step process for conducting a needs analysis:

Step 1: Determine purposes on the basis of initiators. Three types of initiating situations may be taking place: performance problems, "new stuff," and mandates. The instructional designer must determine what type of situation initiated the problem, then determine what purposes need to be addressed to develop a solution for the existing problem. Figure 5.2 shows the relationship between the three types of initiators and the needs assessment purposes.

Step 2: Identify sources. The next step is to identify who has the information that is needed and where it is located. What constraints impede access to this information? Which individuals need to know that you are involved in developing a solution to the existing problem?

Step 3: Select tools. Gathering various types of data requires different tools. You must plan carefully so that you select the proper tools to allow you to effectively gather useful data. Conducting interviews, observing employee performance, examining records and outcomes, holding group meetings, and administering questionnaires are tools that can be used.

Step 4: Conduct the needs assessment in stages. Once you identify the purpose (step 1), establish the sources where data will be collected (step 2), and determine the tools to use to collect the data (step 3), you are ready to conduct the needs assessment. Most needs assessments are performed in stages; that is, data are collected and analyzed, then a determination is made as to whether additional information is needed. Additional information may be needed from the identified sources if you determine that the collected data are inadequate. Inadequate data may be a result of improper sources or data-collection tools. If so, you may need to revisit steps 2 and 3.

Step 5: Use the findings for decision making. The information gathered during the needs assessment is used to develop an appropriate solution.

Smith and Ragan's Three Needs Assessment Models

Smith and Ragan (1999) said that instructional designers must learn to be "clever investigators" who can clearly analyze the learning context. They stated that analyzing the learning context involves two steps: (a) "the substantiation of a need for instruction to help learners reach learning goals" and (b) "a description of the learning environment in which the instruction will be used" (p. 31). They said that a needs assessment helps determine whether the need for new instruction exists.

Smith and Ragan (1999) outlined three needs assessment models: discrepancy-based needs assessment; the problem-finding, problem-solving model; and the innovation model. Instructional designers use the *discrepancy-based needs assessment model* when learning goals are already identified and instruction related to these goals is being offered. Five phases are carried out with this approach:

1. List the goals of the instructional system.
2. Determine how well the identified goals are already being achieved.
3. Determine the gaps between "what is" and "what should be."
4. Prioritize gaps according to agreed-upon criteria.
5. Determine which gaps are instructional needs and which are most appropriate for design and development of instruction. (pp. 32–35)

The *problem-finding, problem-solving model* is used when "someone in management or administration; some member of the constituency, such as parents, clients, or community leaders; or some employees or students have identified that a problem exists in the organization's achieving its mission" (Smith & Ragan, 1999, p. 35). This model has four steps: (a) Verify that a problem exists, (b) establish whether the problem is caused by employee performance (in a training environment) or learner achievement (in an educational environment), (c) determine whether the performance or achievement problem can be eliminated by learning, and (d) find out whether instruction is currently being offered (pp. 35–36).

The *innovation model* is used to examine "changes or innovations in the educational system or organization" to determine whether adding new learning goals is necessary to account for the changes or innovations. This model has four steps:

1. Determine the nature of the innovation or change.
2. Determine the learning goals that accompany this innovation.
3. If you have a choice of goals, determine whether these goals are appropriate and high priority in the learning system.
4. Begin learning environment analysis design activities (i.e., start the next phase of the instructional design process).

With this model, including the stakeholders (e.g., teachers or trainers; managers or administrators) is extremely important because one outcome could be the addition of or a change in organizational goals (Smith & Ragan, 1999).

Needs Analysis Procedure

Although the needs analysis approaches described in the previous section employ different tactics, they share an outcome: to provide useful data that an instructional designer can use to create the best possible solution to help solve an existing problem, meet a given need, or bring about a desired change. To gather the appropriate data, the designer must conduct a thorough needs analysis by using various data-gathering tools and answering some fundamental questions.

Determination of the Desired Change

The first step in a needs analysis is to determine what change is being requested. As mentioned, the desired change could be in behavior, skill, or attitude. You will want to locate information that can help you answer the following questions:

- What problem exists or what change is being requested?
- Who is being asked to change?
- What is currently taking place in this environment with this individual or individuals?

Typically, the client who hired you will be able to provide either the information needed to answer these questions or access to such information. In most cases, your client will specifically tell you what change is desired and who the individuals are who are being asked to change. This information can be gathered through an interview. In addition, through an interview, the client will be able to provide insights into what is currently taking place in the environment where the individual or individuals are being asked to change. However, because the client's opinion about what is occurring will be biased, you should also observe the environment personally, rather than relying solely on the client's description.

Not all instructional design projects will be this straightforward. On occasion, you may be asked to observe what is taking place in an organization and to determine the type of change that needs to occur. This type of activity is often associated with the field of human performance technology (HPT). According to the International Society for Performance Improvement (ISPI, 2004), HPT focuses on analyzing outcomes to identify the causes for a gap between the current and desired performance levels. Once the causes are identified, an intervention is developed to bridge the performance gap. The focus of HPT is on human performance that is typically related to activities that occur in industry and business settings.

The Party Requesting the Desired Change

After developing a clear understanding of the existing problem or the requested change, you must understand who is asking for the change. This factor is extremely important to understand because it will help you determine the type of intervention needed, the emotional and political climate of the situation, and the level of support that is present and that will most likely be needed for a change to take place. To come to an understanding of these elements, you will need to answer the following question:

- Who identified the problem or is requesting this change?

This information is generally easy to obtain. Often, the client who hired you wants the change to occur. However, additional stakeholders might be interested in having the change occur. Talking to additional stakeholders to clarify how they feel about the problem or the requested change may be difficult, though.

Implementation Location for the Desired Change

Determining where the desired change will occur is another important element to consider. Doing so will help you better understand the context of where an intervention will need to take place. You will need to answer this question:

- Where will the solution or change need to occur?

Again, the client is the best source of information. In most cases, the answer will be obvious (e.g., a school, the workplace). Visiting this location can help you gain a solid understanding of the environment but may not always be possible. If not, researching the environment will be extremely important.

The Intervention

Once you have the data that allow you to understand the entire context—what the desired change is, who is requesting the change, who is being asked to change, and where the change needs to occur—you must determine whether instruction is the most appropriate intervention. You will need to answer the following question:

- Is instruction the most appropriate means for solving the problem or bringing about the desired change?

The client will be relying on you to determine the answer. You will find no steadfast rules on whether instruction is the most appropriate intervention because each instructional design situation is different. Instruction is most appropriate when a change in skill or knowledge is desired. On the basis of the information you gathered through your needs analysis, you will need to determine an appropriate intervention. Keep in mind that you may want to offer your client more than one type of intervention. Allow your client to be part of the decision-making process, but remember that, as mentioned, he or she will be relying on you to make the final decision.

A properly conducted needs analysis contributes significantly to how successful the entire instructional design process will be carried out. A thorough identification of the problem that needs to be addressed will lead to development of an effective and efficient solution.

Evaluation of the Success of a Needs Analysis

How do you know when you have successfully conducted a needs analysis? How do you know that the gathered data accurately describe the problem or the change that needs to take place (thus helping you develop an appropriate solution)? One method used to evaluate the success of a needs analysis is to determine whether the solution that was developed and implemented helped bring about the desired change. In other words, did performance improve? This *summative* evaluation activity, although extremely important, poses serious problems if it is the only evaluation method used. The most serious problem is that it is conducted long after the needs analysis and consequently does not provide corrective feedback. It is an "all-or-nothing" method. It helps to determine whether you have succeeded or you have failed. Therefore, one good practice is to use *formative* evaluation activities throughout the needs analysis process, in addition to this summative activity.

An important formative evaluation activity to use is sustained communication between you and the client during the entire needs analysis process. Gathered data should be shared periodically with the client during this process. This formative evaluation activity helps ensure that you are gathering accurate data by presenting the client with opportunities to provide feedback. The frequency of this communication depends on the nature of the project and the client's availability. Thus, no standard frequency can be recommended. Nevertheless, in general, communicating at least once a week with your client is usually desirable. You must realize, though, that consistently communicating with some clients can be difficult.

Another formative evaluation activity is to share data and interpretations of the data with a member of the target audience for whom the change is designed (or with someone who has had a similar experience, although this situation is not as ideal). Doing so can help you determine whether what you have found matches what the individual perceives is taking place. If the data and interpretations seem familiar and appropriate to these individuals, the needs analysis was most likely successful. This process is referred to as a *member check*. It is a comparison method of evaluation that comes from a qualitative research paradigm. Member checking is discussed in more detail in Chapter 7.

SUMMARY

Numerous needs analysis methods are available to instructional designers. Popular approaches to needs analysis include those outlined by Mager, Morrison et al., Rossett, and Smith and Ragan. Although these methods are carried out differently, they share the goal of providing an instructional designer with data that help inform and influence the design and development of an effective and efficient solution. This solution will help solve a problem or bring about some type of change, typically an improvement in performance—in knowledge, skills, or attitudes.

A needs analysis is conducted by using various data-gathering tools to help answer fundamental questions such as the following:

- What problem exists or what change is being requested (including who is being asked to change and what is currently taking place)?
- Who identified the problem or is requesting this change?
- Where will the solution or change need to take place?

- Is instruction the most appropriate means for solving the problem or implementing the desired change?

The success of a needs analysis is determined by using a combination of formative and summative evaluation techniques to determine whether the instructional designer created the best possible solution to help solve an existing problem, meet a given need, or bring about a desired change. A properly conducted needs analysis contributes significantly to the success of the entire instructional design process.

CONNECTING PROCESS TO PRACTICE

1. You are the lead instructional designer recently hired for a large-scale project. Your client has asked you to describe why a needs analysis is important to the success of the project. What do you tell your client? Do not assume your client knows what a needs analysis is.

2. Several perspectives on needs analysis were discussed in this chapter. What key elements for conducting a needs analysis do these perspectives have in common? How do these perspectives differ?

3. Describe an instructional design scenario in which you believe a formal needs analysis would not need to be conducted.

4. You have been hired to work on an instructional design project for a company that owns several nursing home facilities in California. Your client has indicated to you that incidents of complaints from people living at the nursing homes have risen steadily during the past 6 months. The client wants the residents to have comfortable living experiences. Therefore, a solution that will help reduce the number of complaints is needed. Your client is not sure, however, what needs to be done. A variety of issues could be contributing to the problem. Your task is to conduct a needs analysis to determine what type of solution may be necessary. Describe how you would conduct a needs analysis in this situation. Include the steps you would take, the data you would gather, how you would analyze the information, and how you would report the findings to your client, which would include what you think needs to be done.

5. Is conducting a needs analysis appropriate for preparing instruction for a K–12 setting? How might a person conduct a needs analysis for instruction to be delivered in a third-grade classroom?

RECOMMENDED READINGS

Dick, W., Carey, L., & Carey, J. O. (2001). *The systematic design of instruction,* (5th ed.). New York: Addison-Wesley/Longman.

Kaufman, R., Rojas, A. M., & Mayer, H. (1993). *Needs assessment: A user's guide.* Englewood Cliffs, NJ: Educational Technology Publications.

Mager, R. F. (1997). *Making instruction work, or skillbloomers* (2nd ed.). Atlanta, GA: Center for Effective Performance.

Mager, R. F., & Pipe, P. (1997). *Analyzing performance problems: Or you really ought a wanna* (3rd ed.). Atlanta, GA: Center for Effective Performance.

Morrison, G. R., Ross, S. M., & Kemp, J. E. (2004). *Designing effective instruction* (4th ed.). New York: Wiley.

Rossett, A. (1995). Needs assessment. In G. Anglin (Ed.), *Instructional technology: Past, present, and future* (2nd ed., pp. 183–196). Englewood, CO: Libraries Unlimited.

Rossett, A. (1999). Analysis for human performance technology. In H. D. Stolovitch & E. J. Keeps (Eds.), *Handbook of performance technology: Improving individual and organizational performance worldwide* (pp. 139–162). San Francisco: Jossey-Bass.

Seels, B., & Glasgow, Z. (1998). *Making instructional design decisions* (2nd ed.). Upper Saddle River, NJ: Merrill/Prentice Hall.

Smith, P. L., & Ragan, T. J. (1999). *Instructional design* (2nd ed.). New York: Wiley.

REFERENCES

International Society for Performance Improvement. (2004). What is human performance technology? In *HPT—Human performance technology.* Retrieved August 4, 2005, from http://www.ispi.org

Mager, R. F. (1997). *Making instruction work, or skillbloomers* (2nd ed.). Atlanta, GA: Center for Effective Performance.

Morrison, G. R., Ross, S. M., & Kemp, J. E. (2004). *Designing effective instruction* (4th ed.). New York: Wiley.

Rossett, A. (1995). Needs assessment. In G. Anglin (Ed.), *Instructional technology: Past, present, and future* (2nd ed., pp. 183–196). Englewood, CO: Libraries Unlimited.

Smith, P. L., & Ragan, T. J. (1999). *Instructional design* (2nd ed.). New York: Wiley.

Chapter 6

CONDUCTING TASK ANALYSIS

Key Terms

Content analysis
(page 106)

Subject matter analysis
(page 106)

Subject matter expert
(SME) *(page 107)*

Task analysis
(page 106)

I often do a task analysis when creating self-paced training. To facilitate this, I go into the factory with a technician and my notepad. I also have an associate go with us to shoot video of the tasks to be performed. I observe the technician performing the tasks that are required for the training and take judicious notes throughout the training. While I take notes, my colleague will shoot video of the tech performing the tasks. This video is a great tool to document the procedures and helps me later ensure I've captured everything, as I can go back through the procedure repeatedly. This video also helps when I have questions. I can show the particular piece I have questions about to the technician and get further details about the task. Once I have completed observing, and have double-checked the process and procedure using the video, I validate the procedures with the technician and the tool owner. I begin categorizing the tasks from simple knowledge tasks to complex performance tasks. Once this is completed, I begin looking at the tasks independently and bundling them into like tasks by subject. For example, if several tasks are related to safety, I'll put them together. I continue looking for common themes until all tasks are categorized. Using this process helps later when I'm defining the goals and objectives.

—*Jona Titus,*
Senior Training Specialist,
Intel Corporation,
Hillsboro, OR

Guiding Questions

- What is task analysis?
- What important information is gathered during a task analysis?
- What do experts in instructional design recommend about conducting a task analysis?
- What is the final outcome of a task analysis?
- How can an instructional designer evaluate the effectiveness of a task analysis?

Chapter Overview

After a needs analysis is conducted to determine whether instruction should occur, who is requesting the instruction, and in what environment the instruction needs to take place, instructional designers commonly conduct a task analysis. Task analysis is a critical component in the instructional design process because it provides important information about the content and tasks that will form the basis for the instruction being developed. According to many instructional design experts, task analysis is often considered the most important part of the instructional design process. (Jonassen, Hannum, & Tessmer, 1989; Morrison, Ross, & Kemp, 2004; Richey, Klein, & Nelson, 2004).

In this chapter, we describe various methods for gathering information about the type of content and activities that need to be included in the instruction. Various task analysis approaches that instructional design experts use are introduced and explained. We also suggest how an instructional designer can evaluate the effectiveness of a task analysis.

What Is Task Analysis?

Instructional designers must have a clear understanding of what learners are to know or be able to accomplish by participating in instruction. Coming to this understanding requires identifying the type of content that will make up the instruction and in what sequence this content should be provided. The systematic process instructional designers use to determine this information is typically called **task analysis.**

ID INSIGHT

Task Analysis by Any Other Name Is Still Task Analysis

Shakespeare's Juliet said, "That which we call a rose by any other name would smell as sweet." In other words, a rose is still a rose no matter what it may be called. The same can be said about the various terms instructional designers use to refer to task analysis, such as **content analysis** and **subject matter analysis.** Despite the different names, each refers to what is most commonly called the *task analysis process,* and the goal remains the same: to gather information about the content and tasks that need to be part of the instruction being developed.

Morrison et al. (2004) wrote that a task analysis solves three problems for an instructional designer:

1. It defines the content required to solve the performance problem or alleviate a performance need. This step is crucial since most designers work with unfamiliar content.
2. Because the process forces the **subject matter expert (SME)** to work through each individual step, subtle steps are more easily identified.
3. During this process, the designer has the opportunity to view the content from the learner's perspective. Using this perspective, the designer can often gain insight into appropriate teaching strategies. (p. 78)[1]

Jonassen, Tessmer, and Hannum (1999) provided a slightly expanded view of what instructional designers are trying to determine when they conduct a task analysis. Jonassen et al. wrote that a task analysis helps determine the following:

1. The goals and objectives of learning;
2. The operational components of jobs, skills, learning goals or objectives, that is, to describe what task performers do, how they perform a task or apply a skill, and how they think before, during, and after learning;
3. What knowledge states (declarative, structural, and procedural knowledge) characterize a job or task;
4. Which tasks, skills, or goals should be taught, that is, how to select learning outcomes that are appropriate for instructional development;
5. Which tasks are most important—which have priority for a commitment of training resources;
6. The sequence in which tasks are performed and should be learned and taught;
7. How to select or design instructional activities, strategies, and techniques to foster learning;
8. How to select appropriate media and learning environments; and
9. How to construct performance assessments and evaluation. (p. 3)

Popular Approaches to Task Analysis

Instructional design scholars and practitioners have developed numerous approaches to task analysis. These approaches vary according to the context surrounding the instruction that needs to be developed. Most approaches have similar elements, although their procedures may differ slightly. All

[1]Reprinted from Morrison, Ross, and Kemp, *Designing Effective Instruction*, 4th ed. 2004. Reprinted with permission by John Wiley & Sons.

share one goal: determining the type of content and skills that need to be included in the instruction. The various approaches to task analysis are important to understand as you develop your own understanding of how this process is accomplished.

Jonassen, Hannum, and Tessmer's Approach

According to Jonassen and colleagues (1989), task analysis is a "process of analyzing and articulating the kind of learning that you expect the learners to know how to perform" (p. 3). These researchers asserted that the task analysis process consists of five discrete functions: (a) inventorying tasks, (b) describing tasks, (c) selecting tasks, (d) sequencing tasks and task components, and (e) analyzing tasks and content level. These functions consist of the following activities:

- *Inventorying tasks:* Identifying tasks or generating a list of tasks that need to be developed for instruction
- *Describing tasks:* The process of elaborating the tasks identified in the inventory
- *Selecting tasks:* Prioritizing tasks and choosing those that are more feasible and appropriate if a large number of tasks is involved
- *Sequencing tasks and task components:* Defining the sequence in which instruction should occur in order to successfully facilitate learning
- *Analyzing tasks and content level:* Describing the type of cognitive behavior, physical performance, or affective response the tasks require

Morrison, Ross, and Kemp's Three Techniques

Morrison and colleagues (2004) stated that the content required for instruction is influenced by the goals derived during a needs analysis and the information gathered during a learner analysis. The needs analysis provides instructional designers with a focus and the overall breadth of the instruction that needs to be developed. The learner analysis provides an understanding of the learner's knowledge and background related to the content. The combination of the needs and learner analyses provides a starting point for the instructional designer to determine the scope and sequence of the content to be included in instruction. The result of a task analysis is used to provide input for developing instructional objectives.

Three techniques for analyzing content and tasks are provided by Morrison et al. (2004): topic analysis, procedural analysis, and the critical incident method. *Topic analysis* is used to help analyze cognitive or declarative knowledge. A topic analysis provides two types of information: the content that will make up the instruction and the structure of the content components. These components can be facts, concepts, principles and rules, procedures, interpersonal skills, or attitudes. Conducting a topic analysis is much like creating an outline: You start with the major topic and work your way down to subordinate information associated with the major topic.

Procedural analysis is used to analyze tasks by identifying the steps required to complete them. In conducting a procedural analysis, the instructional designer typically walks through the steps with a SME, preferably in the environment (or as close as possible to the actual environment) where the task will be performed. The result of a procedural analysis is typically a flowchart that identifies the substeps that need to occur for the learner to accomplish the task.

The major element of the *critical incident method* is an interview. The interview allows the instructional designer to gather important information about the conditions under which an individual successfully and unsuccessfully accomplished a task. Flanagan (1954) developed this method during World War II to help determine why military pilots were not learning how to fly correctly. The pilots were interviewed to determine the conditions that were present when successful and unsuccessful missions were performed. They were asked three types of questions:

1. What were the conditions before, during, and after the incident?

    a. Where did the incident occur?
    b. When did it occur?
    c. Who was involved?
    d. What equipment was used and what was its condition?

2. What did you do?

    a. What did you do physically (e.g., grabbed the rudder)?
    b. What did you say and to whom?
    c. What were you thinking?

3. How did this incident help you reach or prevent you from reaching your goal? (Flanagan, 1954, as cited in Morrison et al., 2004, pp. 91–92)

The interview process in the critical incident method allows the instructional designer to identify knowledge and skills that an individual (the SME) uses to accomplish a task. The information identified during the interview can be combined with that derived from a topic or procedural analysis to provide a better understanding about the content and tasks that are to be part of the instruction (Morrison et al., 2004).[2]

Dick, Carey, and Carey's Instructional Analysis

Dick, Carey, and Carey (2001) wrote that the process of identifying the skills and knowledge that should be included in instruction is complex. They called this process *instructional analysis:* "Instructional analysis is a set of procedures that, when applied to an instructional goal, results in the identification of the relevant steps for performing a goal and the subordinate skills required for a student to achieve the goal" (p. 38). They separated this process into two parts. In the first part, the instructional designer determines the major components of the instructional goal through goal analysis. The second part involves how each step of the instructional goal can be further analyzed to identify subordinate skills learners must have to meet the instructional goal.

The instructional analysis process can begin once the instructional goal has been identified. Dick et al. (2001) wrote that the instructional designer should start the instructional analysis process by asking, "What exactly would learners be doing if they were demonstrating that they already could perform the goal?" (p. 37). This question keeps the focus on what learners should be able to accomplish by participating in instruction rather than on just the content of the instruction. This focus is called a *goal analysis procedure.* The results of a goal analysis are the classification of the kind of learning that will occur and a visual representation (e.g., a flowchart) that displays the specific steps (and substeps) a learner should take to achieve an instructional goal. Various goal analysis procedures are available to the instructional designer.

The second part of the instructional analysis process is referred to as the *subordinate skills analysis.* The purpose of this analysis is to identify the appropriate set of subordinate skills that a learner will need in order to perform a specific step that helps him or her meet an instructional goal. Dick et al. (2001) identified several techniques for conducting a subordinate skills analysis; the hierarchical approach and cluster analysis are two examples. The instructional designer should select a particular technique according to the type of knowledge that is needed to meet the instructional goal.

---

[2]Reprinted from Morrison, Ross, and Kemp, *Designing Effective Instruction*, 4th ed. 2004. Reprinted with permission by John Wiley & Sons.

Smith and Ragan's Analysis of the Learning Task

Smith and Ragan (1999) referred to task analysis as *analysis of the learning task*. They stated,

> The process of task analysis transforms goal statements into a form that can be used to guide subsequent design. Designers expend a great deal of effort in obtaining as clear a description and as thorough an analysis as possible of the learning task. (p. 63)

They listed five steps to perform during learning-task analysis:

1. Write a learning goal.
2. Determine the types of learning of the goal.
3. Conduct an information-processing analysis of the goal.
4. Conduct a prerequisite analysis and determine the type of learning of the prerequisites.
5. Write learning objectives for the learning goal and each of the prerequisites. (p. 63)

The result of a learning-task analysis is a list of the goals that describe what learners should know or be able to accomplish as a result of the instruction. Included in the list are the prerequisite skills and knowledge learners will need in order to achieve these goals.

A key element of this approach is the information-processing analysis of the goal (step 3). Such analysis allows the instructional designer to determine the content that is needed for the instruction. Smith and Ragan (1999) stated that when instructional designers conduct an information-processing analysis, they are attempting to identify the mental and physical steps an individual must take to complete the learning task. These researchers stated that although information-processing analysis is not the only approach to examining and dissecting the task, "it seems to be the easiest, most straightforward approach to take" (p. 69).

Task Analysis Procedure

The different approaches described in the previous section share the goal of gathering information about the content and tasks that will make up the instruction that needs to be developed. Each approach has a specific set of techniques that help to accomplish this goal. Describing the techniques of each approach in great detail is beyond the scope of this book; you will most likely study these approaches and their techniques in depth during more advanced instructional design courses, specifically a course on task analysis.

The SME

In most task analysis procedures, instructional designers work with a subject matter expert (referred to as a *SME*; pronounced "smee" or "ess-em-ee"). A SME is an individual who is an expert in the content area for which the instruction is being developed. SMEs play a critical role in the task analysis process by providing insights into what the content should be composed of and how it should be sequenced.

The Subject Matter Expert

One element that all the approaches emphasize is the need for a SME to be part of the task analysis process. The SME's job is to help the instructional designer gather the information about the content and tasks that is necessary to develop the instruction. In some instances, the instructional designer may also be the SME because of his or her expertise in the subject area.

Task Analysis Document

With all task analysis procedures, the result is a document, created by the instructional designer, that depicts the content and tasks. This document can take several forms. The two most common are outlines of the content and flowcharts that depict the tasks and subtasks that the learner will need to accomplish (see Figures 6.1 and 6.2).

Influencing Factors

The task analysis approach that an instructional designer will use depends on the context that surrounds the instruction that needs to be developed. A major factor influencing the selection of the approach is the goal of the instruction. The goal of the instruction will relate to the type of content and tasks for which the instruction is being developed. For example, if the goal of instruction is for learners to know how to change a flat tire, the task analysis approach that should be used will be best suited for analyzing procedural tasks. An important point to remember about task analysis is that no single approach works for every situation. Successful instructional designers are able to select the proper approach on the basis of the context and the

FIGURE 6.1

Resulting Task Analysis Document: Outline Format

Teaching a dog to touch his or her nose to the end of a stick is a skill that can lead to many other tricks, such as closing an open door.

Please keep in mind that this example is provided to illustrate a relatively simple task that most people can identify with. In providing this example, we do not intend to minimize the role of instructional designer to that of someone who solely creates training that deals with dogs. We recognize that most tasks you will analyze will not be as simplistic and follow such a strictly behavioristic approach. As an instructional designer, you will be involved in analyzing many complex behaviors, such as the performance of a cardiac catheterization by a doctor.

1. **Obtain the necessary supplies.**
   a. Training clicker
   b. Dog treats
   c. Yardstick
   d. Plastic lid from a yogurt container (or a similar-size, round, flat object)
   e. Adhesive to attach lid to the end of the yardstick
2. **Get ready to train your dog.**
   a. Break the treats into small pieces.
   b. Place the treats in your pocket or in an easily accessible place.
   c. Put the clicker in your dominant hand.
   d. Find a comfortable area where you and your dog will not be distracted.
3. **Train your dog to respond to the clicker.**
   a. Have your dog in front of you.
   b. Click the clicker one time.
   c. Immediately give your dog a treat.
   d. Repeat steps b and c several times until your dog recognizes that he or she will receive a treat each time he or she hears the clicker.
      i. An attentive dog means the dog recognized that a click will be followed by a treat.
   e. Stop the activity for at least 15 minutes.
   f. Repeat steps a through c.
4. **Train your dog to "touch."**
   a. After you think your dog recognizes that he or she will receive a treat each time he or she hears a click, a new step can be added.
      i. Typically, you will not attempt this step until at least 1 day has passed.
   b. Make sure you have plenty of small pieces of dog treats.
   c. Put your clicker in your hand.
   d. Have your dog in front of you.

(continued)

FIGURE 6.1

Resulting a Task Analysis Document: Outline Format (*continued*)

    e. Touch the palm of your hand to your dog's nose and at the same time click the clicker and say, "Touch."

    f. Immediately give your dog a treat.

    g. Repeat this process several times.

    h. Touch the palm of your hand to your dog's nose and say, "Touch" at the same time.

       i. Do not use the clicker.

    i. Immediately give your dog a treat.

    j. Repeat this process several times.

    k. Move back at least 1 foot from your dog.

    l. Hold out your hand to the side with your palm open.

       i. Your hand should be at the level of your dog's height.

    m. Say, "Touch."

       i. Your dog should move and touch his or her nose to your palm.

         (1) Immediately give your dog a treat and praise.

         (2) If your dog does not touch his or her nose to your palm, you may need to move your hand closer to his or her nose and attempt the process again or go back to step e if moving your palm closer to his or her nose does not work.

       ii. Repeat steps l and m several times.

5. Train your dog to touch a round lid on the end of a yardstick.

    a. Attach the round lid to the end of the yardstick.

    b. Make sure you have plenty of small pieces of dog treats.

    c. Put your clicker in your hand.

    d. Have your dog in front of you.

    e. Hold out the yardstick with the lid on the end of it.

    f. Touch the lid to your dog's nose and say, "Touch" at the same time.

    g. Immediately give your dog a treat.

    h. Repeat this process several times.

    i. Move back at least 1 foot from your dog.

    j. Hold out the stick with the lid on the end.

    k. Say, "Touch."

       i. Your dog should move and touch the lid with his or her nose.

       ii. If your dog does not do this, repeat steps e through h.

    l. Immediately give your dog a treat and praise.

    m. Repeat this process several times.

    n. Move back several feet and hold out either your palm or the yardstick and give the command "Touch."

       i. Immediately give a treat and praise when the dog touches your palm or the stick.

       ii. Eventually move the target higher and lower to challenge the dog.

FIGURE 6.2

Resulting Task Analysis Document: Flowchart Format

This flowchart depicts the process of sending an e-mail in Microsoft Outlook.

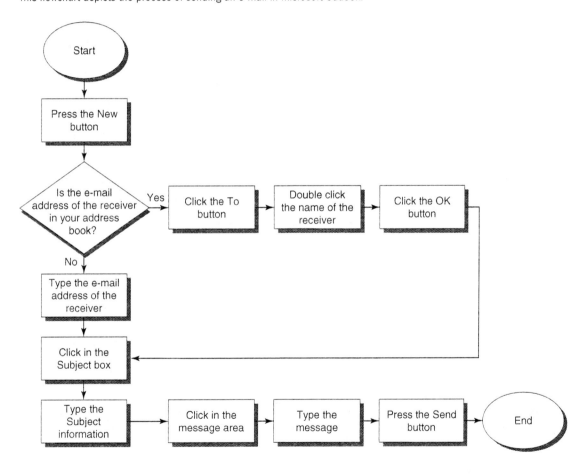

instruction that needs to be developed and to modify the approach to meet their particular needs.

Evaluation of the Success of a Task Analysis

How do you know that you have conducted a successful task analysis? How do you know that you correctly analyzed the content and tasks that will be part of the instruction that needs to be developed? One of the most effective methods

PROFESSIONALS IN PRACTICE

Our task analysis is based on the skills a person must have to successfully install, implement, and modify our software in his or her business setting. Setting up a computer-based telephone system is an unforgiving assignment. Our task analysis starts at the bottom (installation and configuration) and works upward toward the ultimate goal (dial tone, or a working automatic call distribution system, for example). Typically, we rely on flowcharting to map out the expected output of each task and the dependencies of subsequent tasks. Failure to complete a task or incorrect execution of a task quickly becomes apparent.

—Erik Novak,
Distance Learning Course Developer,
Interactive Intelligence, Inc.,
Indianapolis, IN

for determining the success of your task analysis during the design and development of instruction is to ask a SME who was not part of the task analysis to look over what you created and to evaluate it for accuracy and thoroughness. This formative evaluation activity will provide a valuable perspective that you can compare with the data you gathered during your task analysis.

Another method for evaluating the effectiveness of your task analysis is to compare it with the other information gathered during the instructional design process, such as that obtained from the needs analysis and the learner analysis. Do the results of the task analysis match what is known about the goal of the instruction being developed? Have you gathered the information about the content and tasks that is necessary to help learners meet the instructional goal? In addition, what is known about the learners? Have the prerequisite content and skills that need to be included in instruction been correctly identified? Taking a step back from the task analysis results and comparing them with other available information will allow you to evaluate, to some degree, the initial effectiveness of your task analysis.

Finally, a summative evaluation activity you can conduct once the instruction has been implemented is to look at the success of the instruction. Were the learners able to accomplish the instructional goal? If the learners were successful, more than likely your task analysis was conducted effectively.

PROFESSIONALS IN PRACTICE

As director of distance education, I manage a team that works with various faculty members to develop online courses. The typical context in which my team works is one in which a faculty member has taught a course face to face numerous times and for various reasons needs to transition the course into an online format. Because the course has been taught previously, the content has been developed and has been approved by university committees. Formal task analysis is typically not conducted. The instructional designer working with the faculty member does, however, perform a modified task analysis by looking at the content with the faculty member in order to thoroughly understand the content involved in the course. The result is an outline of the content and skills that students will need to be successful in the course.

—Tim Green

SUMMARY

Task analysis is often considered the most critical component of instructional design. Instructional designers must be able to determine the content and tasks for which the instruction is being developed. A properly conducted task analysis will help an instructional designer do so. Instructional designers can take numerous task analysis approaches; however, selection of an approach should be based on the context that surrounds the instruction that needs to be developed. Popular approaches to task analysis include those outlined by Jonassen and colleagues, Morrison et al., Dick et al., and Smith and Ragan. Most task analysis approaches include the use of a SME, who assists the instructional designer by providing guidance on the scope and sequence of the content and tasks that need to be included in the instruction (which in most cases is based on the needs analysis and the learner analysis). The result of a task analysis is a document depicting the scope and sequence of the content and tasks for which the instruction is being developed. Typically, the document will take the form of an outline or a graphical representation such as a flowchart. The effectiveness of a task analysis is often evaluated during the design and development of the instruction by having a SME who was not involved in the initial task analysis critique the results of the task analysis or by comparing the results with other information gathered during instructional design (e.g., needs analysis or learner analysis). After the results are evaluated and modified (if necessary), they are used to develop specific learning goals and objectives that learners will be expected to meet during instruction.

CONNECTING PROCESS TO PRACTICE

1. Several approaches to task analysis were outlined in this chapter. What key elements for conducting a task analysis do these approaches have in common? How do these approaches differ?

2. Describe an instructional design scenario in which you believe a task analysis would be difficult to carry out.

3. Select a common activity that you do regularly. Conduct a task analysis for this activity.

4. You have been hired by an international telephone company to work on an instructional design project. The client has indicated that more than 100 operators need to be trained how to provide customers, who call a toll-free number, with information about the company's products and services. The operators need to be trained how to access this information through the company's electronic knowledge base and how to provide this information to customers in a timely and accurate manner. How would you conduct a task analysis for this project? Outline the process you would use.

5. How might a high school teacher conduct a task analysis when he or she is preparing instruction on the causes of World War II, which will be delivered in the teacher's advanced placement history class?

RECOMMENDED READINGS

Chipman, S. F., Schraagen, J. M., & Shalin, V. L. (2000). An introduction to cognitive task analysis. In J. M. Schraagen, S. F. Chipman, & V. L. Shalin (Eds.), *Cognitive task analysis* (pp. 3–23). Mahwah, NJ: Erlbaum.

Dick, W., Carey, L., & Carey, J. O. (2001). *The systematic design of instruction* (5th ed.). New York: Addison-Wesley/Longman.

Jonassen, D. H., & Hannum, W. H. (1995). Analysis of task analysis procedures. In G. J. Anglin (Ed.), *Instructional technology: Past, present, and future* (2nd ed., pp. 197–209). Englewood, CO: Libraries Unlimited.

Jonassen, D. H., Hannum, W. H., & Tessmer, M. (1989). *Handbook of task analysis procedures.* New York: Praeger.

Jonassen, D. H., Tessmer, M., & Hannum, W. H. (1999). *Task analysis methods for instructional design.* Mahwah, NJ: Erlbaum.

Mager, R. F., & Pipe, P. (1997). *Analyzing performance problems: Or you really oughta wanna* (3rd ed.). Atlanta, GA: Center for Effective Performance.

Morrison, G. R., Ross, S. M., & Kemp, J. E. (2004). *Designing effective instruction* (4th ed.). Hoboken, NJ: Wiley.

REFERENCES

Dick, W., Carey, L., & Carey, J. O. (2001). *The systematic design of instruction* (5th ed.). New York: Addison-Wesley/Longman.

Flanagan, J. C. (1954, July). The critical incident technique. *Psychological Bulletin,* 5(4), 327–358.

Jonassen, D. H., Hannum, W. H., & Tessmer, M. (1989). *Handbook of task analysis procedures.* New York: Praeger.

Jonassen, D. H., Tessmer, M., & Hannum, W. H. (1999). *Task analysis methods for instructional design.* Mahwah, NJ: Erlbaum.

Morrison, G. R., Ross, S. M., & Kemp, J. E. (2004). *Designing effective instruction* (4th ed.). Hoboken, NJ: Wiley.

Richey, R. C., Klein, J., & Nelson, W. (2004). Developmental research: Studies of instructional design and development. In D. Jonassen (Ed.), *Handbook of research for educational communications and technology* (2nd ed., pp. 1099–1130). Bloomington, IN: Association for Educational Communications and Technology.

Smith, P. L., & Ragan, T. J. (1999). *Instructional design* (2nd ed.). Hoboken, NJ: Wiley.

Chapter 7

ANALYZING THE LEARNERS

Key Terms

Changing differences
(*page 131*)

Changing similarities
(*page 131*)

Diagnostic teaching
(*page 122*)

Entry competencies
(*page 127*)

Learner characteristics
(*page 133*)

Learner-centered
environments (*page 122*)

Learning styles (*page 127*)

Member check (*page 136*)

Motivation (*page 125*)

Stable differences
(*page 130*)

Stable similarities
(*page 129*)

Universal design for
education (*page 133*)

Learner analysis is difficult in the company I work for. We have a diverse group of people with varied education levels and performance abilities. For this reason, when I am considering implementing a new training project or program, I may not always be able to complete a learner analysis for all the individuals who may use the training. I try to identify the key users of the new training material and the skill sets they should have. One method I use is surveying. Once the tasks have been identified, I ask a random sample of technicians whether they know how to complete the task or know the answer to the knowledge questions. I clarify with the technicians that I am asking this question only to get an understanding of the general knowledge of the people who will be required to complete the tasks. Such questioning also helps me identify whether additional training information may be required, such as job aids, one-on-one training, and so forth.

—Jona Titus,
Senior Training Specialist,
Intel Corporation,
Hillsboro, OR

Guiding Questions

- What does an instructional designer need to know about the learners for whom he or she is creating instruction?
- How can the common attributes of a group of learners be determined?
- What common attributes among a group of learners are most important for an instructional designer to determine?
- How can the data collected about the learners be organized into a useful format?
- How can an instructional designer determine whether his or her learner analysis is accurate?

Chapter Overview

A corollary activity to task analysis is learner analysis. Determining the learners' approach to the instruction, including their prerequisite knowledge, skills, and attitudes toward the task, is an important part of effective design and development. In this chapter, we describe various methods of determining and articulating learner predispositions, knowledge, and skills. The approaches that various instructional design experts take are also presented and explained. In addition, we offer not only suggestions for formatting the gathered data to make it useful during instructional design and development, but also recommendations of methods for evaluating the effectiveness of a learner analysis.

Analysis of Learners

Creating an instructional intervention that the intended audience cannot or will not use is pointless. Therefore, understanding the target audience of learners and determining in advance what they can and will do is an essential element of any instructional plan. To understand the target audience, you must conduct some form of preliminary evaluation. Learner analysis is considered a critically important component of the instructional design process.

At one time, most educators perceived the learner as an "empty vessel." He or she was without knowledge, and teaching was considered the act of "filling up" students with facts, procedures, and concepts. This approach has long since fallen into disfavor; most educators now perceive learners as individuals who come to each instructional situation with a variety of background experiences that affect the new experience. To prepare instruction appropriately requires consideration of the learners' prior knowledge, viewpoints, and perceived needs.

Bransford, Brown, and Cocking (2000) described the importance of **learner-centered environments,** in which careful attention is given to the skills, knowledge, beliefs, and attitudes that learners bring to an instructional situation. This concept fits well with that of **diagnostic teaching** (Bell, O'Brien, & Shiu, 1980), in which instructional problems are approached through the development of a thorough understanding of the conceptual and cultural knowledge students bring with them to the educational environment.

Nearly everyone would agree that instructional design requires some understanding of the learner, but gaining such understanding through a trustworthy, reliable process can be a challenge. No single, correct method of learner analysis exists for every instructional designer to use.

Some aspects of learner analysis are easily quantifiable, and gathering these data is relatively simple. For example, accurately determining physical characteristics such as age and gender is easy. However, cultural and psychological information can be far more difficult to define.

Although carefully considering the cultural and psychological aspects of the target audience is important, the many variables involved in determining in advance precisely what will be "culturally appropriate" or "psychologically optimal" instruction are beyond anyone's control. At best, the most thorough learner analysis is still a matter of taking a "best guess" at how the instruction should be designed to work efficiently and effectively for the target audience.

A number of theoretical constructs and recommended practices can help an instructional designer conduct the best possible learner analysis. Approaching the task by making use of these constructs and practices can significantly improve the chances of determining what type of instruction will work for the target audience.

Human Needs

Before looking at the intended audience as a group of learners, you should recognize them as a group of *human beings*. Basic human wants and needs must be addressed before any instructional intervention is attempted. Although providing for each of these needs is not the instructional designer's role, you should at least be familiar with how to gauge an individual's or a group's instructional readiness at this essential level.

One of the most popular theoretical constructs addressing the issue of human needs is Maslow's *hierarchy of needs* (Figure 7.1; Maslow, 1968). According to Maslow's theory, at any given time a person's behavior is determined by his or her needs. The hierarchy of needs is typically depicted as a pyramid that has at its base general physiological comforts such as hunger and thirst. Once these bodily comforts are met, the more abstract needs of knowledge, aesthetics, and self-fulfillment may be addressed. At the pinnacle of the hierarchy is the ability to help others find self-fulfillment (*transcendence;* Orlich, Harder, Callahan, Trevisan, & Brown, 2004).

An example of addressing the learners' needs according to Maslow's hierarchy would be ensuring that the learners are not particularly hungry when they participate in instruction (in schools, this issue may be addressed through a free lunch or breakfast program; in a corporate setting, it may be addressed by providing snacks or a meal as part of the instructional event). Once you establish that the intended audience's needs are met to the point at which they are ready to receive instruction, you must determine what content the learners are prepared for and how best to deliver the content to keep all participants active and interested.

FIGURE 7.1

Maslow's Hierarchy of Needs

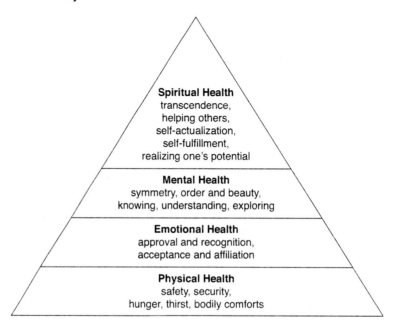

Captive Audience or Willing Volunteers?

For any instructional activity, participants can be divided into two categories: captive audiences and willing volunteers. *Captive audiences* are the people who receive a mandate to receive the instruction (e.g., in the United States children are required to attend school; they are a captive audience). *Willing volunteers* participate in the instructional activity because they are motivated to do so without a mandate: Taking courses for pleasure or pursuing an advanced degree is most often an instructional activity in which individuals choose to participate. You must be able to distinguish between captive audiences and willing volunteers because the two groups can behave differently toward the instruction presented (you rarely hear an adult who has chosen to take a course in painting at a local community college ask, "Why are we doing this?" whereas grade-school pupils in a state-mandated mathematics class ask that question frequently).

Determining the learners' motivations to participate in the developed instruction can greatly improve its effectiveness. **Motivation** is a complicated subject that deserves continued study; we discuss only its basic elements in this section. Motivation can essentially be divided into two classes: intrinsic and extrinsic. If learners enjoy the instruction for its own sake and take pleasure in the activity, the motivation is said to be *intrinsic*. If learners participate in the instruction because they anticipate a reward beyond the instruction itself (e.g., they are paid, or completing the instruction allows them to do something they truly enjoy), the motivation is said to be *extrinsic* (Malone & Lepper, 1987). The question that must be answered during learner analysis is "What motivates the target audience to participate in this instruction?" Determining what makes the students participate can help shape the presentation of the instruction in a way that learners will find most acceptable and appealing.

Popular Approaches to Analyzing Learners

A number of respected instructional design scholars have addressed the issue of learner analysis. The elements common to and unique among these approaches are worth examining as you begin to develop your own learner analysis methodology.

Mager's Approach

As mentioned previously, Robert F. Mager is an author of instructional design texts that have been popular for decades. His approach to learner analysis is a good place to start. Mager (1997)[1] recommended the following procedure:

1. Begin with the realization that a learner analysis is a working document that will not be published or seen by anyone other than yourself and perhaps other members of the instructional design team. You need not organize the content into specific categories.
2. Write down everything you think you know about the target audience. If doing so seems challenging, begin with trigger questions such as the following: "Why are they taking this course?" "Do they want to be in this course?" "What training and experience do they have in relation to the subject matter?"
3. Describe the range of learner characteristics whenever possible.

In addition, according to Mager, when you are conducting a learner analysis, be sure to do the following:

- Take care to describe the learners as they are, not as you would like them to be.

---

[1] ©1997, The Center for Effective Performance, Inc., 1100 Johnson Ferry Road, Suite 150, Atlanta, GA 30342. www.cepworldwide.com 800-558-4237. Reprinted with permission. All rights reserved. No portion of these materials may be reproduced in any manner without the express written consent from The Center for Effective Performance, Inc.

- Describe people, not institutions or policies.
- Describe the differences among the learners as well as the similarities.
- Remember that you are creating a working document that can be amended during the development process.

Mager (1997) recommended analyzing and articulating the following data about the target audience:

1. Age range
2. Sex distribution
3. Nature and range of educational background
4. Reason(s) for attending the course
5. Attitude(s) about course attendance
6. Biases, prejudices and beliefs
7. Typical hobbies and other spare time activities
8. Interests in life other than hobbies
9. Need-gratifiers (rewards that would work)
10. Physical characteristics
11. Reading ability
12. Terminology or topics to be avoided
13. Organizational membership
14. Specific prerequisite and entry-level skills already learned (p. 103)[2]

A common approach to learner analysis is to "ask the students themselves" by generating and distributing a survey or questionnaire. However, Mager (1997) asserted that questionnaires are *not* a useful source of information about the target audience:

> Questionnaires are not a useful source of information about your students. Why izzat, you may wonder? It's because it takes a great deal of skill and time to prepare a questionnaire that will elicit the type of information you may want. Items have to be drafted, and they absolutely must be tested and then revised, and maybe tested again, before one can have any assurance at all that the questionnaire will work. And people with this specialized skill are rare. If they are skilled in questionnaire development, they are not likely to be working in a training department. (p. 102)[3]

Mager's statement about questionnaires is open to debate. Powerful arguments can be developed for and against the use of questionnaires. Instructional

---

[2-3]©1997, The Center for Effective Performance, Inc., 1100 Johnson Ferry Road, Suite 150, Atlanta, GA 30342. www.cepworldwide.com 800-558-4237. Reprinted with permission. All rights reserved. No portion of these materials may be reproduced in any manner without the express written consent from The Center for Effective Performance, Inc.

ID INSIGHT

Taking a Cue from Actors

When an actor studies for a role, he or she reviews what the character says about him- or herself, what the other characters say about him or her, and how the stage directions describe his or her actions. Instructional designers targeting a specific group may want to apply a similar approach by examining what members of the target audience say about themselves, what others say about the target audience, and what performance evidence is available about the target audience (e.g., grades in previous courses or projects completed in other instructional settings). Comparing the perceptions and reports of different sources about the same subject is sometimes referred to as *triangulation* by social scientists.

designers must consider the potential problems and benefits of this popular strategy before deciding whether to use it.

Heinich, Molenda, Russell, and Smaldino's Approach

Heinich, Molenda, Russell, and Smaldino (2002) took a different approach. They suggested that the learner analysis should focus on three aspects of the target audience: general characteristics, specific **entry competencies,** and **learning styles:**

- *General characteristics:* General characteristics include demographic information, such as the learners' ages, physical abilities, and socioeconomic status; the learners' cultural identification or shared values; and the amount of previous experience with the content to be covered. All this information can help the designer make informed decisions about how to prepare and deliver the instruction.

- *Specific entry competencies:* Prior knowledge necessary for learners to succeed with the instruction is critically important to the success of any instructional design project (e.g., creating instruction on how to conduct research on the Internet is pointless if the target audience does not know how to use a mouse).

- *Learning styles:* The psychological predilections of individuals affect what they find to be attractive and effective instruction. Gardner's (1993) aspects of intelligence (verbal–linguistic, logical–mathematical, visual–spatial, musical–rhythmic, bodily–kinesthetic, interpersonal, naturalist, and existentialist) and Gregorc's "mind styles" (concrete-sequential, concrete-random, abstract-sequential, and abstract-random; Butler, 1986) are examples of explanations about how people prefer to approach and deal with problem solving and instruction. Knowledge of these preferences may help the designer create instruction that the target audience can easily understand and accept.

ID INSIGHT

Learning Styles

One hot topic among educators is learning styles. The basic premise is that all individuals can approach learning challenges in a different way, but these approaches are not necessarily idiosyncratic; they can be categorized into common "styles." Arthur Ellis (2001) wrote:

> Most styles advocates stress the idea that each of us receives and processes information differently, and because this is so, teachers should make every attempt to know how students learn best. The logic of this thought dictates to us that although styles are different, they are equal. The argument goes that intelligence and ability are equally but differentially distributed among human beings. Typical school assignments tend to discriminate in favor or against certain learners. But the issue may not be one of ability if one person learns much and another little from, say a lecture presentation. It may be that the lecture format is simply more suited to one person's learning style (auditory, for example) than to another's. What this implies is that otherwise capable people are left behind in many cases because the approach to learning is inappropriate, not because they are incapable of learning the idea. (p. 151)

Popular instruments of styles assessment include the Myers–Briggs Type Indicator, the Learning Styles Inventory, the Sternberg–Wagner Self-Assessment Inventory, and the Embedded Figures Test (Ellis, 2001).

At present, little evidence suggests that designing instruction to meet the specific learning styles of individuals increases their academic achievement (Ellis, 2001). However, awareness that learners apprehend information differently should remind anyone responsible for designing instruction to provide a number of activities that stimulate learners' thinking in different ways.

Dick, Carey, and Carey's Method

Dick, Carey, and Carey (2001) listed the following factors as useful information about the target population:

- Entry behaviors (similar to Heinich et al.'s entry competencies)
- Prior knowledge of the topic area
- Attitudes toward the content and the potential delivery system
- Academic motivation
- Educational and ability levels
- General learning preferences
- Attitudes toward the organization giving the instruction
- Group characteristics

Two items from this list—attitudes toward the content and the potential delivery system, and attitudes toward the organization giving the instruction—are important reminders to take into consideration the impressions and prejudices the learners may have about the instructional content, the method of instruction, and the group providing the instruction. These impressions can have a tremendous impact on the effectiveness of the instruction. Furthermore, the learners' receptiveness to the instruction can be improved by recognizing and addressing their preexisting attitudes, by either capitalizing on positive impressions or addressing early on the concerns raised by negative impressions.

Smith and Ragan's Approach

Smith and Ragan (1999) approached learner analysis by suggesting that the designer categorize learners by their stable and changing similarities and differences:

- *Stable similarities:* The concept of **stable similarities** refers to the idea that learners are generally "configured" similarly (the eyes and ears are located in the same location, as are legs and arms; most learners convert oxygen to carbon dioxide through respiration). Perhaps more important to an instructional designer is knowledge of the perceptual similarities among human beings. For example, human beings can see only what is in their visual field, and the eyes have a mechanism for blocking out visual stimuli altogether (the eyelid); human hearing, however, does not need to be directed (no "field of hearing" exists; we hear everything around us whether or not we direct our attention toward the noise), nor can humans block hearing. Humans have no "*ear*lid"). As another example,

PROFESSIONALS IN PRACTICE

We don't usually have the luxury of doing a formal learner analysis. For live classes, we create a list of prerequisites that a person should have before attending. If someone attends without the prerequisites, he or she may be in for a rough ride. We are extremely specific about prerequisites. Following are several examples:

- Have experience with graphical user administration tools on a data or voice network
- Have installed Windows NT or Windows 2000 and service packs
- Be able to establish a Windows 2000 LAN connection
- Have a current working knowledge of a fourth-generation programming language or an event-driven language (e.g., Visual Basic, C, C++, PowerBuilder, Delphi, Basic, or another procedural language) and have built an application using tools associated with that language

If we are building an online class, the same criteria apply.

—Erik Novak,
Distance Learning Course Developer,
Interactive Intelligence, Inc., Indianapolis, IN

healthy human vision systems can read static text (this ability is called *scanning*), and they can follow movement within their visual field (this ability is called *tracking*), but they cannot do both at the same time (although the vision system can switch between these two tasks in microseconds, which coincidentally causes considerable fatigue). The way human vision works is something anyone designing instructional multimedia should consider.

- *Stable differences:* According to the concept of **stable differences,** any group of learners can be divided into subgroups that are inherently different from the larger group. These differences may be physical (such as gender or age), psychological (including differing learning styles and intelligence levels), or psychosocial (Smith and Ragan described these as personality traits that affect an individual's performance in a learning environment).

- *Changing similarities:* Certain types of human development have been studied extensively and researchers' observations indicate that processes like physical, intellectual, and language development are by and large the same for all people. These processes are considered **changing similarities**. For example, children develop physical dexterity more slowly than they do intellectual and language skills (a typical 6-year-old can describe the activity of creating a toy parachute and can discuss why the parachute slows the descent of the object to which it is attached, but the child probably will not have the dexterity necessary to assemble the parachute). An instructional designer can use knowledge of human development to prepare lessons and activities that are most appropriate for the learner.

- *Changing differences:* Knowledge, values, skills, beliefs, and motivations change with time, and they combine uniquely for each individual. These **changing differences** may be the most difficult elements for which an instructional designer must effectively prepare. Nonetheless, you should recognize that a number of changing differences come into play when you are considering a group of learners.

PROFESSIONALS IN PRACTICE

Changing Differences

When I taught eighth-grade English, I would meet with the seventh-grade teachers each summer to learn about the students who would be entering my class in the fall. It was important to hear about individuals and the group as a whole in order to prepare coursework and activities. However, I knew that the vast physical and emotional changes that many of the students would go through over the summer would alter both individuals and the group dynamic. I used the information the seventh-grade teachers provided, keeping in mind that the students I would meet in the fall would be 3 months older and would have summer experiences that might change their values and perceptions.

—Abbie Brown

ID INSIGHT

Universal Design for Education

Universal design for education, or *universal design for learning*, is an outgrowth of the universal design movements in architecture (Curry, 2003; Howard, 2003). Federal legislation, including the Architectural Barriers Act of 1968 and the Americans with Disabilities Act of 1990, supports a universal design approach that makes all situations accessible to the most learners possible. Taking into consideration that physical and intellectual ability, cultural and ethnic background, and socioeconomic status can affect how people perceive and process information, the universal design for education movement seeks to create environments and instructional contexts that provide equal access to the resources necessary for academic success (Curry, 2003):

> When schools introduce universal design, student diversity becomes a powerful component of the education environment. But implementing the universal design framework goes beyond accommodating individual learners. Because it makes education environments seamlessly and inherently functional for almost all students, universal design minimizes the need for individual accommodations. (pp. 56–57)

Keep in mind that universal design for education is not only about accommodating learners who are mentally or physically disabled, but also about providing appropriate activities and challenges for gifted and talented students. Universal design for education strives to provide appropriate instructional opportunities for all learners in a way that goes beyond attaching "add-on" activities after the instructional design is completed (Howard, 2003). Instructional designers must be aware of the needs of diverse learners and plan activities that welcome meaningful participation by all members of the target audience. Following the principles of universal design for education can help make the planning process easier and the final product more efficient and effective for all participants.

Morrison, Ross, and Kemp's Approach

Morrison, Ross, and Kemp (2004) approached learner analysis by creating a list of the following personal and social characteristics of learners:

- Age and maturity level
- Motivation and attitude toward the subject
- Expectations and vocational aspirations (if appropriate)
- Previous or current employment and work experience (if any)
- Special talents
- Mechanical dexterity
- Ability to work under various environmental conditions, such as noise, inclement weather (for those working outdoors), or high elevations (p. 60)[4]

Morrison et al. (2004) also recommended analyzing the characteristics of *nonconventional learners*. These researchers suggested that special attention be paid to the needs of culturally diverse learners and learners with disabilities. Designing with diverse learners in mind has become a popular topic. One approach that is gaining approval in the field is the **universal design for education,** in which instruction is planned by accounting for the active participation of learners who are culturally and physically diverse.

Learner Analysis Procedure

All the approaches described previously have one premise in common: They stress the need to gather information about the target audience in order to create instruction that is effective, efficient, and appealing for that specific group. Likewise, in all the approaches, the instructional designer is reminded that some types of data are more useful than others for determining appropriate instruction and that even the most careful analysis will result in taking a "best guess" at the learners' skills and needs. Another element common to most learner analysis approaches is the recognition that members of any group will range in ability and interest. Keeping all this in mind, the instructional designer must create a useful working document that describes the target audience. Numerous possibilities for creating such a document are available, two of which are as follows:

1. A chart of **learner characteristics** data
2. A fictitious profile of the average member of the target audience

[4]Reprinted from Morrison, Ross, and Kemp, *Designing Effective Instruction*, 4th ed. 2004. Reprinted with permission by John Wiley & Sons.

TABLE 7.1

Learner Ability Chart

		Learners	
Data Type[a]	**Challenged**	**Average**	**Gifted and Talented**
Reading ability			
Maturity level			
Mechanical dexterity			

[a]The abilities listed were chosen from those described in Mager's (1997) and Morrison, Ross, and Kemp's (2004) approaches to learner analysis for illustration purposes only. The actual abilities chosen for a specific chart depend on the goal of and the context for the instruction.

Charting Learner Characteristics Data

Charting learner characteristics data involves deciding what data to gather and creating a chart that illustrates the range of the learners' abilities (Table 7.1). Typically, instructional designers define the range by describing the average learner, the challenged learner, and the gifted and talented learner. An *average learner* is the typical participant, the person who is most similar to the largest portion of the target audience. The *challenged learner* is an individual who does not have all the entry competencies of the average learner; the challenged learner may also have some differing physical abilities or learning characteristics. The *gifted and talented learner* is an individual with exceptional skills or abilities in all or part of the instructional content; this person may have had more training in the area or may excel naturally.

Creating a Fictitious Profile of the Typical Learner

Another method of compiling the data gathered about the target audience is to create a fictitious profile of a "typical" member of the group (Figure 7.2). Doing so requires a little creativity; the learner must be created from the data provided plus some fictional elements (such as a name).

Comparing the Learner Ability Chart and the Learner Profile

Both charting and creating fictitious profiles have strengths and weaknesses. On the one hand, charts are handy references that provide at-a-glance information, but they are usually more clinical and can lead to a less humanistic approach to designing instruction. Also, charts imply that the information is perfectly reliable, even though learner analysis is not an exact science.

FIGURE 7.2

Learner Profile

This profile describes characteristics similar to those listed in Table 7.1, but some embellishments were added to give the example personal characteristics that a designer can relate to on a human level. Separate profiles can be created to describe challenged learners and gifted and talented learners.

> Shirley is 24 years old with a bachelor's degree in liberal arts from a local university. She is married and has a toddler son. She is concerned about spending too much time at work, away from her family. Shirley reads at a ninth-grade level (above average nationally, average for college graduates). She is a competent computer user and types about 60 words per minute.

On the other hand, profiles are far less clinical, creating a target human being for whom to design instruction. However, the information is less readily accessible than that in a chart, and the creative embellishments may prove more distracting than productive. The instructional designer's job is to find the proper balance between clinical data and creative interpretation that works for the context of the assignment.

ID INSIGHT

User-Centered Design

Specialists in human–computer interaction (HCI) often discuss the need for a user-centered design approach. The essential premise of user-centered design is that learner (or user) analysis should be an ongoing activity throughout the process of designing and developing software. Consideration for the end user's characteristics—"gathering, analyzing and specifying user personas, their tasks, their work environment, and usability and [user interface] requirements" (Seffah, 2003)—must be a part of the designer's thinking from beginning to end. An essential part of user-centered design is usability testing. Put simply, usability testing is an analysis method whereby observers watch individuals or groups use the product to complete a set of prescribed tasks. The problems the subjects encounter in completing the tasks indicate where product revision needs to occur.

(continued)

> "I remember watching a group of graduate students design an interactive kiosk display. In the prototype, a little bell sound accompanied the "Next" button that took the user to a new screen. During usability testing, the students learned that the bell sound was not helpful; the team observed that many of the end users assumed the bell indicated a problem, and they stopped using the software as soon as they heard the bell. Fixing this problem made the final product far more "usable" and effective.
>
> —*Abbie Brown*
>
> User-centered design is intended as a way of looking at the entire software development process in terms of the end user instead of in terms of the programmer or the machine. Keeping the end user in mind is the key to learner analysis. A user-centered design approach is often useful for designing instruction in general and learner analysis in particular.

Evaluation of the Success of a Learner Analysis

After you conduct a learner analysis, how do you know that the results of the analysis are accurate? How do you know that the gathered data have helped you create the best possible instruction? The only sure way to know is to compare the learner analysis results with information on the students who participate in the instruction and to listen to what students have to say about the instruction after they have completed it. Doing so is an important summative evaluation activity that will help you determine the best course of action for subsequent learner analyses.

One way to evaluate the learner analysis during the design and development of the instruction (part of a formative evaluation) is to conduct a **member check.** Member checking is a comparison method of evaluation; the interpretations drawn from the gathered data are shared with a peer who has similar experience with developing instruction for a population like the one for whom you are designing instruction. If the data and interpretations seem familiar and appropriate to the person with similar experiences, the learner analysis was successful.

A member check can also be conducted with someone from the target audience. Asking a member of the target audience whether the profile developed seems appropriate (asking, essentially, "Is this you?") can be helpful in determining the success of the analysis.

SUMMARY

Careful consideration of the target audience helps ensure that the instructional design is effective and efficient for that audience. Learner analysis is a critically important component of any instructional design project. Although many educators once considered students to be "empty vessels" to fill with knowledge, the current perception is that students come to each instructional episode with their own skills, knowledge, and attitudes. No single, correct method of learner analysis exists. Some learner data are easily quantifiable (e.g., age); some data are difficult to quantify (e.g., cultural perspective). Even the most thorough learner analysis is a matter of taking a "best guess" about the target audience. Knowing precisely how the learners will react to new instruction is not possible. However, a number of theoretical constructs can help the instructional designer conduct an effective learner analysis. At the most basic level, the instructional designer can determine in advance whether the learners' basic human needs are being met. The designer can also determine whether the learners are choosing to participate in the instruction or are under some obligation to do so. Popular approaches to learner analysis include those outlined by Mager, Heinich et al., Dick et al., Smith and Ragan, and Morrison et al. Most experts agree that considering the entire range of the target audience is important when you are conducting a learner analysis: The learners who are high achieving and those who are challenged must be considered, as well as the learners who are "average." Two possible procedures for organizing learner analysis data are to create a chart of the data and to use the data to create a fictitious learner profile. Determining the accuracy and effectiveness of the learner analysis is an important evaluation activity. Comparing data and conclusions drawn with those of other educators who work with the same or similar populations is part of a formative evaluation. Gathering data about student reactions to the instruction and interpreting these data is an important summative evaluation activity.

CONNECTING PROCESS TO PRACTICE

1. Do you agree with Mager's statement that questionnaires are *not* a useful source of information about learners?
2. Several perspectives on learner analysis were described in this chapter. What key elements do these perspectives have in common?

3. You are an instructional designer for a large corporation. How would you conduct a learner analysis for a new course on maintaining good customer relations that every sales representative will be required to take?

4. What are the differences among learner analysis approaches for K–12, university, and workplace instruction?

5. You are the instructional designer for a university library and have been assigned the task of creating computer-based instruction on how to find and retrieve journal articles from an electronic database. This instruction will be delivered by using the Internet. What learner analysis processes will you use before you begin to design the instruction?

RECOMMENDED READINGS

Bransford, J. D., Brown, A. L., & Cocking, R. R. (Eds.). (2000). *How people learn: Brain, mind, experience, and school*. Washington, DC: National Academy Press.

Mager, R. F. (1997). *Making instruction work, or skillbloomers* (2nd ed.). Atlanta, GA: Center for Effective Performance.

Norman, D. A. (1988). *The design of everyday things*. New York: Currency Doubleday.

REFERENCES

Bell, A. W., O'Brien, D., & Shiu, C. (1980). Designing teaching in the light of research on understanding. In R. Karplus (Ed.), *Proceedings of the Fourth International Conference for the Psychology of Mathematics Education, Berkeley, CA* (pp. 20–27). Nottingham, UK: International Group for the Psychology of Mathematics.

Bransford, J. D., Brown, A. L., & Cocking, R. R. (Eds.). (2000). *How people learn: Brain, mind, experience, and school*. Washington, DC: National Academy Press.

Butler, K. A. (1986). *Learning and teaching style: In theory and in practice* (2nd ed.). Columbia, CT: Learner's Dimension.

Curry, C. (2003). Universal design accessibility for all learners. *Educational Leadership, 61*(2), 55–60.

Dick, W., Carey, L., & Carey, J. O. (2001). *The systematic design of instruction* (5th ed.). New York: Addison-Wesley/Longman.

Ellis, A. K. (2001). *Research on educational innovations* (3rd ed.). Poughkeepsie, NY: Eye on Education.

Gardner, H. (1993). *Multiple intelligences: The theory in practice.* New York: Basic Books.

Heinich, R., Molenda, M., Russell, J., & Smaldino, S. (2002). *Instructional media and technologies for learning* (7th ed.). Upper Saddle River, NJ: Merrill/ Prentice Hall.

Howard, J. (2003). Universal design for learning: An essential concept for teacher education. *Journal of Computing in Teacher Education, 19*(4), 113–118.

Mager, R. F. (1997). *Making instruction work, or skillbloomers* (2nd ed.). Atlanta, CA: Center for Effective Performance.

Malone, T. W., & Lepper, M. R. (1987). Making learning fun: A taxonomy of intrinsic motivations for learning. In R. E. Snow & M. J. Farr (Eds.), *Aptitude, learning, and instruction: Vol. 3. Cognitive and affective process analysis* (pp. 223–253). Hillsdale, NJ: Erlbaum.

Maslow, A. H. (1968). *Motivation and personality.* New York: Van Nostrand.

Morrison, G. R., Ross, S. M., & Kemp, J. E. (2004). *Designing effective instruction* (4th ed.). New York: Wiley.

Orlich, D. C., Harder, R. J., Callahan, R. C., Trevisan, M. S., & Brown, A. H. (2004). *Teaching strategies: A guide to effective instruction* (7th ed.). Boston: Houghton Mifflin.

Seffah, A. (2003). Human-centered design skills and patterns for software engineers' education. *Interactions, 10*(5), 36–45.

Smith, P. L., & Ragan, T. J. (1999). *Instructional design* (2nd ed.). New York: Wiley.

CREATING INSTRUCTION

Planning, Designing, and Implementing the Intervention

8 Developing Instructional Goals and Objectives

9 Organizing Instruction

10 Creating Learning Environments and Producing Instructional Activities

The needs, task, and learner analyses described in the previous section help you determine what kind of instructional intervention is best for your learners. The next step is to decide how to best organize the events that make up the instructional intervention. In Chapters 8, 9, and 10, we describe the principles, processes, and practices of setting instructional goals and objectives, organizing instruction, and selecting appropriate instructional activities.

In Chapter 8, we explain how instructional designers create instructional goals and objectives, which determine what students will do during the instruction. Chapter 9 provides an introduction to the principles, processes, and practices of organizing instruction, which helps the designer determine the scope and sequence of the activities in which the learner will engage. In Chapter 10, we describe the variety of learning environments and instructional activities that may be incorporated into an instructional design. These goals, objectives, sequences, and activities are the elements of the instructional design to which the learners will be directly exposed.

Chapter 8

DEVELOPING INSTRUCTIONAL GOALS AND OBJECTIVES

Key Terms

"ABCD" approach
(*page 146*)

Affective knowledge
(*page 152*)

Bloom's taxonomy
(*page 151*)

Cognitive, affective, and
psychomotor domains
(*page 147*)

Declarative knowledge
(*page 152*)

Enabling objectives
(*page 147*)

Functional analysis system
technique (FAST)
(*page 149*)

Gagne's hierarchy of
intellectual skills
(*page 151*)

Performance objectives
(*page 146*)

Performance technology
approach (*page 146*)

Procedural knowledge
(*page 152*)

Subordinate skills analysis
(*page 146*)

Terminal objective
(*page 147*)

I begin setting the instructional goals and objectives when I am completing the front-end analysis. At this time, I can get a clear understanding of the goals and objectives of the person requesting the training. Because I've categorized the tasks required for the training into knowledge and performance activities, I can then verify these objectives once the task analysis is completed and add goals and objectives to the training. Often, I will have a large list of potential goals and objectives. Once I have my list, I work with the content expert and pare down the goals and objectives to a few key items, making sure to include a good balance of knowledge and performance objectives.

—Jona Titus,
Senior Training Specialist,
Intel Corporation,
Hillsboro, OR

Guiding Questions

- What is an instructional goal?
- What is an instructional objective?
- How do instructional goals and objectives differ?
- How does an instructional designer begin writing or identifying instructional goals?
- How does an instructional designer create instructional objectives?

Chapter Overview

Determining goals is an essential part of instructional design and development. Defining specific instructional objectives is more often than not a critically important consideration as well. In this chapter, we explain the difference between instructional goals and instructional objectives and examine a variety of approaches instructional design experts use to define and develop them. Common methods of describing learning outcomes are presented, as are methods of evaluating the success of goal setting and objective specification.

Instructional Goals and Objectives

My goal is simple. It is a complete understanding of the universe, why it is as it is and why it exists at all.

—Stephen Hawking

Creating any form of instruction without first setting goals for it is pointless. The instructional intervention must be designed to *do something*—to cause a change in the learner's knowledge, skill, or attitude—otherwise, it is nothing more than a toy, a collection of artifacts, or an aimless discussion or presentation.

The Difference Between Goals and Objectives

Instructional goals and instructional objectives are different. An instructional *goal* can be a general statement about the intention of the instruction—for example, "Students will become better writers." An instructional *objective*, however, is usually much more specific about how and to what degree the instruction will affect the learners. If the instructional goal is "Students will become better writers," one instructional objective might be "Upon completing the lesson, students will produce a traditional, 'five-point' essay with a recognizable introductory paragraph that includes a thesis statement, three paragraphs supporting the thesis statement, and a concluding paragraph that restates the thesis."

An instructional goal can be used as an organizing topic for subordinate instructional objectives. For example, the instructional goal "Students will recognize and value the behaviors of a healthy lifestyle" might serve as the organizing topic for a number of specific instructional objectives (see Figure 8.1).

FIGURE 8.1

Example of an Instructional Goal and Subordinate Objectives

Notice that all the objective statements include active verbs (*describe, predict, create, produce*).

Goal	Students will recognize and value the behaviors of a healthy lifestyle.
Objective 1	Students will *describe* the differences between complex and simple carbohydrates.
Objective 2	Students will *predict* the consequences of including too many simple carbohydrates in their diet.
Objective 3	Students will *create* an appropriate exercise plan for themselves on the basis of their personal requirements.
Objective 4	Students will *produce* a personal daily schedule that includes sufficient time for rest and recreation.

The example goal and objectives listed in Figure 8.1 all have one thing in common: They focus on what the learner will do upon completing the instruction. Keep in mind that this approach to designing instruction is a key component of instructional *systems* design. Other approaches to instructional design might not put as much emphasis on specific, observable learner outcomes and thus may not require objectives written in this manner.

Some designers believe that important outcomes of instruction are difficult to define and measure (Morrison, Ross, & Kemp, 2004). In fact, some designers would go so far as to say generating goals and objectives through traditional, systems methods is not a useful pursuit. This perspective would be in keeping with a postmodern philosophy that suggests that instruction should not necessarily be designed on the premise of a positivist worldview. The learner may deem the instruction successful because it accomplishes personal goals and objectives that the designer cannot determine in advance. We would argue that regardless of an individual's view, by definition, a design must have some goal defined at the outset, and instructional design is not an exception.

The development of instructional goals and objectives depends on the type and purpose of the instruction you are creating. Creating instruction on how to fly a fighter jet requires specific objectives that have demonstrable outcomes. However, creating instruction about the history of flight may not require objectives written according to a systems approach.

Popular Approaches to Setting Goals and Objectives

Mager's Approach

The approach to developing learning objectives that instructional designers use most often was created by Robert F. Mager. Mager's approach is designed to generate **performance objectives** and is inextricably connected to behavioristic instructional design applications. Mager (1997) recommended using three components to write learning objectives:

1. *Action:* Identify the action the learner will be taking when he or she has achieved the objective.
2. *Conditions:* Describe the relevant conditions under which the learner will be acting.
3. *Criterion:* Specify how well the learner must perform the action.

According to Mager (1997), a learning objective is "a description of a performance you want learners to be able to exhibit before you consider them competent" (p. 3). Dick, Carey, and Carey (2001) and Heinich, Molenda, Russell, and Smaldino (2002) took similar approaches, focusing on the actions, conditions, and criteria.

Dick, Carey, and Carey's Approaches

Dick and colleagues (2001) suggested that goals and objectives are determined through one of two approaches: Either they are prescribed by a subject matter expert (SME), or they are determined by a performance technology approach. SMEs may be called on to work with the instructional designer to articulate the appropriate goals and objectives for an instructional design project. In contrast to a SME's prescription of goals and objectives, in a **performance technology approach,** they are derived from the data gathered during a needs analysis. According to Dick et al., once the goals are established, a **subordinate skills analysis** should be conducted to determine the specific performance objectives for the instruction.

"ABCD" Approach

Heinich et al. (2002) described the **"ABCD" approach** to creating well-stated objectives. *ABCD* stands for audience, behavior, conditions, and degree:

- *Audience:* Identify and describe the learners.
- *Behavior:* Describe what is expected of the learners after they receive instruction.

FIGURE 8.2

Example of Terminal and Enabling Objectives

Topic	Magnetic attraction
General purpose	To acquire knowledge and understanding of the properties of magnetic materials
Terminal objective	To describe the general properties of magnetic materials
Enabling objective	To discriminate between magnetic and nonmagnetic materials

- *Conditions:* Describe the setting and circumstances in which the learners' performance will occur.
- *Degree:* Explain the standard for acceptable performance.

Heinich et al. also classified objectives as belonging to one of four domains: cognitive, affective, motor skill (psychomotor), and interpersonal. The unusual domain in this scheme is the interpersonal domain. Skills that are "people centered," such as teamwork, administration, and selling ability are separated from the more traditional **cognitive, affective, and psychomotor domains** and given a place of their own.

Morrison, Ross, and Kemp's Approach

Morrison et al. (2004) discussed the idea of terminal and enabling objectives (Figure 8.2). A **terminal objective** is the major objective for an instructional intervention, articulating "the overall learning outcomes expressed originally as the general purpose for a topic" (p. 116).[1] The **enabling objectives** are supporting descriptions of observable behaviors or actions that indicate that the terminal objective has been achieved.

Goal Setting

Goals describe the intention of the instruction. According to Mager (1997), "A goal is a statement describing a broad or abstract intent, state or condition" (p. 33). In general, goals cannot be directly perceived. For example, the statement "Students will appreciate classical music" is a reasonable instructional

[1]Reprinted from Morrison, Ross, and Kemp, *Designing Effective Instruction*, 4th ed. 2004. Reprinted with permission by John Wiley & Sons.

goal, but it does not have specific observable features. The students may be listening, but how do you determine whether they are appreciative?

Regardless of any lack of visible evidence, setting goals for instruction is a critically important part of the instructional design process. Writing goals is often relatively easy if you are starting with a "clean slate"—a situation in which no instructional interventions have been attempted and no past practices have been established. However, you are rarely offered a completely clean slate when you are designing instruction. Often, a number of established instructional interventions are in place, and people may have lost sight of the original goals for this instruction. Instructional designers almost always work within an organizational structure with its own idiosyncratic demands. More than likely, tradition, politics, and the decision makers' predilections will be critical factors in determining the goals for any instructional design project (Dick et al., 2001).

To gain some sense of what the goals are for an instructional situation, you may have to begin by working backward, using the established practices

PROFESSIONALS IN PRACTICE

When I taught eighth-grade English, I traditionally ended the year by having my classes read Shakespeare's *As You Like It.* The goal was to build students' confidence with a difficult text (we did so through activities that included "translating" passages into modern language and acting out and illustrating scenes from the play). One year, I had a particularly difficult group of students; I decided not to read *As You Like It* with the group because I believed the goal of building their confidence would not be met—I thought that trying to do something so ambitious with this particular group might have the opposite effect.

When the students discovered that I was not planning to read Shakespeare with them in the spring, they expressed deep disappointment. I learned from them that my former students considered reading a Shakespeare play in eighth grade a rite of passage. Even though I did not believe this activity was an appropriate way to address one of my goals for this particular group of students, I did it anyway because the students would have felt "cheated" if I had not. I realized that one goal for this activity was not something that I had created, but that had grown out of the student community.

—Abbie Brown

FIGURE 8.3

A Simple FAST (Functional Analysis System Technique) Chart

as a foundation for articulating the larger goals. One method of determining instructional goals in this manner is to apply the **functional analysis system technique (FAST)** to create a FAST chart (Thornburg, 1998).

FAST charting was developed in the field of value engineering, where it is used to decrease costs, increase profits, and improve quality (for more on this topic, visit the Society of American Value Engineers' Web site—www.value-eng.com—or SAVE International—www.value-eng.org).

When you create a FAST chart to determine the goals for instruction, you generate verb–noun pairs to describe the specific activities that apply directly to the outcome of the instruction (e.g., "Write poem"; "Fix sink"). The abstraction of the verb–noun pairs is increased with each successive description of the activity (putting the verb–noun pairs on adhesive notes makes rearranging them as the need arises particularly easy). A simple example can be seen in Figure 8.3.

In the sample FAST chart shown in Figure 8.3, "Maintain health" is the goal derived from the action of brushing your teeth. To some individuals, this goal may be obvious, but to many people, brushing their teeth is such an ingrained activity that they lose sight of the fact that the larger goal is maintaining a healthy body. The FAST chart technique is particularly helpful when an established or expected set of instructional activities is part of standard practice and you as the instructional designer are trying to determine why those activities are important.

Translation of Goals into Objectives

Just as a goal is the intention of the instruction, an objective is the intended outcome of each instructional activity. The intended outcome can be described as what the learner will be able to do upon completing the instruction. Determining the intended outcome in advance is an important step in the design process if student success will ultimately be measured against specific evaluation criteria or a standard. Clearly stating instructional objectives

PROFESSIONALS IN PRACTICE

In our software company, the process for setting instructional goals and objectives is driven by advances in technology. Every new product release or upgrade has an impact on the person who ultimately uses the software. Instructional goals and objectives are dictated by the product characteristics. Our course developers are in daily contact with software engineers so that they can determine the following factors:

- What has changed?
- Who will be affected by the change?
- What other systems are affected by the change?
- What is the best way to impart knowledge about this concept?

—*Erik Novak,*
Distance Learning Course Developer,
Interactive Intelligence, Inc.,
Indianapolis, IN

also makes producing instruction that meets with the approval of everyone involved easier for the design team. Smith and Ragan (1999) wrote,

> Objectives are valuable to all members of the learning system. They aid the designer since they provide a focus of the instruction, guiding the designer in making decisions about what content should be included, what strategy should be used, and how students should be evaluated. The specification of clear objectives is especially critical when a number of individuals—such as designers, content experts, graphic artists, and programmers—are working together to produce instruction. In these situations, learning objectives serve as a concrete focus of communication. (p. 84)

The instructional designer must keep in mind that a well-stated instructional objective describes an observable or a measurable action performed by the learner. The objective should describe what the learner might be observed doing that he or she could not do prior to the instruction. A typical "rookie mistake" is to write an objective that is just a description of the instructional activity. The example "Students will view a 30-minute videotape on the basics of photography" is *not* a well-written instructional objective; a better example would be "After viewing a 30-minute videotape

FIGURE 8.4

Bloom's Taxonomy of Educational Objectives: Cognitive Domain

Evaluating the value of material for a given purpose

Synthesizing something new from given material

Analyzing material by breaking it down into its components to understand its organizational structure

Applying learned material in new and concrete contexts

Comprehending new material

Knowing previously learned material

on the basics of photography, students will demonstrate their ability to choose the correct f-stop setting for a variety of lighting conditions."

We cannot discuss creating instructional objectives without referring to **Bloom's taxonomy** (Bloom, Engelhart, Furst, Hill, & Krathwohl, 1956). Since the mid-1950s, educators have used Bloom's taxonomy as a common point of reference for setting instructional objectives:

> Perhaps the taxonomy's greatest contribution has been in the development of a professional language. Teachers and administrators who describe and analyze instruction know that terms such as *knowledge level* and *higher levels of learning* will be understood by educators everywhere. (Orlich, Harder, Callahan, Trevisan, & Brown, 2004, p. 92)

Bloom's taxonomy is divided into three domains—cognitive, affective, and psychomotor—which are described in more detail in Chapter 3. Educators use the cognitive domain (Figure 8.4) most often, no doubt because cognition is usually the focus of formal education.

The headings of Bloom's taxonomy can be used to write performance objectives. Objectives that begin with phrases such as "Students will *know* . . . ," "Students will *apply* . . . ," and "Students will *evaluate* . . ." are reasonably well understood by educators because the taxonomic description of the active verbs in these phrases creates a common understanding among individuals familiar with the taxonomy. The wording used in the levels of the three domains (cognitive, affective, and psychomotor) is a good place to start when you are writing objectives.

Another theoretical construct popular among instructional designers and useful for determining instructional objectives is **Gagne's hierarchy of**

FIGURE 8.5

Gagne's Hierarchy of Intellectual Skills
In this hierarchy, you start at the bottom (discrimination) and work up to problem solving.

> **Problem solving.** Students are asked to determine if the platypus is a mammal or a bird.
>
> **Rule or principle.** The defined concepts are restated into general rules about how to decide if an animal is a mammal or a bird.
>
> **Defined concept.** Students use their observations of mammals and birds to determine the differences between mammals and birds.
>
> **Discrimination.** Students look at various mammals and birds.

intellectual skills (Gagne, 1985; Zook, 2001). Gagne took an approach to the domains of instruction similar to that of Bloom's taxonomy, but with important differences. Gagne divided what can be learned into three categories: **declarative knowledge** (verbal information), **procedural knowledge** (motor skills, intellectual skills, and cognitive strategies), and **affective knowledge** (attitudes). He stated that five types of learning outcomes are possible: intellectual skill, cognitive strategy, verbal information, motor skill, and attitude. Gagne's hierarchy of intellectual skills (the skills most often addressed through instruction) states that a progression can be followed to bring a student to the point of being able to solve problems on his or her own. The four steps in this progression are discrimination, defined concept, rule or principle, and problem solving (see Figure 8.5).

Traditionally in instructional design, a goal is a general statement of the educators' intentions; an objective is a specific instance of the goal in action. If the goal is "Students will develop social skills," specific objectives may include "Students will say *please* and *thank you* at the appropriate times" and "Students will hold the door for each other as they enter and exit the building."

Articulating instructional goals is important; they are the written embodiment of the intention behind the instructional intervention. Using instructional goals to create instructional objectives can be equally important, particularly if the effectiveness of the instruction and the achievement of the learners will be measured against a set of standards or a list of specific evaluation criteria. Well-stated objectives help everyone involved in creating and supporting the instructional event by providing focus for the instructional activities.

PROFESSIONALS IN PRACTICE

I personally do not like setting strict instructional goals and objectives. Because each learner is different from others, we cannot make something that is "one size fits all." As Prensky (2001) stated, such an approach was the old paradigm. Because learning is an active process, it shows an adaptive nature. For me, setting strict objectives does not seem realistic. Instead, I like to define more general goals and objectives. Moreover, strict goals and objectives put learners in a passive mode. While talking about their instructional system building process, Prensky stated, "The words 'objective,' 'learn,' and 'know how to' were banned, replaced with imperative action verbs like 'build,' 'get through,' 'repair,' and 'rescue'" (p. 14). I can't be that radical, but I like this approach. Moreover, while defining the goals and objectives, I must not focus on only individuals—the organizational structure and culture must also be considered. Such consideration is necessary because individuals live in this social setting, so the issues about individuals should not be isolated from their environments.

On the basis of my experience, I can say that the results of learner, task, and needs analyses almost always yield the general goals and objectives of the instruction.

—*Kursat Cagiltay,*
Professor,
Department of Computer Education and Instructional Technology,
Middle East Technical University,
Ankara, Turkey

Evaluation of the Success of Instructional Goal Setting and Objective Specification

The specified instructional goals and objectives should be supported by the data gathered during learner and task analyses. The question to answer about the goals and objectives is this: "Do these goals and objectives direct us to create instruction that supports the identified population of learners in gaining skill with the tasks that have been identified?" In traditional instructional design, taking time to consider whether the goals and objectives that were developed have truly grown out of the learner and task analyses is important.

Another approach to evaluating the success of the specified goals and objectives is to compare them against each other. As the project takes shape, the designer determines whether the objectives are appropriate by continuing to ask him- or herself whether the objectives support the goals. Conversely, at the same time, to determine whether the instructional goals are appropriately articulated, the designer asks him- or herself whether the goals realistically reflect the objectives.

SUMMARY

Goals and objectives define the intention of the instruction. An instructional goal is a general statement about the ultimate intention of the instruction. An instructional objective is a more specific statement about how and to what degree the instruction will affect the learners. The objective should describe an action taken by the learner at the conclusion of the instructional event that an observer can empirically measure.

Goals must be articulated in order to create instruction. Objectives, however, are subordinate to goals and may or may not be necessary to an instructional design. Objectives are critically important if the learners are to be evaluated on the basis of standards or specific criteria. However, if learners will not be evaluated in this manner and if, for example, the instruction is intended to foster creativity or critical thinking, writing specific instructional objectives may be inappropriate.

Popular approaches to goal and objective writing include Mager's development of performance objectives (determining the action, conditions, and criterion), Dick et al.'s dual approaches of determining goals and objectives by either consulting SMEs or taking a performance technology approach (deriving goals and objectives from the data gathered during needs and task analyses), Heinich et al.'s ABCD (audience, behavior, conditions, degree) approach, and Morrison et al.'s terminal and enabling objectives.

Novice instructional designers must realize that most often they will be creating instruction for organizations that have their own traditions and political necessities; instructional objectives may be well articulated, whereas the instructional goals may not be written down. Missing or poorly articulated instructional goals may be determined by using a FAST chart and working from a specific instructional objective back to a general goal.

Writing instructional objectives can be facilitated through the use of hierarchies or taxonomies that define the types and levels of instructional outcomes. Bloom's taxonomy and Gagne's hierarchy of intellectual skills are reference tools popular among educators.

When evaluating the success of writing instructional goals and objectives, the instructional designer must consider one critically important question: "Will the goals and objectives lead to the creation of instruction that is appropriate and effective for the learners?" Constant comparison of the goals with the objectives (and vice versa) can help make the final instructional product truly useful.

CONNECTING PROCESS TO PRACTICE

1. Several methods for determining goals and objectives were introduced in this chapter. What key elements do these methods have in common? What are some of the essential differences among them?

2. You have been asked to create a 6-week unit on writing poetry for a high school English class. How would you determine the appropriate goals and objectives for this task?

3. In which organizational settings are instructional designers most likely to use Gagne's hierarchy instead of Bloom's taxonomy?

4. You are the instructional designer in the human resources department of a midsize corporation. You have been assigned the task of creating instruction that addresses the appropriate use of corporate expense accounts. What factors may affect the goals you set for this instruction?

5. Your employer wants to be sure that everyone in the organization knows CPR (cardiopulmonary resuscitation). What goals might you derive for instruction that supports this knowledge?

6. You are teaching a group of 10-year-olds how to play soccer. You want them to improve their ball-passing skills. What goals and objectives might you set for your instruction?

RECOMMENDED READINGS

Bloom, B. S., Engelhart, M. D., Furst, E. J., Hill, W. H., & Krathwohl, D. R. (1956). *Taxonomy of educational objectives: The classification of educational goals. Handbook I: Cognitive domain.* New York: McKay.

Gagne, R. (1985). *The conditions of learning* (4th ed.). Philadelphia: Holt, Rinehart & Winston.

REFERENCES

Bloom, B. S., Engelhart, M. D., Furst, E. J., Hill, W. H., & Krathwohl, D. R. (1956). *Taxonomy of educational objectives: The classification of educational goals. Handbook I: Cognitive domain.* New York: McKay.

Dick, W., Carey, L., & Carey, J. O. (2001). *The systematic design of instruction* (5th ed.). New York: Addison-Wesley/Longman.

Gagne, R. (1985). *The conditions of learning* (4th ed.). Philadelphia: Holt, Rinehart & Winston.

Heinich, R., Molenda, M., Russell, J., & Smaldino, S. (2002). *Instructional media and technologies for learning* (7th ed.). Upper Saddle River, NJ: Merrill/Prentice Hall.

Mager, R. F. (1997). *Goal analysis: How to clarify your goals so you can actually achieve them* (3rd ed.). Atlanta, GA: Center for Effective Performance.

Morrison, G. R., Ross, S. M., & Kemp, J. E. (2004). *Designing effective instruction* (4th ed.). Hoboken, NJ: Wiley.

Orlich, D. C., Harder, R. J., Callahan, R. C., Trevisan, M. S., & Brown, A. H. (2004). *Teaching strategies: A guide to effective instruction* (7th ed.). Boston: Houghton Mifflin.

Prensky, M. (2001). *Digital game-based learning.* New York: McGraw-Hill.

Smith, P. L., & Ragan, T. J. (1999). *Instructional design* (2nd ed.). New York: Wiley.

Thornburg, D. D. (1998). *Brainstorms and lightning bolts: Thinking skills for the 21st century.* San Carlos, CA: Thornburg Center.

Zook, K. (2001). *Instructional design for classroom teaching and learning.* Boston: Houghton Mifflin.

Chapter 9

ORGANIZING INSTRUCTION

Key Terms

Curriculum *(page 161)*
Dale's cone of experience *(page 164)*
Distance education *(page 161)*
Enactive experiences *(page 165)*
Events of instruction *(page 163)*
Generative (instructional event) *(page 164)*

Iconic experiences *(page 165)*
Job aids *(page 171)*
Learning management system (LMS) *(page 169)*
Lesson plans *(page 161)*
Program of study *(page 161)*
Programmed instruction *(page 168)*

Scope and sequence *(page 160)*
Supplantive (instructional event) *(page 164)*
Syllabus *(page 161)*
Symbolic experiences *(page 165)*
Units (of instruction) *(page 161)*

I work in an ethnically diverse middle school and therefore have many second-language learners. My goals and objectives must meet state standards, but they must also meet the significantly different needs of all my students. Therefore, I have to structure my lessons to fit the class. In social studies, I incorporate a variety of strategies, including GLAD (guided language acquisition and development) strategies, when introducing new cultures and concepts. Lessons always begin by activating background knowledge, getting students to make the connections between their world and the ancient world. Repetition is a key factor to success, and we do chants and sing songs to help remember what has been learned. Prior to a new lesson, we discuss the previous lesson and watch as each lesson builds on the next in order to better grasp the ancient cultures that we study.

—Jody Peerless,
Sixth-grade teacher,
Washington Middle School,
La Habra, CA

Guiding Questions

- How does organizing content and learning activities help an instructional designer?
- What is a curriculum?
- What are the events of instruction?
- What is the continuum of learning experiences?
- What are the various methods of instructional delivery?

Chapter Overview

Designing the best instruction possible involves organizing instructional activities to create a satisfying and effective learning experience. Doing so is particularly important when the content to be covered is sizable (e.g., year-long training; multiple years of study for a degree; an entire K–12 curriculum). The activities of any one lesson must often fit appropriately into a larger educational scheme. Understanding how these larger schemes work and how to develop such a scheme allows the instructional designer to deliver better instruction.

Organizing content allows the designer to see the depth and breadth of the content to be covered, while organizing instructional activities allows him or her to see the range of methods used to communicate the content to the learner. A course of study organized by the content to be covered and the activities used to cover it is called a curriculum. A curriculum for any course of study is described by its scope and sequence, the instructional events and learning experiences it encompasses, and the methods by which these events and experiences are delivered.

Scope and Sequence of Instruction

The **scope and sequence** of instruction encompasses a wide range of possibilities. Instruction can be designed to incorporate many activities during a long time period (e.g., a program of study leading to a graduate degree), a single activity in a brief period (e.g., the instructions on the back of a packet

ID INSIGHT

Curriculum

The word *curriculum* is Latin. Its original meaning is related to racing and racecourses. According to the *Oxford Latin Dictionary* (Glare, 1983), a curriculum is a race, a lap in a race, or a racetrack. Today, the word *curriculum* is used to refer to the organization of a course of study. A curriculum can be thought of as the set of markers necessary to define a course.

of instant soup), or anything between. The instructional designer determines the scope and sequence of the activities on the basis of the goals and objectives he or she has developed through needs, task, and learner analyses.

In K–12 settings, people most often think in terms of curricula, units, and lesson plans. The **curriculum** is the entire scope of what is to be learned from beginning (prekindergarten) to end (12th grade); a curriculum is therefore most often measured in years. **Units** are measured in months or weeks; they are large sets of activities that relate to a specific theme (e.g., oceanography or Greek myths). **Lesson plans** contain the specific, day-to-day activities that compose a unit. The activities articulated in lesson plans are measured in hours or minutes.

In college and university settings, people think in terms of programs of study, syllabi, and classes. A **program of study** is the entire set of courses that, once completed, leads to the conferring of a degree (e.g., bachelor of arts, master of science). A **syllabus** is the scope and sequence description for a single course (usually one semester long), and classes are the individual meetings held regularly throughout the semester. (Classes are sometimes referred to as *lessons* in postsecondary education, particularly in the case of nonsynchronous **distance education,** when students and the instructor do not meet at a specific time on a specific day but instead complete assignments that include presentations, reading, and responding within a given period, usually a week or a few days.)

In nonacademic settings such as business or government, instruction may be approached in terms of competencies and certifications. These institutions may organize instructional activities in terms of courses or study guides that support individuals in improving work-related skills or achieving passing scores on professional certification examinations.

According to Orlich, Harder, Callahan, Trevisan, and Brown (2004), sequencing instruction serves one of two essential purposes: to isolate a piece of knowledge (a concept or principle) to help students comprehend its unique characteristics, or to relate the concept or principle to a larger organized body of knowledge. Determining the scope of instruction serves the essential purpose of placing some restriction on just how much of any topic will be covered as part of the instruction.

For any instructional event, both the scope (the amount of information) and the sequence (the order in which the information will be presented) must be determined. Regardless of how the instruction is organized and divided, some scope and sequence must be developed at the outset to determine what is to be taught and the order in which it will be presented.

Levels of Organization: Macro, Micro, Vertical, and Horizontal

Curriculum expert George Posner (1995) described organizing instruction by *macro and micro levels* and by *vertical and horizontal dimensions*. Macro and micro levels are relative terms when used in connection with instructional organization. According to Posner, the broadest macro level refers to educational levels (e.g., the difference between elementary and secondary education). The micro level at its most specific refers to the relationships among concepts, facts, or skills within lessons. Posner's descriptions of horizontal and vertical dimensions of instruction help clarify the difference between *scope* and *sequence*. If you think of a program of study laid out sequentially (like a time line), the *sequence* of study is the vertical dimension (e.g., first grade, second grade, third grade). The horizontal dimension describes the *scope*—that is, all the various concurrent and integrated activities. According to Posner, "The aspect of curriculum organization that describes the correlation or integration of content taught concurrently is termed *horizontal organization*. The aspect of curriculum organization that describes the sequencing of content is termed *vertical organization*" (p. 124).

Organizational Structures: Content and Media

Posner (1995) stated that only two basic methods can be used to organize a curriculum or program of study. Instruction can be organized by using either a *content* or a *media* structure. In content structure, the instruction is organized by the concepts, skills, or attitudes students are to acquire (as described by the instructional objectives). In a media structure, the instruction is organized by the activities, methods, and materials used to teach the concepts, skills, or attitudes described by the instructional objectives.

Events of Instruction

Associated with Posner's micro level organization of instruction is determining the order of the activities within a given lesson, which are commonly known as the *events of instruction*. These events are discrete activities that work best in a specific order. The most elemental series of instructional events consists of an introduction, a body (a variety of activities related to the content), a conclusion, and an assessment (Smith & Ragan, 1999). As an example, consider Figure 9.1, an example of a K–12 teacher's daily lesson plan. The activities and evaluation sections are labeled with the four elemental events of instruction.

FIGURE 9.1

Example of a K–12 Teacher's Daily Lesson Plan

Background: A class of 24 second-grade students

Goal: To understand the concept "Air takes up space"

Objective: By the end of the lesson, students will be able to describe how a parachute works.

Activities:

Introduction

1. *Introductory discussion:* Remind students about making scientific observations and introduce the new concept.

Body

2. *Toy parachutes:* Using clothespins, string, and paper towels, students create their own parachutes.
3. *Sailboat submarines:* Using walnut shells, toothpicks, construction paper, and glue, students create small sailboats.

Conclusion

4. *Summative discussion* about air: Ask students to think of other demonstrations of the concept "Air takes up space."

Assessment

Evaluation: Students were asked to devise their own demonstrations for the concept "Air takes up space." Acceptable responses range from . . .

The eminent instructional designer and scholar Robert Gagne (1916–2002) theorized that designers must consider nine **events of instruction** (1985):

1. Gain the learners' attention.
2. Inform learners of the objective.
3. Stimulate recall of prior learning.
4. Present the stimulus.
5. Provide guidance for the learners.
6. Elicit learner performance.
7. Provide feedback.
8. Assess learner performance.
9. Enhance retention and transfer (varied practice and reviews).

To put this theory into practice, you must create at least one instructional activity for each of the events described. The order of the activities makes a difference in the effectiveness of the instruction. Careful consideration of instructional events is analogous to the consideration that goes into a well-planned meal: The order of dishes served affects the overall experience.

Although the events of instruction are most often described in terms that make the teacher seem to be the active participant and the learners passive recipients of instruction, this situation is not the case. Both directed and open-ended learning environments have carefully planned instructional events. In both environments, students may take an active role in each instructional event. Smith and Ragan (1999) observed that each instructional event can be viewed as having two aspects: the **supplantive**, supplied by the instruction, and the **generative**, generated by the student. For example, during an introduction event, the instructor may present activities intended to gain the learner's attention, but the learner must activate his or her attention to participate effectively. Likewise, during the body of a lesson, the instructor may present the activities, but the learner must actively participate by doing such things as focusing his or her attention, using learning strategies, and offering and responding to feedback. The events of instruction should be considered a reciprocal process in which instructors and students make contributions that lead to an effective learning experience.

Continuum of Learning Experiences

All learning experiences can be placed on a continuum. At one end of this continuum are the experiences in which the learner acquires skills, concepts, and attitudes by participating in a concrete, real-world activity. As an extreme example of this type of learning experience, a person may learn to swim by being thrown into deep water; the only option available short of drowning is for the person to determine how to stay afloat and propel him- or herself. At the other end of this continuum are the experiences in which the learner is exposed to skills, concepts, and attitudes through completely contrived, or abstract, activity. An extreme example of this type of learning experience would be for a person to learn to swim by only having someone describe it—without the person's getting near water.

Most instructional activities fall somewhere between the two extremes of this concrete–abstract continuum. One of the most popular methods of categorizing learning activities within this continuum is **Dale's cone of experience** (Figure 9.2; Dale, 1969; Heinich, Molenda, Russell, & Smaldino,

FIGURE 9.2

Dale's Cone of Experience

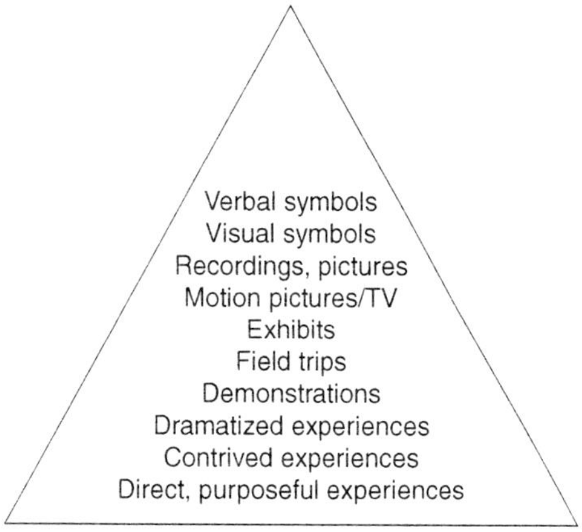

Verbal symbols
Visual symbols
Recordings, pictures
Motion pictures/TV
Exhibits
Field trips
Demonstrations
Dramatized experiences
Contrived experiences
Direct, purposeful experiences

2002). At the base of Dale's cone are direct, purposeful experiences (real-world activities), simulations, and dramatizations. In the middle of Dale's cone are film or video presentations, pictures and photographs, and audio recordings. At the top of the cone are visual and verbal symbols (text and speech).

The psychologist Jerome Bruner (1966) described learning experiences as one of three types: enactive, iconic, or symbolic. **Enactive experiences** are at the base of Dale's cone. As Bruner said,

> We know many things for which we have no imagery and no words, and they are very hard to teach to anybody by the use of either words or diagrams or pictures. If you have tried to coach somebody at tennis or skiing or to teach a child to ride a bike, you will have been struck by the wordlessness and the diagrammatic impotence of the teaching process. (p. 10)

Iconic experiences fall in the middle of Dale's cone. The iconic experience "depends upon visual or other sensory organization and upon the use of summarizing images" (Bruner, 1966, p. 10). Iconic experiences offer explanations through symbols or representations.

Symbolic experiences are those at the top of Dale's cone. In symbolic experience, the entire communication is conducted by using sounds and signs that have no direct association with the actual event (languages are symbolic communication systems—the words we speak or read may arbitrarily represent concepts and real things, but they do so by completely artificial means). Bruner (1966) pointed out that symbolic systems can convey a tremendous amount of information compactly and efficiently. For example, scientists and poets convey vast amounts of information through symbols and words. Consider Einstein's equation $E = mc^2$ and the first line of Robert Frost's "Nothing Gold Can Stay": "Nature's first green is gold." Each is a brief expression that carries a tremendous amount of information to individuals who know how to interpret the symbols, in the case of Einstein's theorem, and symbolism, in the case of Frost's words. "Enacting" the content of either expression would take a long time.

Instructional designers use Dale's cone of experience and Bruner's descriptions to analyze the characteristics of various activities so that they can make informed decisions about the use of such activities within an instructional plan. One good idea is to use a wide range of enactive, iconic, and symbolic activities to provide students with a variety of learning opportunities.

Enactive, iconic, and symbolic activities have unique instructional strengths. For example, enactive activities generally provide students with more opportunities to synthesize and apply what they are learning; however, these activities can be expensive to produce and time consuming to participate in. Symbolic activities can easily be controlled to focus on the most

PROFESSIONALS IN PRACTICE

For a few years, I taught a judo class at The Bank Street School for Children. I had taught judo in a number of settings before that. There is a traditional method of teaching judo and an established curriculum for the sport. However, at Bank Street I had to organize things a little differently to suit a special group of students. Judo is normally a highly physical activity and is generally taught in an enactive manner: Students observe the instructor in action and try out the movements by practicing with peers. My students at Bank Street were particularly verbal in their approach to learning, and after the first meeting it became obvious to me that some portion of class time had to be devoted to more symbolic experience (in this case, discussion) in order to make the enactive experiences meaningful for this particular group.

—Abbie Brown

important aspects of the instructional content and are best used when time is limited, but they seldom offer students an opportunity to explore the content details in a deeply meaningful manner.

Understanding where learning experiences fall on the continuum between concrete and abstract helps answer questions such as these:

How does this activity help students apply the content to situations outside the learning environment?

How quickly can students learn important content features from this experience?

Instructional Delivery

Methods of Instructional Delivery

Instructional events and learning experiences can be organized for a variety of delivery methods. The most popular are the traditional in-person approach (classroom teaching), programmed instruction, and distance education.

Classroom Teaching. Most people are familiar with classroom teaching through personal experience. In the United States, the traditional approach to organized instruction consists of one teacher who works with a group of students who are similar in age and in experience with the subject matter to be taught. This format is the basis of the K–12 "grade" system; the assumption is that most students in a given grade are similar in age and have similar experiences with school subjects (e.g., someone in third grade is assumed to have satisfactorily completed the first and second grades). This approach extends to postsecondary settings, in which groups of students take a class with one or a few instructors; students in that class must meet the prerequisites (i.e., completion of specific courses, or status as an undergraduate or a graduate student) for the class before they can participate. Other groups that use classroom teaching, such as businesses and military organizations, follow this approach as well, grouping students by experience and ability to work with one or a few instructors.

The roots of current classroom teaching practice can be traced to Joseph Lancaster (1778–1838), an English educator who created a unique set of manuals that detailed the organization and management of group instruction (Saettler, 1990). Although instructional methods have changed considerably, Lancaster's physical models for organization continue to heavily influence classrooms.

The setup of a traditional classroom is a number of desks and chairs for students, generally organized to face a chalkboard, whiteboard, or projection screen. A teacher directs the instructional activities, offering and receiving feedback from students as the lesson progresses.

Programmed Instruction. **Programmed instruction** is an arrangement of content materials that allows a student working independently to form responses and receive feedback on the responses (receiving positive reinforcement for correct responses). The feedback and reinforcement come from the instructional media, not from a live instructor or facilitator. Although forms of programmed instruction have been part of teaching since the days of ancient Greece (Saettler, 1990), it became particularly popular in the 1960s, mainly as a result of noted behavioral psychologist B. F. Skinner's work. Skinner described a need for the refinement of "teaching machines," automated methods of providing instruction that would allow a multitude of learners to work through content at a personal pace. With the advent of affordable computing systems and software that allows nonprogrammers to create software with relative ease (e.g., Authorware, Director, Flash, HyperStudio, and ToolBook), programmed instruction has increased. A number of programmed-instruction software programs, often referred to as *skill-and-drill programs,* teach everything from basic reading to preparation for the Graduate Record Examinations.

Instruction, not the technology used to deliver it, is the focus of programmed instruction. Highly effective programmed instruction can be designed and delivered without computing tools. For instance, the book *Bobby Fischer Teaches Chess,* by Fischer, Margulies, and Mosenfelder (1972), is an example of excellent programmed instruction that makes sole use of the printed page.

Distance Education. The most common perception of distance education is that of a traditional classroom experience (one teacher, many students) translated into a communications environment that allows students to participate without having to congregate in a specific geographic location. Distance education may be *synchronous* (everyone who is involved participates within a specified time period by means of videoconferencing or online chat) or *asynchronous* (everyone who is involved participates at a time of his or her choosing, sharing messages through an online discussion board, postal letters, or e-mail messages). Asynchronous distance education may also be delivered in the form of programmed instruction, which allows the student to review the material at an individualized pace without the need (or support) of a teacher or peer group.

With the ubiquity of inexpensive computing tools and telecommunications, and the extensive networking of colleges and universities, Internet-based distance education has become a particularly popular topic among educators (Simonson, Smaldino, Albright, & Zvacek, 2003).

In a distance education setting, all instructional activities are delivered through some type of communications medium that links geographically remote participants. One example is Web-based "courseware" such as Blackboard or WebCT. Courseware, sometimes referred to as a **learning management system (LMS),** is essentially a computer-based empty classroom that an instructor may fill with assignments and presentations; online message boards and chat areas are a part of the courseware, facilitating communication among participants.

Distance education provides a number of advantages for education and training. Students need not travel to a classroom, and in asynchronous situations they may participate at a time that works best for them. However, an interesting opposition of forces is at work in distance education. Although more students demand distance education options, most of them say they do not want to learn at a distance—that a live instructor and the presence of learning-group peers is important to them (Simonson et al., 2003).

Two Categories of Instructional Delivery

The methods of instructional delivery can be thought of as belonging to two categories: those that involve immediate feedback to both the student and the instructor and those that offer immediate feedback to the student alone.

Immediate Feedback to Both Students and the Instructor. In instructional settings such as a traditional classroom or distance education, the students and instructors communicate with each other in a way that allows them to adjust their activities according to feedback received. For example, the teacher in a traditional classroom may notice that the students are looking drowsy and decide to take a short break, or the instructor of an online course may receive a number of messages asking for clarification of a particular concept and decide to offer a minilesson covering the concept in more detail.

Immediate Feedback to the Student Alone. Education conducted through programmed instruction does not involve an instructor who adjusts the experience on the basis of learner feedback. The instruction may be programmed to respond to a student's responses, but all possible responses are determined before student participation.

ID INSIGHT

The Hidden Curriculum

Although the content for a course of study can be described in terms of a curriculum, often a *hidden curriculum* accompanies the described curriculum. The content and activities used to teach it combine to create a set of experiences for the learner that causes a change in how he or she relates to the world, or at least the part of his or her world on which the content focuses. For example, young people do not learn just facts and figures while in school; they also learn how to deal with people outside their home environment. This process is referred to as *socialization* and is an important aspect of the school experience. People preparing to enter a profession learn from the hidden curriculum as well. Participating in instructional activities with peers and other members of the professional community reveals the methods, expectations, and actual practices of that community.

Comparison of the Two Categories. Both categories of instructional delivery have strengths and weaknesses. One strength of methods that provide feedback to both the instructor and students is that it can make the experience more personal for each learner; however, this method requires the instructor to do a great deal of work and students to follow a specific schedule for participating in and completing activities. Methods that offer feedback to the student but not the instructor are less personalized but can be offered to a much larger number of learners, all of whom may participate at a time of their choosing and for however long they would like. Choosing the delivery method is therefore a critically important instructional design decision, and the method used affects the selection of activities for purposes of effectiveness and efficiency.

Instructional Activities in Noneducational Situations

Sometimes, instructional activities can be used to improve performance without specifically teaching people new information, skills, or attitudes. Practitioners in the field of human performance technology (HPT) directly address these issues. According to the International Society for Performance Improvement (ISPI; 2004), HPT "has been described as the systematic and systemic identification and removal of barriers to individual and organizational performance."[1]

HPT practitioners use a wide range of interventions drawn from many other disciplines, including behavioral psychology, instructional systems design, organizational development, and human resources management. They stress the analysis of present and desired levels of performance, look for causes of performance gaps, guide the process of eliminating or minimizing the gaps, and evaluate the results.

If analysis of a human performance problem indicates the need for an instructional activity, the goal of that activity is to provide support that fills the performance gap. One type of activity that supports performance is commonly referred to as a *job aid*.

Job Aids

Job aids are devices that relieve an individual of the need to memorize a set of steps or procedures. Often presented in paper or electronic format, job aids do not teach; rather, they support performance. Job aids are typically used when esoteric procedures are necessary to complete a task. The individual understands the task, but the steps involved in completing the task may be difficult to remember. Examples of job aids can be found in public transportation settings where ticketing machines provide instructions for their use and in most business offices where the steps involved in using the photocopier or fax machine are posted.

Effective Instruction

Understanding the organization, scope and sequence, events, learning experiences, and delivery methods of instruction provides the instructional designer with better knowledge about how to organize instructional activities and present them in the most effective way for a particular group of students. It also facilitates creating an instructional situation that accommodates a range of learners, in keeping with the universal design for education ideas introduced in Chapter 7. Understanding the organization of instruction helps the instructional designer with the following tasks:

- Choosing activities that support remediation and extension; using scope and sequence organization to identify appropriate content for students who need either extra support or an extra challenge

---

[1]Reprinted with permission of the International Society for Performance Improvement, www.ispi.org.

- Choosing activities that support different learning styles; selecting a variety of types of enactive, iconic, and symbolic experiences, and using Dale's cone as an organizer
- Selecting activities most appropriate to each instructional event to create an effective series of activities for a given lesson or instructional intervention
- Making available job aids that support the student and allow him or her to focus on the concepts to be learned instead of the steps involved in completing a specific task
- Choosing activities that are best suited to the delivery method, or choosing the best delivery method to meet an individual's or an organization's needs

Every instructional designer's goal is to create effective, efficient, and satisfying learning experiences for each student. Understanding the organization of instruction and making considerate use of a variety of instructional activities can help instructional designers meet this goal.

SUMMARY

The content to be covered and the instructional activities used to convey the content can be organized into a curriculum. A curriculum defines and describes the content to be covered in terms of its scope (amount of information) and sequence (order in which the information is presented). Instructional content can be further organized at the macro level (e.g., elementary versus advanced levels) or the micro level (the relationships among concepts, facts, and skills in any given lesson). Instructional content can also be described as having horizontal and vertical dimensions. The horizontal dimension is the range of content taught concurrently at any one time; the vertical dimension describes the sequence of the content taught through time. The organization of a curriculum can be based on either a content structure (the concepts, skills, or attitudes students are to acquire) or a media structure (the activities, methods, and materials used to teach the content).

The order in which activities are presented in a lesson is referred to as the *events of instruction*. Although instructional events may be described in much more detail, the four basic events are the introduction, body, conclusion, and assessment. Each instructional event has two aspects: the supplantive (which is provided by the activity) and the generative (which is created by the student).

Learning experiences can be said to exist within a continuum that ranges from the concrete (real-world situations) to the abstract (symbolic representation). Jerome Bruner described three types of learning experiences: enactive, iconic, and symbolic. These experiences are divided into more specific instances in Dale's cone of experience.

The methods of delivering instructional experiences include traditional classroom teaching, programmed instruction (the arrangement of content that allows students to work independently while receiving feedback from the instructional presentation), and distance education (students and teachers working in geographically diverse locations). These methods either provide feedback to both the instructor and the students or provide feedback to the student alone.

Noneducational instructional events are a part of the discipline of human performance technology (HPT). A common example of an instructional design that is not intended to teach is the job aid. A job aid supports performance by relieving an individual of the need to memorize a set of steps or procedures.

Understanding the organization, scope and sequence, events, learning experiences, and delivery methods of instruction helps the instructional designer know what is necessary to create effective instruction for a variety of learners—from students who are "average" to those who require either more support or greater challenge.

CONNECTING PROCESS TO PRACTICE

1. You have been asked to design a 2-hour introduction for parents to the children's book section of your local library. What might be the scope and sequence of this instruction?

2. A multinational corporation has hired you as a consultant. The corporation is considering ways to offer business management courses to its employees worldwide. Explain the options for course delivery methods to the chief executive officer (CEO) of the organization.

3. You have been asked to develop a unit on ancient Egypt for fifth-grade students. What enactive, iconic, and symbolic experiences might you include in this unit?

4. You are the instructional designer for a nonprofit organization with a number of volunteer workers. The volunteers are often unfamiliar with the telephone system of the organization, which makes transferring calls difficult for them. What might you do to address this problem?

5. You are the instructional designer for a university. The vice president of the university has asked to meet with you to discuss the possibility of offering a distance education program leading to a bachelor's degree in liberal arts. So that you can make well-considered recommendations, what questions will you ask the vice president?

RECOMMENDED READINGS

Dale, E. (1969). *Audio-visual methods in teaching* (3rd ed.). New York: Holt, Rinehart & Winston.

Posner, G. J. (1995). *Analyzing the curriculum* (2nd ed.). New York: McGraw-Hill.

REFERENCES

Bruner, J. S. (1966). *Toward a theory of instruction.* Cambridge, MA: Harvard University Press.

Dale, E. (1969). *Audio-visual methods in teaching* (3rd ed.). New York: Holt, Rinehart & Winston.

Fischer, B., Margulies, S., & Mosenfelder, D. (1972). *Bobby Fischer teaches chess.* New York: Bantam Books.

Gagne, R. M. (1985). *The conditions of learning and theory of instruction.* New York: Holt, Rinehart & Winston.

Glare, P. G. W. (Ed.). (1983). *Oxford Latin dictionary.* New York: Oxford University Press.

Heinich, R., Molenda, M., Russell, J., & Smaldino, S. (2002). *Instructional media and technologies for learning* (7th ed.). Upper Saddle River, NJ: Merrill/Prentice Hall.

International Society for Performance Improvement. (2004). What is human performance technology? In *HPT—Human performance technology.* Retrieved January 23, 2004, from http://www.ispi.org

Orlich, D. C., Harder, R. J., Callahan, R. C., Trevisan, M. S., & Brown, A. H. (2004). *Teaching strategies: A guide to effective instruction* (7th ed.). Boston: Houghton Mifflin.

Posner, G. J. (1995). *Analyzing the curriculum* (2nd ed.). New York: McGraw-Hill.

Saettler, P. (1990). *The evolution of American educational technology.* Englewood, CO: Libraries Unlimited.

Simonson, M., Smaldino, S., Albright, M., & Zvacek, S. (2003). *Teaching and learning at a distance: Foundations of distance education* (2nd ed.). Upper Saddle River, NJ: Merrill/Prentice Hall.

Smith, P. L., & Ragan, T. J. (1999). *Instructional design* (2nd ed.). New York: Wiley.

Chapter 10

CREATING LEARNING ENVIRONMENTS AND PRODUCING INSTRUCTIONAL ACTIVITIES

Key Terms

Advance organizers
(page 198)

Direct teaching *(page 183)*

Directed learning
environment *(page 181)*

Graphic organizers
(page 190)

Indirect teaching
(page 183)

Instructional games
(page 185)

Just-in-time teaching
(page 193)

Open-ended learning
environment *(page 182)*

Prescriptions *(page 178)*

Scaffolding *(page 185)*

Simulations *(page 185)*

Our instructional plans, for both classroom-based and online learning, are based on the idea that hands-on exposure to our software early and frequently provides the best skill building and knowledge retention. I developed a little model called "See It, Read It, Do It," which reflects this idea well. First, an instructor can demonstrate an idea or a concept. Then, there might be some associated reading or video/animation observation of the concept or its supporting concepts. Finally, the student begins the task(s) actively, with either the real software or a simulation of it in the online world. All instructional activities have a real-world counterpart.

—Erik Novak,
Distance Learning Course Developer,
Interactive Intelligence, Inc.,
Indianapolis, IN

Guiding Questions

- How are instructional activities defined?
- How does an instructional designer choose appropriate and effective instructional activities?
- How are learning environments defined and differentiated?
- Which instructional activities are supported by grounded theory and research?

Chapter Overview

Creating learning environments and producing activities that carry out instructional goals and objectives is one of the most exciting and challenging aspects of instructional design. The novice instructional designer should be familiar with the types of possible learning environments as well as the various instructional activities that can be used within these environments.

Development of Instruction

After the goals of the instructional event are determined (in traditional systems design situations, objectives would also be specified) and an organizational strategy (a lesson plan, unit, program of study, or curriculum) is devised, the interactions and events in which the learners will engage must be developed. Such interactions and events are what the learners participate in to gain new knowledge, skill, or insight.

The instructional designer recommends specific activities on the basis of the information gathered through needs, task, and learner analyses and through the development of goals and objectives. This process is similar to how a medical doctor might prescribe treatment for a patient after forming a diagnosis. In fact, the activities an instructional designer recommends are sometimes referred to as **prescriptions.** At the heart of any instructional design are the activities prescribed for the learners. Technically, an instructional designer could avoid all other aspects of preparing an instructional intervention *except* preparing activities, although this approach would never be recommended.

Consider, as an example of instructional design in action, how school-teachers incorporate activities into their instructional designs. Teachers in elementary and secondary schools typically develop daily lesson plans that are divided into five parts: background, goals, objectives, activities, and evaluation (see Figure 10.1). As with any instructional design, the lesson plan includes information about the learners, goals and objectives set by the instructor, and evaluation procedures to determine whether the goals were met. Although the activities in which the students participate are just one part of the lesson plan, *they are the only part that causes learning to occur.*

Teaching Pitfall

One pitfall to avoid when you are designing instruction is using activities you are comfortable with because they were used when you were a student.

FIGURE 10.1

A K–12 Teacher's Daily Lesson Plan

Background: A class of 24 second-grade students. The students have been in school for 2 months and have studied the natural phenomena of magnetism and liquid surface tension through empirical observation. The general concept "Air takes up space" needs to be introduced by using empirical observation techniques to which the class has become accustomed.

Goal: To understand the concept "Air takes up space."

Objectives: By the end of the lesson, students will be able to describe how a parachute works. Students will also perform a demonstration called "Sailboat Submarines" and describe why the top of the sailboat does not get wet when it is submerged.

Activities:

1. *Introductory Discussion:* Students are reminded about making scientific observations and are introduced to the concept that even though humans do not usually perceive air around them, it is matter that takes up space.

2. *Toy Parachutes:* Using clothespins, string, and paper towels, students create their own parachutes. After they see a sample parachute and create their own, students test their parachutes out on the playground. This testing is followed by a discussion of how the parachute works (specifically, how the paper-towel-and-string configuration causes the air to slow the descent of the clothespin).

3. *Sailboat Submarines:* Using walnut shells, toothpicks, construction paper, and glue, students create small sailboats. The boats are then "sailed" underwater in a large tank by submerging them within an upside-down clear plastic cup. Sailing is followed by a group discussion on why the boat "sails" did not get wet when they were submerged.

4. *Summative Discussion* about air: Students are asked to think of other demonstrations of the concept that air takes up space.

Evaluation: Students are asked to create their own demonstrations of the concept "Air takes up space." Acceptable responses range from simple reconfigurations of the activities (e.g., flying an airplane underwater) to new and original demonstrations of the concept.

People often teach as they were taught or in a manner that supports their preferred learning style (Cruickshank, Bainer, & Metcalf, 1999). Almost everyone who has attended high school or college has experienced a common method of instruction: an advance reading assignment (e.g., chapters from a textbook), a course presentation by the instructor, assignment of a paper that synthesizes the information from the reading and the presentation, and preparation for a test on the same material. Nothing is wrong with these activities; however, they are only a few of many possibilities. If you are reading this book as part of a course assignment, you are probably comfortable with the traditional instructional activities that include listening to lectures and studying textbooks (you would not be reading this book if you had not mastered techniques for achieving success with these types of assignments). As an instructional designer, you must think *beyond* what worked for you personally and consider what will work best for your target audience.

Learning Environments

A *learning environment* is the milieu in which the instructor, the content, and the learners are placed. A learning environment is the context in which instruction occurs. More than just a physical setting, a learning environment is shaped by the type of instruction that needs to occur, and it is influenced by the attitudes and preferences of the individuals who organize and operate the environment.

Four Perspectives on the Design of Learning Environments

In their book, *How People Learn: Brain, Mind, Experience, and School,* Bransford, Brown, and Cocking (2000) described four ways in which learning environments can be designed: learner centered, knowledge centered, assessment centered, and community centered (Figure 10.2):

In *learner-centered environments,* the focus is on the attitudes, skills, knowledge, and beliefs that students bring to an instructional setting. In such an environment, the instructor uses information about how the learners relate to the content, as well as information about the learners' preconceived ideas or misconceptions, to create situations in which the learners generate new (and, it is hoped, improved) perceptions of the content.

In *knowledge-centered environments,* the focus is on the information and activities that help learners develop an understanding of disciplines. In such an environment, learners are exposed to well-organized knowledge in order to facilitate planning and strategic thinking.

In *assessment-centered environments,* the focus is on providing opportunities for feedback and revision. In this type of environment, testing and critiquing are used to provide learners with opportunities to rethink and revise their ideas.

FIGURE 10.2

Bransford, Brown, and Cocking's Four Types of Learning Environment Designs

In *community-centered environments,* the focus is on people's learning from one another and contributing to larger societies whose members share common interests or goals. In this type of environment, the connections between the instructional setting and the outside world are used to give the content greater meaning and place it in a more global context.

Keep in mind that these environments are not mutually exclusive. Bransford et al. (2000) described them as working together, and they can be used to express the various perspectives through which any instructional situation might be viewed.

Directed and Open-Ended Learning Environments

Hannafin, Land, and Oliver (1999) described two primary types of learning environments: directed and open ended (Table 10.1). In a **directed learning environment,** the instructional designer has determined specific learning objectives and prescribes structured activities in which participants meet the objectives to demonstrate that they have learned. Most people are familiar with directed learning environments through personal experience. Traditional classrooms are directed learning environments organized around the practice of teaching content in increments through highly structured activities to meet externally generated objectives.

TABLE 10.1

Directed and Open-Ended Learning Environments Compared

Directed Learning Environments	Open-Ended Learning Environments
Content is broken down and taught in increments.	Opportunities are set up for students to manipulate, interpret, and experiment.
Detection and mastery of specific concepts is simplified.	Concepts are linked to everyday experience.
Structured teaching–learning strategies are used.	Information is explored by looking at "the big picture." Flexible understanding is encouraged, and appreciation for multiple perspectives is fostered.
Learning is promoted through specific activities and practice.	Learning is promoted by supporting the individual learner's personal connections to the material.
Internal learning is activated by carefully directing external conditions.	Cognition and context are linked.
Mastery is achieved by producing "correct" responses.	The importance of understanding through trial and error is stressed.

Source: Adapted from "Open Learning Environments: Foundations, Methods, and Models," by M. Hannafin, S. Land, and K. Oliver, in *Instructional Design Theories and Models: A New Paradigm of Instructional Theory* (pp. 115–140), edited by C. M. Reigeluth, 1999, Mahwah, NJ: Erlbaum. Copyright 1999 by Lawrence Erlbaum Associates. Adapted with permission.

An **open-ended learning environment** differs from a directed learning environment in that the learning goals and the method of pursuing the goals are determined in one of three ways (Hannafin et al., 1999):

1. Presenting the learner with a complex problem along with a specific task to complete
2. Presenting the learner with a complex problem to explore (with no specific task to complete)
3. Helping the learner articulate a personalized problem to be solved or explored

In both directed and open-ended learning environments, instructional goals are established, but only directed learning environments require the creation of specific instructional objectives. Directed and open-ended learning environments have different strengths. Open-ended learning environments can be especially useful in promoting divergent thinking and are helpful when multiple perspectives are valued. In contrast, directed learning environments are particularly useful in situations in which a variety of learners need to develop the same or similar knowledge, skills, or attitudes.

The differences between directed and open-ended learning environments echo two views of what a learner is. An instructor may perceive a learner as either a passive receiver of information or an active participant in constructing his or her knowledge (Table 10.2).

Cruickshank and colleagues (1999) distinguished between direct (or expository) teaching and indirect teaching. **Direct teaching** places the instructor in the center of all activity. The instructor presents specific information and decides exactly what students will do and when they will do it. Direct teaching is most commonly used in directed learning environments.

Indirect teaching places the instructor in a more peripheral position during learning activities. The instructor offers support and guidance while students approach an assigned problem in the ways that seem best to them. This approach is often used in open-ended learning environments. A common expression that illustrates the two possibilities is the teacher as either "the sage on the stage" (direct) or the "guide on the side" (indirect).

Most educators perceive learners as being at some point on a continuous scale from completely passive (*they need guided through everything*) to completely active (*they can find everything on their own*). These educators recognize that learners fall somewhere between these two extremes; therefore,

TABLE 10.2

Differences Between Passive Reception and Active Participation

Passive Reception	Active Participation	Timing
Presentations (lectures, performances)	Simulations and games	The student must keep up with the pace set by the activity.
Displays (textbooks, static Web sites, bulletin boards, dioramas)	Problem-based learning	The student may proceed at his or her own pace.

learning activities are almost never exclusively directed or open ended. For example, a good problem-based (primarily open-ended) learning activity will not only allow students to participate in their own research and analysis, but also provide them opportunities to obtain information presented by experts in a directed manner—both of which will lead to solving the problem. In any sequence of instruction that extends beyond a single instructional activity, making use of both direct and indirect approaches is possible. For example, an instructor may spend most of his or her time as "the guide on the side" as students solve a prescribed problem, while on occasion he or she may use direct teaching methods by making presentations or lecturing on a specific topic to provide specific information that may help in solving the problem.

Problem-Based Learning. Problem-based learning (PBL) activities are open-ended learning situations. Students are usually presented with a problem that needs to be solved and are then encouraged to develop a solution to the problem by using the resources and tools available to them. Once the problem is presented to the class, students work in small groups, deciding how to approach the problem and what information is necessary to form a reasonable solution. Students then conduct research individually, returning to the group later to share findings and apply them to developing a solution. In the final phase of a PBL activity, students reflect on both the problem and their methods of developing a solution, summarizing and synthesizing what they have learned (Albion, 2003). As students engage in solving carefully contrived problems, they develop and refine their understanding of the subject matter in a highly personal and meaningful way.

As an example, a PBL approach is used in some master of business administration (MBA) programs. Students are told at the beginning of a semester that they must submit their answer to a specific question by the end of the semester. The question may be something like "Should company X acquire company Y?" Students then spend the semester engaging in research to learn more about the problems involved in answering the question, determining the best solution, and presenting their findings in such a way as to convince other individuals that their course of action is best.

According to Hannafin and colleagues (1999), any open-ended learning environment should include four components to support the learners:

1. *Enabling contexts:* Articulated perspectives that influence how the approaches are planned and resources are interpreted
2. *Resources:* A range of sources (print, electronic, human) that provide information about the problem

3. *Tools:* The means for engaging and manipulating resources and ideas
4. *Scaffolding:* Processes that support individual learning efforts

These four components are critically important in creating an effective and truly educational PBL situation.

Instructional Simulations. Learning through simulation has long been part of human experience. **Simulations** are, in essence, evolving case studies that allow participants to examine issues and problems that arise in a specific situation (Gredler, 2004). In a simulation, participants make decisions that affect the situation and experience the results of their decisions in an environment that does not affect the real world. For the most part, instructional simulations are open-ended learning activities.

Simulation as an educational tool is particularly appealing for situations in which physical safety is an issue. Activities that allow individuals to play out situations without placing anyone at risk have a long and honorable history. As an example, astronauts practice space walks in pools that simulate the conditions they will encounter in outer space; such practice is much safer than letting new astronauts experiment with space walking for the first time when they are in orbit around the Earth. Proponents of simulations as an educational activity argue that humans have a natural tendency to learn through mimesis, that a simulation offers a safe environment in which to explore possibilities, and that humans need opportunities to experiment with decision making before actually entering certain professional arenas. For example, the personnel at California's San Onofre Nuclear Generating Station regularly review and explore the best methods of dealing with emergencies by staging simulated crises in a room designed to look exactly like the control center of the plant. Simulations can also be useful instructional activities for promoting better, more informed decision making regardless of the relative safety of the real-world event (Brown, 1999). Students seem to gain experience as multidimensional problem solvers while they are engaged in instructional simulations (Brown, 1999; Gredler, 1996).

Instructional Games. Instructional games are a subset of instructional simulations. A *game* is an activity in which participants abide by specified rules as they strive (often competing against others) to achieve a specific goal (Heinich, Molenda, Russell, & Smaldino, 2002). According to Gredler (2004), games can support four instructional purposes:

1. To practice or refine knowledge or skills
2. To identify gaps or weaknesses in knowledge or skills

PROFESSIONALS IN PRACTICE

When I was a public school teacher, I was a member of the executive council of my union. I was involved with negotiating a contract between teachers and the local board of education. Both sides agreed to facilitate the process by undergoing training from the Harvard Negotiation Project. One of the first tasks the project instructors had all of us do was participate in a simulation game in which we had to work on coming to an agreement over prices and wages for a fictitious community. Although I can barely remember the scenario or the rules, I clearly remember the lessons learned about combating the problem instead of combating the opposing team. That activity helped all of us as we entered into a particularly difficult contract negotiation.

—*Abbie Brown*

3. To review or summarize the content presented
4. To illustrate and develop new concepts among concepts and principles

Using games as instructional activity has a number of advantages: Games keep the learner interested in repetitious tasks (e.g., memorizing), well-designed games are fun to play and attractive to the learner, and game play can provide a relaxed atmosphere for learning. However, games can also distract the learner from focusing on the content if they are poorly designed or create an atmosphere of intense competition (when the goal of winning the game eclipses that of learning the content; Heinich et al., 2002).

Depending on the construction and application of an instructional game, it may be oriented toward either a directed or an open-ended environment. One particularly popular game adaptation is based on the television show *Jeopardy!* Within a directed learning environment, such a game can be an engaging and effective content review activity.

Research Support for Instructional Practices

An instructional designer's job includes making decisions about the instructional activities that are to be used to help learners meet specific goals and objectives. When an instructional designer is making these decisions without falling into the cycle of only teaching the way he or she was taught, where should the designer begin? One of the most valuable ways to think about these questions is to look at the literature on effective teaching. In doing so, the instructional designer should explore the following question: "What instructional practices and process have been validated by research data?"

Three major research studies or research meta-analyses give specific guidance in answering this question. The results of these studies can assist instructional designers in selecting appropriate and effective instructional activities. First, one of the earliest and most helpful meta-analyses was conducted by Joyce and his colleagues. They proposed systems of instruction (which they called *models*) that have research validation (Table 10.3). These models work better than other processes in accomplishing certain learning outcomes (goals). Joyce and colleagues proposed four categories of models: personal, information processing, behavioral, and social. More than 20 models that have substantial research validation are presented in their book: *Models of Teaching* (Joyce, Weil, & Calhoun, 2004).

A second meta-analysis of research-supported teaching practices appeared in 1993 when Ellis and Fouts published their first analysis involving innovations in education. The second edition of their book (1997) included the results of meta-analyses of 12 educational innovations. They proposed viewing the research on teaching practices on three research levels: basic, comparative, and evaluative. Level I (basic) is pure research conducted in a laboratory. The purpose is to establish a "theoretical construct or idea as having some validity"

TABLE 10.3

Joyce and Colleagues' Models of Teaching Validated by Research

	Model		
Personal	**Information Processing**	**Behavioral**	**Social**
Nondirective teaching	Inductive thinking	Mastery learning and programmed instruction	Partners in learning (dyads to group investigation)
Concepts of self	Attainment of concepts	Directed instruction	Role playing
	Scientific inquiry and inquiry training	Simulations	Jurisprudential inquiry
	Memorization		Adaptation to individual differences
	Synectics		
	Advance organizers		
	The developing intellect		

(Ellis, 2001, p. 20). The research conducted at this stage is extremely useful, but it must be validated with continued research. This research has typically led to theories about learning, which are often then developed into programs or instructional methods. Level II (comparative) research is designed to "test the efficacy of particular programs or instructional methods in educational settings. Educational researchers who are interested in applying theories and procedures developed at the pure or basic level generally conduct such studies" (Ellis, 2001, p. 22). The research at this level is conducted in educational settings to determine the effectiveness of these particular instructional methods or programs. Level III (evaluative) research is designed to determine the efficacy of instructional methods or programs at a much larger level, rather than in an isolated educational setting. Large-scale implementation of an instructional model or program is studied to examine its overall effects on various stakeholders (e.g., learners, instructors, customers).

Ellis (2001) continued this analysis. His work indicates that few educational innovations have sufficient research validation (levels II and III) to prove their effectiveness. He identified a few clear winners (teaching practices with research validation) and a few clear losers (teaching practices with little or no clear research validation) but said most educational innovations have mixed research support. The 12 educational innovations he analyzed are as follows:

1. Standards setting
2. Self-esteem and self-efficacy
3. Brain research
4. Teaching for intelligence
5. Thinking skills programs
6. Whole-language learning
7. Elements of styles: learning, thinking, and teaching
8. Curriculum integration
9. Cooperative learning
10. Success for all and schoolwide reform
11. Direct instruction
12. Authentic and performance assessment

Marzano, Pickering, and Pollock (2001) also conducted a meta-analysis of teaching practices research. In their book, *Classroom Instruction That Works: Research-Based Strategies for Increasing Student Achievement,* they proposed that teaching is rapidly becoming more of a science. The evidence examined so far indicates that specific types of teaching practices have strong effects on student achievement and that these practices work well with all types of subject matter. We use Marzano et al.'s work to organize the recommended instructional activities in the following section.

Activities Based on Proven Effective Practices

Probably as many kinds of specific learning activities have been created as instructors exist. Every teacher has a few activities that have become his or her favorites through habit or a history of success. As a novice instructional designer developing your own repertoire of instructional activities, be sure to experiment with those that have the most potential to positively affect your students' achievement. As mentioned previously, Marzano et al.'s (2001) categories of instructional strategies were proved through research to have a strong effect on student achievement. These nine categories are as follows:

1. Identifying similarities and differences;
2. Summarizing and note taking;
3. Reinforcing effort and providing recognition;
4. Homework and practice;
5. Nonlinguistic representations;
6. Cooperative learning;
7. Setting objectives and providing feedback;
8. Generating and testing hypotheses;
9. Questions, cues and advance organizers. (p. 146)

Prescribing activities that use these general strategies should therefore lead to a more successful and effective instructional design. Following is Marzano et al.'s (2001) list, expanded with descriptions and specific examples of activities that can be prescribed.

Identifying Similarities and Differences

The ability to determine how things are alike and different is critically important to most forms of understanding. Specific instructional activities that can facilitate this process include the following:

- *Examples and nonexamples:* The essential instructional strategy activity that explores similarities and differences is the provision of examples and nonexamples. Simply describing what something is, is not

TABLE 10.4

Simple Classification Chart

Orders of the reptile class of animals		
Lizards	**Snakes**	**Turtles**
Gecko	Boa constrictor	Box turtle
Iguana	Cobra	Painted turtle

sufficient; also illustrating what something is *not* (e.g., "A noun is a person, place, or thing. A noun is *not* an action word or a descriptive word") is extremely important.

Classifying. Classifying requires organizing various elements, objects, or concepts according to their similarities. Marzano et al. (2001) posited that one of the critical tasks of classifying is identifying the rules that govern category relationship. Activities that support skill in classifying include the following:

- *Graphic organizers:* A visual display that illustrates the classification of information can help students better understand the similarities and differences among various elements, objects, or concepts (Table 10.4). Venn diagrams are popular **graphic organizers** for displaying sets and subsets (Figure 10.3).
- *Scattergrams:* An example of an instructional activity that requires students to organize information according the similarities of the components is a scattergram (Figure 10.4). The instructor provides a randomized display of the various elements, objects, or concepts that are the topic of study and asks students to organize them according to their similarities. Students may do this activity on their own, as a class, or in small groups. Although usually no single method of organizing the data is correct, a critically important aspect of this activity is the discussion of why students organized things as they did (which allows for clarification and guidance from the instructor and from peers).
- *Analogies, metaphors, and similes:* Another activity in which the similarities and differences of elements, objects, and concepts is explored is the development of analogies ("A is to B as C is to D"), metaphors

FIGURE 10.3

Simple Venn Diagram Showing Sets and Subsets

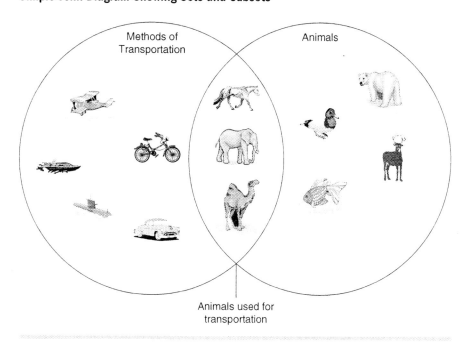

Methods of
Transportation

Animals

Animals used for
transportation

FIGURE 10.4

Scattergram of Terms and Labels Used in the Order of the Reptile Class of Animals

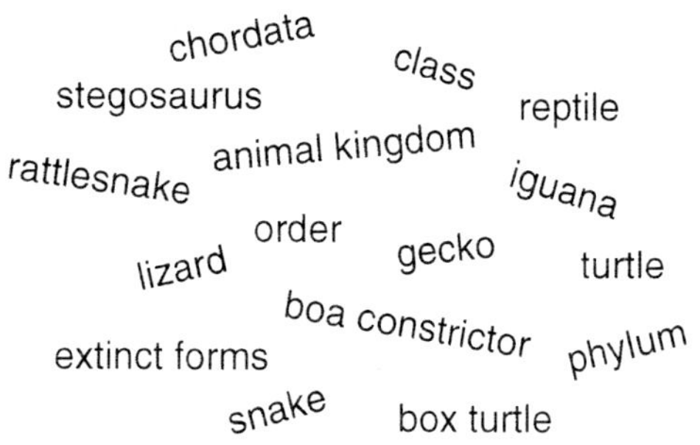

chordata

class

stegosaurus

reptile

rattlesnake   animal kingdom

iguana

order   gecko   turtle

lizard

boa constrictor   phylum

extinct forms

snake   box turtle

PROFESSIONALS IN PRACTICE

When teaching multimedia production, I often ask students to develop a simile that compares the production process to the student's previous experiences. Asking students to complete a sentence such as "Multimedia production is like . . ." often results in deeply insightful statements that, when shared with the entire class, cause everyone to understand multimedia production a bit better than they did before. This exercise often increases my understanding of how better to describe the process as well.

—*Abbie Brown*

("A is D"), and similes ("A is like D"). Exploration of analogies, metaphors, and similes can encourage students to draw on their personal experiences to better understand new information.

Summarizing and Note Taking

Often considered study skills and seldom addressed as part of an instructional design after high school, summarizing and taking notes have proved to be highly effective instructional activities for both adolescent and adult learners. Activities that facilitate summarizing and note taking include the following:

- *"Ten and two"*: Common wisdom among experienced instructors is the rule of "ten and two" (10 minutes of presentation, 2 minutes of synthesis). During formal instruction, the teacher schedules a brief, relatively informal review and synthesis activity after about 10 minutes. Students may turn to a neighbor and discuss the information presented, or they may review and compare their notes. After this review and synthesis, the instructor invites questions and offers clarifications on the material presented.

- *Reflective writing:* Students may be asked to generate a written response to the information presented. Doing so gives students an opportunity to reflect on and make personal connections with the material. As with the "ten and two" activity, reflective writing should be followed by a question-and-answer period.

- *Reciprocal teaching:* In a reciprocal teaching activity, small groups of students teach each other the content dictated by the instructional goals and objectives. One student takes the role of group leader and directs the discussion, but all members of the group are responsible for reviewing, clarifying, and summarizing the information.

- *Revision of and addition to notes:* An effective instructional activity that is often overlooked is the revision of notes taken during presentation. Students work individually or in small groups to revise and add to their notes in order to summarize and synthesize the material.

Reinforcing Effort and Providing Recognition

Critically important to student success is the belief that effort ultimately enhances achievement. Students who believe in the importance of effort are much more likely to succeed. Finding ways to recognize and reward effort is therefore an activity that can increase the efficiency and effectiveness of an instructional design. One method of doing so is as follows:

- *Pause, prompt, and praise:* The pause, prompt, and praise activity can be extremely important in helping students achieve success, but it cannot be scheduled precisely into an instructional design. If the instructor notices one or more students struggling with a task, the students are asked to pause and discuss the problems they have encountered. The instructor then offers a prompt, suggesting a way of working around or through the problem. If the students succeed by implementing the suggestion, the instructor offers praise for a job well done.

ID INSIGHT

Just-in-Time Teaching

Just-in-time teaching, or *just-in-time instruction,* has become a popular concept among educators. It is a strategy whereby direct instruction is provided according to the immediate needs students express or indicate during a lesson or work period. **Just-in-time teaching** is adaptive; the instructor may choose from a number of short lessons prepared in advance, or he or she may improvise a brief lesson. The just-in-time approach makes use of direct teaching methods within an indirect teaching environment. The instructor takes the role of facilitator, providing short lessons that cover content the students request.

Rewards and Symbols of Recognition. An instructional design may have methods of rewarding and recognizing student success built into it. Students may receive tokens (small prizes), or they may see their names highlighted in a place of honor. These extrinsic rewards do not diminish intrinsic motivation if they are given for accomplishing specific performance goals (Marzano et al., 2001).

Homework and Practice

Research indicates that homework and practice increase achievement and learning (Marzano et al., 2001). A natural, intuitive assumption is that the more an individual practices, the better he or she becomes with just about anything. Assigning activities that promote repeated practice is a recommended component of most instructional designs. Such activities include the following:

- *Speed and accuracy reporting:* For instruction that has skill development as one of its goals, requiring students to keep track of their speed and accuracy is a good idea. Each student should keep a progress chart.
- *Homework:* Assigning activities to be completed outside formal class time can extend learning opportunities and give students a chance for more practice. Assuming the instruction requires multiple class meetings, homework assignments should include a clear statement of the purpose and outcome of the assignment so that students know why they are performing the task and what they should focus on. Feedback on homework assignments must be given during subsequent class meetings; offering feedback greatly increases the effectiveness of homework as an instructional activity.

Nonlinguistic Representations

According to one popular psychological theory, known as *dual coding*, humans store information in two forms: linguistic and imagery (Marzano et al., 2001; Pavio, 1990). The *imagery* mode is a combination of mental pictures, physical sensations (touch, taste, smell), kinesthetic associations, and sound. The *linguistic* mode is most commonly used to present instructional material (through the use of lectures, assigned reading, and question-and-answer sessions). However, research indicates that the more people use both linguistic *and* imagery modes, the better they are able to analyze and recall information. Nonlinguistic representations include the following:

- *Illustrations and animations:* The results of research by psychologists like Richard Mayer (2001) suggest that recall is enhanced when learning activities include graphics and animated sequences that illustrate the content. Some evidence suggests that memory for pictures is generally better than memory for words; this phenomenon is referred to as the *picture superiority effect* (Anglin, Vaez, & Cunningham, 2004). However, animations should be used judiciously because research also indicates that they are effective primarily as attention-getting devices or when the learners are not novices with the content and have some knowledge about how to attend relevant cues and details provided by animation (Anglin et al., 2004).

- *Graphic organizers:* Graphic organizers, discussed previously in this chapter, are a combination of the linguistic and imagery modes because they use words and phrases organized in descriptive patterns (Figure 10.5).

- *Sound:* The use of sound effects and nonspeech audio (music, background noises) can have a profound effect on learners' recall. Sound cues support the acquisition, processing, and retrieval of new information in a variety of ways (Bishop & Cates, 2001). The National Public Radio programs that incorporate background noises and sound effects are good examples of how nonlinguistic sound can be used to enhance the presentation of information in a way that stimulates the listener's ability to attend to and recall the information presented.

- *Kinesthetic representation:* Creating physical models or working with manipulative representations (such as the Cuisenaire rods used in elementary math classes) can help learners interpret and understand information through the sense of touch and movement.

FIGURE 10.5

Graphic Organizer Illustrating the Convoluted Family Relationships in the Legend of King Arthur

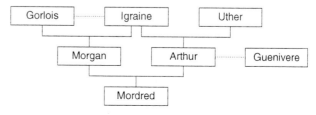

Cooperative Learning

Having students work together to accomplish a task is popular, and research suggests that cooperative learning is an effective and efficient instructional activity (Ellis, 2001; Marzano et al., 2001). Cooperative learning experts David Johnson and Roger Johnson (1999) outlined five defining elements of cooperative learning: positive interdependence (everyone working together to succeed), face-to-face promotive interaction (offering help and praise to group members), individual and group accountability (each member contributing to the group's success), interpersonal and small group skills (communication, decision making, conflict resolution), and group processing (reflecting on how the group functions and how its functioning can be improved). Cooperative learning activities are particularly helpful to learners who are low and middle achievers when the groups comprise heterogeneous combinations of students who are low, middle, and high achieving. All indications are that cooperative learning works best when groups are kept relatively small (three or four students per group). The best cooperative learning activities are well structured and have clearly defined goals and expectations. However, because cooperative learning is particularly popular, this type of activity should not be overused at the expense of independent practice and skill development.

Setting Objectives and Providing Feedback

In Chapter 8, we discussed the importance of developing instructional goals and the common practice of creating instructional objectives to accompany these goals. Although setting instructional objectives (determining the expected outcome of the instructional activity) promotes efficient instruction, in some cases, setting objectives may cause the instruction to be too efficient and thus limit the learner. Research indicates that objectives carefully specified by the instructional designer may cause a decrease in students' general learning. Students may focus so completely on the specified objective that they do not explore the material in a way that allows them to develop broader or deeper understanding of the general topic (Marzano et al., 2001; Walberg, 1999). If the goal is for students to develop a personalized, broader, and deeper understanding of a topic, they should be encouraged to personalize the instructional goals by creating their own learning objectives. The instructor should then work with the students, providing feedback on how well their objectives align with the instructional goals and whether each student is meeting his or her personal objectives. Activities that support setting objectives and providing feedback include the following:

- *Contracts:* A popular activity that supports setting personalized learning objectives is the student contract. Students work with the instructor to develop individualized learning contracts, stating objectives that relate to both the instructional goals and the students' personal interests, strengths, or weaknesses.

- *Critique sessions:* In critique sessions, the instructor, other students, or groups of students offer feedback about whether the individual or group is accomplishing stated objectives. Group-to-group critique sessions are particularly effective as part of cooperative learning activities. Feedback should be a combination of positive and corrective; formal critique sessions often follow a format that offers three categories of feedback: "What I see" (statements of exactly what the reviewer perceives), "What I like" (statements of what the reviewer is positively impressed with), and "What I think needs improvement" (statements of what the reviewer finds problematic).

Generating and Testing Hypotheses

Having students make predictions and conduct experiments based on the predictions is a good way to improve student achievement (Marzano et al., 2001). Two methods are used to generate hypotheses: inductive reasoning and deductive reasoning. *Inductive reasoning* is the process of drawing new conclusions from available information. *Deductive reasoning* is the process of using general rules (heuristics) to predict a future action or event. In generating hypotheses as a classroom activity, students may use inductive reasoning, deductive reasoning, or a combination of both. However, students must explain their thinking (perhaps even explain whether they are working inductively or deductively) to gain the greatest benefit from any hypothesis-generation activity. Although creating and testing hypotheses is most often associated with science, this activity can be used in many other content areas. For example, high school students studying the short story form might be asked to predict the outcome of a story. As another example, adults learning a specific administrative process might be asked to predict the follow-up tasks involved after completing the process. Hypothesis-generating activities cause students to explore the content of the lesson more thoroughly; such activities can also prompt students to think more about their own thinking process (metacognition), which helps them become better decision makers and problem solvers.

Questions, Cues, and Advance Organizers

The strategies of introducing a topic by asking questions about the topic and by providing some type of preview of the topic (cues and **advance organizers**) are intended to help students retrieve what they already know that is related to the topic and to prepare them to receive new information in the best frame of mind. Research on questions, cues, and advance organizers indicates they are an effective and efficient instructional activity (Marzano et al., 2001). Three general rules apply to all question, cue, and advance organizer strategies:

1. The focus should always be on what is important about the topic (as opposed to what is unusual about the topic).

2. Questions and cues that require students to analyze information produce more learning than do questions that require simple recall.

3. After posing a question, teachers should wait briefly before accepting students' responses; doing so can increase the depth of the responses (teachers are typically instructed to slowly count to three mentally before accepting students' responses).

Advance organizers can take various forms. Before proceeding with instruction, teachers may do the following:

- Encourage students to skim the content
- Tell a brief story that relates to the content
- Provide an agenda or outline to students
- Provide a graphic organizer to students
- Give students a writing prompt related to the content

The activities described in this section are only a sample of the myriad activities that are used for instruction. However, these activities have some research-based support for their use.

SUMMARY

The activities in which learners participate to gain knowledge, skill, or insight are the single most important part of an instructional design. Instructional designers prescribe specific activities on the basis of the information gathered during task, learner, and goals analyses. One point to be mindful of is that most people will naturally recommend the instructional activities that they learned from or that best fit their preferred learning style. However, an instructional designer does not have the luxury of prescribing only the activities that he or she prefers. The number and order of the activities prescribed define the scope and sequence of the instruction. The two primary types of learning environments are directed and open ended. Directed learning environments are those in which the instructional designer determines specific learning objectives and prescribes structured activities in which participants meet the objectives to demonstrate that they have learned. Open-ended learning environments either present learners with a complex problem to complete or explore, or help the learner determine a personalized problem to be solved or explored. Problem-based learning and instructional simulations are examples of open-ended learning situations. Instructional games, a subset of simulations, are an activity that may be applied in either directed or open-ended environments. Instructional activities that have a strong research base to prove their efficacy include identifying similarities and differences; summarizing and note taking; reinforcing effort and providing recognition; homework and practice; nonlinguistic representations; cooperative learning; setting objectives and providing feedback; generating and testing hypotheses; and questions, cues, and advance organizers.

CONNECTING PROCESS TO PRACTICE

1. A hospital administrator has contracted you to develop instruction for new volunteers on how to work with patients and their families. What type of learning environment would you recommend establishing for this group?

2. As the instructional designer for a large corporation, you have been assigned the task of creating a 90-minute workshop on office safety and emergency preparedness. What activities might you include in this workshop?

3. You are a fifth-grade schoolteacher. One district objective for all fifth-grade students is to be able to correctly identify the nouns, verbs, adjectives, and adverbs used in a paragraph of expository text by the end of the school year. What activities might you prescribe for your students throughout the school year to help them meet this objective?

4. A professor of American history would like her students to develop a better understanding of what life was like in Chicago during the Roaring 20s. What instructional activities might you recommend to her?

RECOMMENDED READINGS

Bransford, J., Brown, A. L., & Cocking, R. R. (2000). *How people learn: Brain, mind, experience and school.* Washington, DC: National Academy Press.

Hyerle, D. (1996). *Visual tools for constructing knowledge.* Alexandria, VA: Association for Supervision and Curriculum Development.

Marzano, R. J., Pickering, D. J., & Pollock, J. E. (2001). *Classroom instruction that works: Research-based strategies for increasing student achievement.* Alexandria, VA: Association for Supervision and Curriculum Development.

National Public Radio. (n.d.). *Audio archives.* http://www.npr.org.

REFERENCES

Albion, P. R. (2003). PBL + IMM = PBL^2: Problem based learning and interactive multimedia development. *Journal of Technology and Teacher Education, 11*(2), 243–257.

Anglin, G. J., Vaez, H., & Cunningham, K. L. (2004). Visual representations and learning: The role of static and animated graphics. In D. H. Jonassen (Ed.), *Handbook of research for educational communications and technology* (2nd ed., pp. 865–916). Mahwah, NJ: Erlbaum.

Bishop, M. J., & Cates, W. M. (2001). Theoretical foundations for sound's use in multimedia instruction to enhance learning. *Educational Technology Research and Development, 49*(3), 5–22.

Bransford, J., Brown, A. L., & Cocking, R. R. (2000). *How people learn: Brain, mind, experience and school.* Washington, DC: National Academy Press.

Brown, A. (1999). Simulated classrooms and artificial students: The potential effects of new technologies on teacher education. *Journal of Research on Computing in Education, 32*(2), 307–318.

Cruickshank, D. R., Bainer, D. L., & Metcalf, K. K. (1999). *The act of teaching* (2nd ed.). New York: McGraw-Hill.

Ellis, A. K. (2001). *Research on educational innovations* (3rd ed.). Larchmont, NY: Eye on Education.

Gredler, M. (1996). Educational games and simulations: A technology in search of a (research) paradigm. In D. H. Jonassen (Ed.), *Handbook of research for educational communications and technology* (pp. 521–540). New York: Simon & Schuster/Macmillan.

Gredler, M. (2004). Games and simulations and their relationships to learning. In D. H. Jonassen (Ed.), *Handbook of research for educational communications and technology* (2nd ed., pp. 571–581). Mahwah, NJ: Erlbaum.

Hannafin, M., Land, S., & Oliver, K. (1999). Open learning environments: Foundations, methods, and models. In C. M. Reigeluth (Ed.), *Instructional design theories and models: A new paradigm of instructional theory* (pp. 115–140). Mahwah, NJ: Erlbaum.

Heinich, R., Molenda, M., Russell, J., & Smaldino, S. (2002). *Instructional media and technologies for learning* (7th ed.). Upper Saddle River, NJ: Merrill/Prentice Hall.

Johnson, D. W., & Johnson, R. T. (1999). *Learning together and alone: Cooperative, competitive and individualistic learning.* Boston: Allyn & Bacon.

Joyce, B., Weil, M., & Calhoun, E. (2004). *Models of teaching* (7th ed.). Boston: Allyn & Bacon.

Marzano, R. J., Pickering, D. J., & Pollock, J. E. (2001). *Classroom instruction that works: Research-based strategies for increasing student achievement.* Alexandria, VA: Association for Supervision and Curriculum Development.

Mayer, R. (2001). *Multimedia learning.* New York: Cambridge University Press.

Pavio, A. (1990). *Mental representations: A dual coding approach.* New York: Oxford University Press.

Walberg, H. J. (1999). Productive teaching. In H. C. Waxman & H. J. Walberg (Eds.), *New directions for teaching practice and research* (pp. 75–104). Berkeley, CA: McCutcheon.

PART **4**

EVALUATING LEARNER SUCCESS AND THE INSTRUCTIONAL DESIGN

Determining the Effect of the Intervention

11 Evaluating Learner Achievement
12 Determining the Success of the Instructional Design Product and Process

Once you decide on the goals and objectives of the instruction and organize the instructional environment and activities, you will need to decide how to measure the learners' development and evaluate the success of the instructional design. Conducting carefully planned evaluation activities helps the instructional designer revise and improve the instructional intervention to better serve the learners.

Chapters 11 and 12 describe the principles, processes, and practices of assessment and evaluation that instructional designers use to determine learner success and the success of the instructional design process. In Chapter 11, we focus on evaluating learner achievement. Chapter 12 covers how to determine the success of the instructional design product and process.

EVALUATING LEARNER ACHIEVEMENT

Key Terms

Assessment *(page 206)*   Instruments *(page 206)*   Norm referenced
Criterion referenced   Learner evaluation   *(page 211)*
(page 211)   *(page 229)*   Reliability *(page 210)*
Evaluation *(page 207)*   Measurement *(page 206)*   Validity *(page 210)*

Students attend our live classes to become certified in the use of our software. Students who are enrolled in our online education program are either already certified or building their skills in related areas. Consequently, a written exam and a practical exam are sufficient to determine whether someone has the knowledge for certification. Informally, our evaluations break down into three categories, although not always neatly:

1. Human reaction to the course (This was great; I learned a lot. This was terrible; I want my money back.)
2. Skills, concept, or knowledge mastery and retention (This is exactly what I need to do my job.)
3. Greatly improved job performance

We use two kinds of formal evaluations to assess whether a student has retained a concept:

1. If the student attended a live class, he or she must first pass a written exam that includes multiple-choice and essay questions.
2. After the written exam, the student must pass a practical exam in which he or she must use our software to successfully configure a telephone system from scratch. Depending on the class the student is taking, he or she must demonstrate knowledge of how to install our software and its related components, configure it, test for a dial tone, demonstrate some programming knowledge to route telephone calls to a person or to allow a user to enter data (a credit card number, for example), and handle the call accordingly. Students enrolled in online classes must pass a written exam that includes multiple-choice, matching, true–false, and fill-in-the blank questions.

—Erik Novak,
Distance Learning Course Developer,
Interactive Intelligence, Inc.,
Indianapolis, IN

Guiding Questions

- What is evaluation?
- How do evaluation and assessment differ?
- What role does evaluation play in the instructional design process?
- What is learner evaluation?
- What types of learner evaluations exist?
- How are learner evaluations designed and developed?
- How does an instructional designer determine when a learner evaluation has been successful?

Chapter Overview

An important part of the instructional design process is determining how well the design worked. Success can (and should) be measured at different stages and for different elements throughout the process. Varied and sustained evaluation helps ensure that the intervention created during the instructional design process meets the needs of everyone involved.

As an instructional designer, you will typically use three major evaluation types: learner, formative, and summative. Each has a specific purpose and distinct techniques; the techniques are procedures used to gather data. An experienced instructional designer should have a solid understanding of these three evaluation types and the techniques associated with each, and be able to design and conduct evaluations using all three. With this fact in mind, we provide, in Chapters 11 and 12, an overview of these three evaluation types as they relate to the instructional design process.

In this chapter, the focus is exclusively on learner evaluation. The goal of this type of evaluation is described, along with the role it plays in instructional design. The development and the implementation of learner evaluations are discussed, as is how to determine whether a learner evaluation has been successful.

Evaluation, Assessment, and Measurement

Two terms related to evaluation are important for you to know: *assessment* and *measurement*. **Assessment** refers to procedures or techniques used to obtain data about a learner or a product. **Measurement** refers to the data collected, which are typically expressed quantitatively (i.e., numbers). The physical devices used to collect the data are referred to as **instruments** (e.g., rating scales forms, observation sheets, checklists, objective tests). **Evaluation** refers to the process for determining the success level of an individual or a product on the basis of data, then making decisions based on this success level. We use the term *evaluation* in this book; in doing so, we are referring to a process that includes assessment and measurement. We also use the term *assessment* to refer to the techniques used during evaluation to gather data.

Purpose of Evaluation

Worthen, Sanders, and Fitzpatrick (1997) wrote that the purpose of evaluation is the "identification, clarification, and application of defensible criteria to determine an evaluation object's value (worth or merit), quality, utility, effectiveness, or significance in relation to those criteria" (p. 5). In essence, evaluation is used to determine the success level of *something;* this *something* is typically an individual or a product, such as a lesson, project, or program (although a process can also be evaluated). A properly designed and implemented evaluation provides an instructional designer with appropriate data that can be analyzed to determine the success level of who or what is being evaluated. Once this level is determined, the designer decides whether changes need to be made. These changes vary according to who or what is being evaluated, and when the evaluation is taking place. Changes could include learner remediation, the redesign of instructional materials, or abandonment of the entire instructional intervention. Changes are made to help improve the likelihood that a learner will achieve a high level of success.

PROFESSIONALS IN PRACTICE

Following is an example of an instructional design project in which two types of evaluation were used and how changes were made as a result of the evaluations. This example should provide a context for where evaluation fits into the instructional design process.

A hospital contracted me to help design and implement an intervention that would aid a particular population of nurses employed by the hospital in passing a mandatory state examination on anatomy and physiology. Each nurse was returning to the profession after an absence of a year or more. On the basis of data provided by hospital administrators and data from analyses (task and learner) that the instructional

(continued)

designer conducted, I determined that a 4-week, self-paced training system delivered through the Internet would be developed and implemented as the intervention. The nurses in this group, who did not pass the examination the first time, would participate in the training so that they could pass a subsequent examination.

Working with a team that included a Web developer, a graphic artist, and two nurse trainers (subject matter experts), I developed the training. As the training was being developed, several nurses were asked to try portions of it. I observed several nurses using the training. In addition to observating them, I solicited feedback from them by conducting a group interview after they had completed parts of the training. I asked several open-ended questions during the group interview, then analyzed my observation notes and the nurses' responses. This formative evaluation revealed that several changes should be made to the training. One such change was to add review quizzes more frequently throughout the content. I implemented this change, along with several others.

Once the training was completely developed, it was piloted with 25 nurses. The results of the training were encouraging: Twenty-two of the nurses passed the examination. On the basis of the learner evaluation results (the high percentage of nurses who passed the examination), the hospital administration mandated that all nurses needing to take the examination would first participate in the training. If the successful results continued, additional training would be developed using the same self-paced, Internet-based format. The nurses who failed the second examination would repeat the training.

Two types of evaluation were used in this instructional design example: formative and learner. Each was used to provide unique data that allowed me to decide how to develop and implement an efficient, effective, and satisfying intervention that helped meet my client's goal.

—Tim Green

Goal of Learner Evaluation

Learner evaluation helps determine the level of performance or achievement that an individual has attained as a result of instruction. This level is established by the extent to which the learner can meet instructional goals and objectives.

In Chapter 8, we discuss in detail what instructional goals and objectives are and how they are developed. As a reminder, instructional goals describe the general intentions of instruction, whereas instructional objectives describe more specific outcomes of what a learner should be able to demonstrate once instruction is complete. An effective and appropriate learner evaluation is based directly on the instructional goals and objectives. In the next section, we describe how to develop such an evaluation.

ID INSIGHT

Formative and Summative Evaluation

Although formative evaluation and summative evaluation are covered formally in Chapter 12, we believe providing a brief discussion of these two evaluation types is important to show how they relate to learner evaluation. Whereas learner evaluation focuses directly on the learner, formative evaluation and summative evaluation focus on the instructional design process and the intervention created as a result of this process.

Morrison, Ross, and Kemp (2004) wrote, "Formative evaluation is quality control of the development process" (p. 242).[1] Such evaluation is used throughout the instructional design process to ensure that the intervention being developed is tested and revised to meet the client's needs. As the name implies, formative evaluation is used as the intervention is forming.

Summative evaluation is conducted at the end of the instructional design process to determine how successful the process was in helping meet the major goals. As the name implies, summative evaluation is used to provide a summary of what occurred.

Although we have described how both formative and summative evaluations do not deal specifically with learner evaluation, learner evaluation can be formative and summative in its approach. What does this mean? As in this chapter, learner evaluation can take place at different times during instruction—typically, prior to instruction, during instruction, and after instruction has been completed. Conducting learner evaluation prior to and during instruction is formative learner evaluation because the goal is to try to determine how learners are progressing. Learner evaluation conducted after instruction is completed is summative learner evaluation because it is used to determine a learner's success. A well-designed learner evaluation will include both formative and summative elements.

[1] Reprinted from Morrison, Ross, and Kemp, *Designing Effective Instruction*, 4th ed. 2004. Reprinted with permission by John Wiley & Sons.

Development of Learner Evaluations

Development of a learner evaluation begins with examining the instructional goals and objectives that were created as a result of the needs and task analyses. The instructional designer examines the instructional goals and objectives to determine what change the instruction is meant to implement. Is it a change in learner knowledge, skill, or attitude? In addition, the instructional designer determines how the success of a learner will be judged. Will a learner be compared with other learners or will a learner's success level be determined on the basis of competence? The answers to these questions will help the instructional designer develop an effective learner evaluation that includes appropriate assessment activities.

Validity and Reliability

Two key concepts are important to understand and keep in mind during development of a learner evaluation: validity and reliability. A learner evaluation is considered to have **validity** if it helps determine whether the learners achieved the intended outcomes of instruction (on the basis of the instructional objectives). In other words, did the learners meet the instructional objectives? A learner evaluation that allows this factor to be determined is considered valid. However, the validity of a learner evaluation (especially a test) is not always easy to determine.

An instructional designer should be familiar with two of the various types of validity: face validity and content validity. *Face validity* involves how a learner evaluation appears. Experts are asked to judge whether they believe the learner evaluation is reasonable, well designed, and likely to be capable of gathering appropriate data. If so, the learner evaluation is said to have face validity.

Content validity is similar to face validity. However, what is being determined in this case is the extent to which the specific intended domain of content is addressed in the evaluation (Carmines & Zeller, 1991, p. 20). For example, test questions should represent the important content or skills that the instruction covered. Evidence of content-related validity is generally determined by having subject matter experts look at the test items and judge the appropriateness of each item and how well the domain is covered. In addition, the instructional designer can create a table of specifications to help determine the content validity.

Reliability is the extent to which a learner evaluation will provide similar results when it is conducted on multiple occasions. If a test is given to the same learner at different times, without the learner's receiving additional preparation, and similar results occur, the test is considered reliable. Various statistical methods can be used to determine reliability; however, they are beyond the scope of this book.

Criterion Referenced and Norm Referenced: Simplified

Most learner evaluations you will help develop will be **criterion referenced** (also referred to as *minimum competency* or *mastery*). A learner evaluation that is criterion referenced indicates that a learner is being judged on the basis of his or her competency level. Competence is determined by specific criteria, such as being able to answer a specified number of questions or to demonstrate certain skills in a specific amount of time. If you have a driver's license, remember that part of earning it involved passing a driving test, which consisted of your demonstrating to an examiner that you could safely operate a car. As you drove the car, the examiner asked you to perform various tasks and checked off how successful you were at completing these tasks. At the end of the driving test, the examiner tallied your score to determine your level of competence. If your score was high enough, you passed the driving test. Passing the test indicated that you had met certain criteria set by the Department of Motor Vehicles or the Secretary of State and that you had therefore demonstrated competence.

A learner evaluation that is **norm referenced** indicates that the results of the evaluation are being used to compare or rank learners. As a student, you are familiar with numerous norm-referenced examinations. Most graduate students are required to take the Graduate Record Examinations (GRE) and include the score as part of the program admissions application. The GRE is designed to provide a spread of test scores that are ranked in comparison with those of other students who have taken the same test. This information assists admission officers in deciding on who to admit into graduate programs.

Although both types of evaluations are useful, criterion-referenced learner evaluations generally provide more useful information. This information can help instructors and instructional designers decide on where a learner may have gaps in his or her learning. Knowing this type of information will allow for changes to be made to instruction that will benefit the learner. A norm-referenced learner evaluation does not measure competence. Knowing how a learner ranks in relationship to other learners does not provide the information necessary to determine how competent the learner is or what changes need to be made to help improve instruction. Therefore, our treatment of learner evaluation in this chapter focuses on criterion-referenced learner evaluation.

The Starting Point: Instructional Objectives

Instructional objectives are a key element in the development of an effective learner evaluation because the evaluation should be derived from the objectives. A direct relationship must exist between the instructional objectives and the learner evaluation. If it does, the learner evaluation will be authentic; in other words, the learner evaluation will help the instructor and the instructional designer determine whether a learner has met the intended instructional outcomes.

Well-written instructional objectives will describe the outcome a learner should be able to achieve after instruction has been completed. Three typical outcomes are possible: a change in the learner's knowledge, a change in the learner's skill, or a change in the learner's attitude. The instructional designer's task is to identify what type of outcome is expected, then develop an assessment technique that will determine whether this outcome has been achieved. Each of these outcome types requires a different approach. In the following sections, we first discuss how to identify the intended outcome; then, we take a look at how each type of outcome can be addressed.

Instructional Objectives and Instructional Outcomes. How can you determine whether the intended outcome of an instructional objective is a change in knowledge, skill, or attitude? Take a look at the action (the verb) that is part of the instructional objective. For example, read the following sentence and identify the action:

> *The learner will be able to list the three major warning signs of a heart attack.*

The action in the instructional objective is *to list*—more specifically, to list the three major warning signs of a heart attack. The outcome of the instructional objective is for the learner to be able to identify when an individual might be having a heart attack.

We have identified the action and the outcome, but what type of outcome is this? To help answer this question, refer to the learning taxonomies we discussed in Chapters 2 and 8. Three types of learning taxonomies were covered: cognitive, psychomotor, and affective. As you look at these taxonomies, does the action seem to fit into one of them? The action fits into the cognitive learning taxonomy (Bloom's taxonomy of the cognitive domain) at the comprehension level. Because it fits into the cognitive domain, the outcome of the instructional objective is a change in the learner's knowledge.

Knowing this information will help you develop an appropriate assessment technique that will determine whether the learner has achieved the outcome. As you gain more experience with instructional objectives, determining whether the intended outcome is a change in knowledge, skill, or attitude will become second nature.

A Change in Knowledge. For a learner to be competent in a given field, he or she must possess fundamental knowledge that relates to that field. For example, a nurse needs to know anatomy and physiology before being able to treat a patient, a mechanic needs to know the different parts of an engine before fixing it, and a basketball referee must know the rules of the game before officiating it. Because knowledge is such an important element in all fields, being able to determine a learner's knowledge level is a critical part of instruction. A learner's knowledge level and whether it has changed as a result of instruction is typically determined through the use of either an objective test or a constructed-response test (Morrison, Ross, & Kemp, 2004). These types of tests are often referred to as *paper-and-pencil tests*.

An objective test includes questions (referred to as *items*), such as true–false, multiple-choice, matching, and short-answer items, that have one correct answer. Constructed-response tests include essay items, which focus on the learner's constructing an answer rather than selecting one that is provided. Objective tests deal with low-level cognitive abilities—knowledge and comprehension—whereas constructed-response tests often deal with higher level cognitive abilities such as application, analysis, synthesis, and evaluation.

Writing well-designed objective or constructed-response tests requires skill that few individuals have mastered. Textbooks and university courses are available that specifically deal with this topic; in this chapter, we provide only a basic treatment of the topic: guidelines for how to develop different types of test items.

Test Development Plan. Millman and Greene (1989) stated that before a test is developed, answers to some questions must be obtained. The combination of these answers will help an instructional designer create a test development plan. This plan will help guide the development and eventual implementation of the test. The questions are as follows:

- What is the purpose of the test?
- Who will be taking the test?

- How much time will be allotted for testing?
- How will the test be administered?
- What will the test cover?
- What sources of content will be used?
- What are the dimensions of the content?
- Which types of item formats are to be used?
- How many items are available in the item pool, and how many need to be constructed?
- What is the appropriate difficulty and taxonomy level for the items?
- How will the items be grouped and sequenced?
- How will the items and test be scored?
- How will the test be evaluated?
- Will an item analysis be performed?
- Will the reliability and measurement error of the test be assessed? (p. 180)

Hopkins (1998) provided guidelines for developing and implementing tests:

- Prepare a table of specifications to guide item development and selection and to maximize content validity.
- Include more items in the first draft of the test than will be needed in the final form.
- Phrase each item so that the content rather than the form of the statement will determine the answer.
- Ensure that the difficulty level of the items is appropriate for the group of examinees.
- Be sure the items reflect several taxonomy levels.
- Ensure that classroom tests are power tests, not speed tests. Learners should be rewarded for their knowledge rather than their ability to take tests.
- Make the reading level relatively easy.
- Use more than one type of item.
- Place all items of a particular kind together on the test.
- Ensure that the directions to the learner are as clear, complete, and concise as possible.

- Prepare answer keys and outline scoring procedures before the actual scoring begins.
- Take every reasonable precaution to ensure excellent testing conditions.
- If the test is to be used for program evaluation, research, or important student decisions, field-test it with a group of comparable students. (pp. 226–230)

Objective Test Items. As mentioned previously, an objective test can include true–false, multiple-choice, matching, and short-answer items. Each type is described next.

TRUE-FALSE ITEMS. True–false items are written as statements that a learner determines to be either correct (true) or incorrect (false). The knowledge tested with a true–false item is limited to factual information (the knowledge and comprehension level of Bloom's taxonomy). Use of true–false items should be minimized because determining whether a learner knew the correct response or guessed it is difficult, if not impossible (i.e., a learner has a 50% chance of guessing the correct answer).

Guidelines for true–false items:

- Use them sparingly, if at all.
- Be sure they are completely true or false.
- Restrict each item to only one thought or idea.
- Make sure they do not require additional qualification or clarification.
- Avoid wording them negatively.

Examples:

- Sacramento is the capital of California.
- An employee who is late to work for more than 3 consecutive days will be terminated.
- At the collegiate level, a player will be disqualified from a basketball game after committing his or her fourth personal foul.

MULTIPLE-CHOICE ITEMS. Multiple-choice items are considered the most useful items in objective tests. Unlike true–false items, multiple-choice items can be used to judge higher level thinking such as application and analysis. A multiple-choice item consists of a stem, alternatives, and distractors. The *stem* is a question or an incomplete sentence. The *alternatives* are the possible answers to the question, which include the correct answer and incorrect answers called *distractors*.

Guidelines for multiple-choice items:

- Ensure that the content is meaningful and does not deal with trivial information; thus, the item should be directly related to an instructional objective.
- Make sure the stem is clearly written and includes only enough information to allow the learner to understand the item.
- Make the stem either a question (ending with a question mark) or a statement (ending with a colon).
- Stick to four alternatives.
- Be sure each alternative is distinct and does not overlap with other alternatives.
- Ensure that the correct answer is clearly the best possible response.
- Do not use irrelevant clues in the correct answer, such as including more words or using more precise wording than that in the distractors.
- Word alternatives to be grammatically consistent with the stem.
- Avoid negatively stated stems.
- Avoid using *all of the above* or *none of the above* as alternatives; *all of the above* can often be simply eliminated by a learner who knows that one of the alternatives is incorrect. *None of the above* does not necessarily indicate that a learner knows the true answer: A learner may correctly choose *none of the above* but be unable to supply the correct answer if asked to do so.
- Randomly select the position of the correct answer.

Examples:

- Norm-referenced learner evaluations are used to:
    - A. determine the competence of learners.
    - B. rank or compare learners.
    - C. assess the skill level of learners.
    - D. make decisions about instructional objectives.

- The primary function of a notary public is to:

    A. act as an impartial witness.

    B. verify the originality of documents.

    C. authenticate the accuracy of a signature.

    D. bear witness to the signing of loan documents.

- Until 1962, Jamaica was a former colony of what country?

    A. Germany

    B. Great Britain

    C. Spain

    D. United States of America

- In which of the following ways could 180 pencils be packaged for delivery?

    A. 10 boxes with 17 pencils each

    B. 13 boxes with 11 pencils each

    C. 15 boxes with 12 pencils each

    D. 19 boxes with 11 pencils each

MATCHING ITEMS. With matching questions, a learner is asked to determine the relationship between two lists of information. The most appropriate use of matching questions is when the information in each column forms a homogeneous group. A few common examples of information that is tested by using matching questions are terms and definitions, events and persons, events and dates, and rules and examples. Matching questions are typically used to test knowledge-level instructional objectives.

Guidelines for matching items:

- Provide extra items in the answer column (the right column) to reduce the chance that a learner will guess successfully.
- Ensure that learners fully understand the rationale for matching the items.
- Number the items on the left; place the options on the right and assign them letters.
- Arrange items and options in a logical order.
- Place all the items and options on a single page, if possible.
- Limit the number of items to 10 to 15.

Example:

	THEORIST	THEORY
_____ 1.	Bruner	A) Cognitive and affective development of children
_____ 2.	Dewey	B) Cognitive growth
_____ 3.	Gagne	C) Component display
_____ 4.	Gardner	D) Conditions of learning
_____ 5.	Pavio	E) Dual coding
_____ 6.	Piaget	F) Gestalt
_____ 7.	Skinner	G) Multiple intelligences
_____ 8.	Vygotsky	H) Operant conditioning
		I) Progressivism
		J) Zone of proximal development

SHORT-ANSWER ITEMS. A short-answer item is a question in the form of a direct question, a specific problem, or an incomplete statement or question (also known as a *fill-in-the-blank item*). It requires a learner to provide a response rather than to identify the correct response from a list of possible answers, thus it helps eliminate guessing. A short-answer item differs from an essay item in that it requires a more concise and constricted answer. Short-answer items are particularly useful when computation is required to determine the answer.

Guidelines for short-answer items:

- Use a direct question rather than a statement.
- Write the question so that the response will be as brief as possible; such brevity will allow the question to be scored more objectively.
- Do not use wording taken directly from materials learners will have read.
- Avoid grammatical or other clues that can give away the correct answer.
- When using incomplete statements or questions, do not delete too much pertinent information. For example, "The major export of _____, _____, and Venezuela is _____" is too vague.

Examples:

- The two major types of graphic file formats used on the Web are called .gif and _____.
- Ian scored 45 out of 47 on a test. What percentage of his responses were correct?
- Which planet is closest to the sun?

Constructed-Response Tests.   Constructed-response tests differ from objective tests because the answers to questions on constructed-response tests do not necessarily have one correct response. Because of this factor, constructed-response tests are considered to be subjective tests and are therefore generally more difficult to score. The major item used in constructed-response tests is the essay question. This type of question allows higher levels of cognition (e.g., analysis, synthesis, and evaluation) to be assessed.

ESSAY ITEMS.   As mentioned, essay questions are useful for determining a learner's higher level cognitive abilities (e.g., analysis, synthesis, and evaluation). Answers to essay items can provide insight into not only a learner's understanding of the content that was taught, but also how well a learner writes. One caution needs to be mentioned, however: A learner with poor writing skills or whose native language is not being used to answer an essay question may be unfairly evaluated as not understanding content that was taught because he or she lacks adequate writing skills. This point should be taken into consideration any time essay items are used.

Guidelines for essay items:

- Ensure that they are carefully focused.
- Use several shorter questions rather than fewer longer questions; doing so will provide a better learner assessment.
- Do not give students a choice of questions to answer; all learners should answer the same questions.
- Inform learners of how the questions will be graded; if spelling is important, let the learners know. Understanding how a question will be graded will help learners focus on what is important. Providing students with a rubric before they complete the essay questions can be helpful.
- Remember that the length of time needed to answer essay questions can vary significantly among learners.
- Allow learners to prepare to take essay tests.

- Before grading, review the major points that should or could be discussed in each answer.
- When grading, read through and grade the same question for each learner before moving on to the next question.
- When grading, have more than one grader.
- When grading, read through the entire answer once and then check it for factual information.

Examples:

- In your opinion, what is the most important element of the instructional design process? Support your answer with at least two examples. (3-page limit; 20 points)
- Describe how behaviorist and constructivist theories could be used to teach an individual how to design and develop a Web site. Treat each theory separately in your answer.

A Change in Skill.   Whether a learner has had a change in skill is evaluated by examining actions or behaviors that can be directly observed. Such evaluation is often called *performance assessment*. Typically what is being examined is a learner's ability to perform a particular task or series of related tasks that compose a particular skill. One example is taking blood from an individual who is donating blood. This general skill can be broken down into a series of precise skills. The learner is being judged not only on his or her ability to meet the general skill, but also on the more precise skills that make up this general skill. Note that what we call the *general skill* can also be considered the instructional goal. The more precise skills would be considered instructional objectives.

Guidelines for evaluating a skill:

- When evaluating a skill, you can evaluate both the process and the product. Determine whether both or just one will be evaluated; generally both are evaluated. The product is the result or outcome of the skill (e.g., a filled vial of blood correctly labeled and stored).
- When evaluating the process, assess the following elements: following a proper series of steps, using tools or instruments properly, completing the skill in a certain time frame.
- When evaluating the product, assess the quality and quantity.
- Evaluate the skill under the most realistic conditions possible.

A learner's change in skill can be evaluated by using a variety of assessment techniques such as direct testing, performance ratings, observations and anecdotal records, and portfolios. Evaluation of a learner's change in skill often involves using more than one of these techniques.

Direct Testing.   Certain skills can be directly tested to determine how well a learner can perform the skill. What is primarily being evaluated is the final outcome (i.e., the product) that is a result of performing the skill. In addition, the process or processes of how the learner performed the skill can be evaluated, which can provide important information about areas in which a learner needs improvement.

Examples of direct testing:

- A nurse drawing blood from a patient
- A postal worker sorting letters
- A track-and-field athlete running the 110-meter-high hurdles
- A carpenter using a power tool

Direct testing process:

- Start by reviewing the task analysis results to determine the steps of the skill that the learner will need to perform. Each step will be the individual criterion on which the learner will be evaluated.
- Determine the level of proficiency that is considered acceptable for the outcome; for example, a track-and-field athlete who is able to run the 110-meter-high hurdles in 14 seconds or less will make the team.
- Determine where the testing will take place; what equipment, materials, and personnel are needed; and what safety precautions should be taken.
- Write the test instructions to inform the learners about how the test will be conducted.
- Establish how the results will be recorded.
- Conduct the test, judge the learner's level of proficiency, and provide feedback to the learner.

Performance Ratings.   Performance ratings and direct testing are similar techniques. However, the main focus of each differs. The focus of a performance rating is on a learner's ability to perform certain actions—not on the product, as in the case of direct testing. Nevertheless, the product resulting from the actions completed during a performance rating is also evaluated—often in terms of both quantity and quality.

Two common techniques used as part of a performance rating are checklists and rating scales. A *checklist* is used to determine the sequence of actions a learner takes while performing a task. No qualitative judgment is made about how well the actions were performed when a checklist is used; all that is determined is whether the action was performed.

A *rating scale* is designed to provide a rating of how well a learner performs different actions. The rating is typically identified on a numerical scale that indicates performance from low to high, poor to excellent, or unacceptable to acceptable. The following rating scale is an example of a *Likert-type scale* (a scale with five options):

1	2	3	4	5
Poor	Below average	Average	Above average	Excellent

When developing a rating scale, you must pilot test it with several learners from the target group (or those who closely resemble the target group) to determine how the scale will work. In addition, if multiple raters are using the scale, they must understand and agree on the scale criteria to achieve consistency in rating the learners (known as *interrater reliability*).

Examples of performance ratings:

- Using cooking techniques to make a soufflé
- Developing black-and-white photographs in a darkroom
- Using interrogation skills to gather information from a suspected felon
- Using debating skills

Performance rating process:

- As with the direct testing technique, start by reviewing the task analysis results to determine the steps of the skill the learner will need to perform. Each step will be a criterion on which the learner will be evaluated.
- Develop the rating scale that will be used:

  1. Typically, include five levels on the rating scale; doing so will help clearly differentiate a learner's performance. Scales of two or three items may also be used.

2. When defining the numerical rating points, use oral descriptions. The descriptions should not overlap.
3. Use clear and distinct wording to express the item to be rated.
4. Include only one idea in each item.

- Pilot test the rating instrument with at least two learners from the target group or from a closely representative group.

Observations and Anecdotal Records.   An anecdotal record is developed as a result of observing a learner perform a skill. Typically, the skill is performed in the exact (or a representative) setting in which it will generally be used. During observation of the skill, notes are taken that reflect how well a learner performed. After the observation, the notes are expanded into a narrative that describes the learner's performance and areas in which the learner needs to improve. For the most useful results, the notes should be written into narrative form soon after the observation.

Using observations and anecdotal records can be time consuming, especially when many learners must be observed. In addition to the time involved, subjectivity can be an issue. Subjectivity can be minimized if the observer directly reports on what he or she sees and avoids interpretation until after completion of the observation. Rubrics and checklists (both described later in the chapter) can also be used during the observation to focus the observer on what he or she should be looking for.

Examples of observation and anecdotal records:

- Observing a student teacher in a classroom
- Observing an instructor conducting a training session
- Following a supervisor for a day to determine how he manages his employees
- Riding along on a shift with a police officer to assess how she interacts with the public
- Closely monitoring a student as he interacts with other students during several class periods

Anecdotal records process:

- Determine the skills on which the observation will focus. Doing so will help guide you during the observation.
- Determine whether recording devices will be used during the observation, such as a video camera or tape recorder. Permission will need

to be obtained from the person being recorded. If other individuals, such as students, coworkers, or customers, will be recorded (whether planned or not), permission must be obtained from each of them as well.

- Obtain permission to observe the learner at the organization; organizations have different policies, and gaining permission to access certain organizations can take days to weeks; prepare for this possibility.
- Decide whether the observation will be announced or unannounced.
- During the observation, take brief and direct notes about what is occurring. Avoid interpreting the events during the observation. Expand on the notes soon afterward.
- Determine whether follow-up observations are necessary; although time consuming and often costly, multiple observations can provide data that will more accurately depict a learner's skill level.
- If multiple individuals will use the rating scale, ensure that they understand and agree on the criteria.

Portfolios. A *portfolio* is a collection of artifacts that depicts a learner's ability. "Well-designed portfolios represent important, contextualized learning that requires complex thinking and expressive skills" (Herman & Winters, 1994, p. 48). The focus of a portfolio is on the products a learner creates as a result of skills he or she has acquired during a given period. Therefore, a portfolio is meant to show the progression of learning that has occurred. It can directly indicate how well the learner is applying skills learned during instruction by indicating areas of strengths and weaknesses. "The goal is to produce richer and more valid assessments of students' competencies than are possible from traditional testing" (Novak, Herman, & Gearhart, 1996, p. 220).

Examples of portfolios:

- A collection of paintings from an artist
- Songs written and performed by a musician
- Short stories written by a novelist
- A collection of products created by a fourth-grade student on a specific topic
- A set of instructional design project examples created by an individual or a group
- The scholarly and creative works (e.g., articles, presentations, multimedia projects) of a university professor

Portfolio process:

- Determine what skills the portfolio will cover and during what time period. The skills should be directly related to the instructional goals and objectives.
- Identify how the artifacts will be evaluated. Rubrics should be developed that provide criteria for judging the quality of the artifacts.
- Clearly identify how the entire portfolio will be evaluated. How will a learner's change in skill be determined?
- Allow the learner, in consultation with the instructor, to determine which artifact samples are included in the portfolio. Typically, a learner and an instructor meet during the development of the portfolio, which allows the instructor to provide feedback to the learner to determine how he or she is progressing.
- Have the instructor judge the completed portfolio.

ID INSIGHT

Rubrics

We mention several times in this chapter that rubrics can be used along with various learner evaluation techniques. What is a rubric? It is an assessment instrument used to evaluate a learner on the basis of the learner's performance of specific criteria. Specifically, a rubric is a printed set of scoring guidelines (criteria) that is used to evaluate a learner's performance or product. Rubrics can be used with knowledge-, skill-, and attitude-related instructional objectives. When a rubric is used to evaluate a learner, he or she is provided with an overall score based on how well he or she performed on the entire mixture of criteria. The rubric also indicates how well the learner performed on individual criteria. A rubric looks similar to a rating scale; however, a major difference is that a rubric is more descriptive. Rubrics also allow a more holistic approach to be taken to evaluate a learner's performance because it reveals the entire learner outcome.

A rubric can work as a guide for learners and instructors. If provided to a learner before instruction, a rubric will guide the learner by helping him or her focus on the specific areas in which he or she will

(continued)

be evaluated. A rubric also helps guide a teacher by focusing him or her on the areas that will be evaluated. Rubrics allow evaluation to be more objective and consistent by clarifying in specific and descriptive terms the criteria to be evaluated. Rubrics provide a much more comprehensive level of detail about how a learner has performed than do rating scales.

Rubrics have become popular, especially with K–12 teachers, because of the standards-based education movement. Many K–12 teachers have turned to rubrics as evaluation tools because they can be matched directly to state standards and instructional objectives; they provide a much greater level of detail (than do letter grades and numerical scores) on how a student is performing; they can save evaluation time (once they are developed; development of rubrics can be time consuming); and they can help make evaluation more objective and consistent. Rubrics are also popular with non-K–12 teachers for most of the same reasons.

Numerous rubric development software and Web sites can be used to help you develop rubrics. One we use, especially when we work with K–12 teachers, is called *Rubricator*. It is a highly robust program that walks the user through the process of developing rubrics. K–12 teachers enjoy Rubricator because it allows them to download state content standards, which allows a teacher to develop rubrics that directly relate to the standards at the grade level at which he or she teaches. You can download a free 30-day trial of Rubricator at www.rubrics.com.

A Change in Attitude. The most difficult outcome to determine is whether a learner has achieved a change in attitude. Attitudes are based on feelings, emotions, and perceptions, which are highly subjective, often subtle, and difficult to evaluate directly. A learner's attitude is typically evaluated by examining his or her behaviors and what he or she says. Assessment techniques used to examine them are observations and anecdotal records, surveys and questionnaires, self-reporting inventories, and interviews.

Examples of attitudes that can change:

- An employee's feelings about a change in policy on accumulating time off for sick leave

- A learner's interest in listening to classical music
- A doctor's attitude toward his or her patients
- A customer's perceptions about a new product
- A learner's eating habits

Observations and Anecdotal Records.   For determining attitude change, observations and anecdotal records work much as they do for determining whether a learner has had a change in skill. An instructor observes a learner in an authentic environment (e.g., classroom, job site) and takes notes on what he or she observes as it relates to affective outcomes (i.e., attitudes and behaviors). For example, an instructor may be looking at how a learner treats others or how enthusiastic a learner may be to participate in a certain activity. Soon after the observation is complete, the instructor expands on the notes to provide a more complete picture of what took place.

Surveys and Questionnaires.   Observations and anecdotal records are often not feasible. Consider the example of healthy eating. After participating in a workshop dealing with losing weight, a learner is expected to change his or her behavior by planning and eating healthy meals that include certain foods. Direct observation of whether the learner's behavior has changed toward certain types of food would be almost impossible to determine through direct observation. An instructor would not have the time (or the inclination) to follow the learner around to see what he or she eats throughout the day. Instead of observing the learner, the instructor can use a survey or questionnaire to gather data about the learner's behavior and attitudes toward healthy foods.

Surveys and questionnaires generally include two types of items: open-ended questions, for which a learner writes answers, and questions with fixed responses, for which a learner chooses the answer that best indicates his or her opinion. Open-ended questions can provide data that require a significant amount of time to analyze; however, the data provided may be highly informative and insightful about the learner. Questions with fixed responses are easier and quicker to analyze. They do not, however, provide the same level of depth that open-ended questions do.

Rating scales are often used in surveys and questionnaires. As a reminder, a rating scale item allows the user to select from several choices—generally from two, three, or five choices. A rating scale that consists of five choices is known as a *Likert-type scale*.

Self-Reporting Inventories. A self-reporting inventory generally consists of a series of structured questions or statements that are to be answered with *yes* or *no:*

- I usually turn in my homework on time.
- Finishing high school is important to me.

Self-reporting inventories are similar to Likert-type or rating scales. Often, self-reporting inventories use Likert-type- or rating-scale formats.

Interviews. Interviews are one of the most widely used assessment techniques. An interview can provide an opportunity for a wide range of topics to be discussed. It can also be a useful technique for allowing a learner to clarify and expand on answers given through other assessment techniques (e.g., a survey or questionnaire). Because of the potential for increased amounts of data to be collected, interviews can take significant amounts of time to analyze.

Unstructured interviews are usually not advisable because too much time is spent on a limited number of topics; in addition, the learner, not the instructor, often determines the topics. A skillful interviewer will develop a series of open-ended questions that guide the interview. He or she will also provide few clues about the correct answers to questions. The interviewer should refrain from being too active in the interview process so as not to help "shape" a learner's responses.

Learner Evaluation and a Change in Attitude. When a learner evaluation is conducted to determine a change in attitude, problems can occur. These problems are related to the responses learners provide on rating scales, on surveys, on questionnaires, on self-reporting inventories, and during interviews. The most common problems are social-desirability responses, self-deception, and semantic problems.

Social-desirability responses are those that a learner gives because he or she believes they are the expected answers (hence, they are "socially desirable" responses). Self-reporting inventories are highly susceptible to social-desirability responses.

Self-deception is a "common adjustment phenomenon in human behavior" in which the "tendency to want to like what we see when we look at ourselves" affects how we respond (Hopkins, 1998, p. 296). A learner may respond in particular ways because he or she wants to appear a certain way and therefore feel good about him- or herself.

Semantic problems deal with the meanings a learner may attach to words. For example, a rating scale may use the words *rarely, seldom, average, frequently,* and *usually* as choices for an item that asks a learner how often he or she chooses to listen to classical music rather than other types of music. As the learner answers this item, he or she wavers between selecting *rarely* or *seldom* because he or she is unsure of the difference.

Implementation of Learner Evaluations

When should a learner be evaluated? A common mistake a beginning instructional designer may make is to think that a **learner evaluation** is performed only at the end of instruction. Although that is an appropriate time to do so, a learner can be evaluated at other times as well. The three most common evaluation times are before instruction begins, during instruction, and at the conclusion of instruction, as was mentioned. Data gathered at these times can provide significantly different information about the learner.

Preinstruction

Evaluating a learner before instruction begins allows data to be gathered about the learner's ability related to the instructional objectives and content that compose the instruction. Such an evaluation will not reveal how well a learner has done, but it can help to determine how well a learner will do. By understanding what a learner knows or does not know about the objectives and content, the instructor will be able to adjust the instruction to help the learner be successful and satisfied.

Depending on the objectives of the instruction, various assessments can be developed to use in a preinstruction learner evaluation. These assessments are commonly referred to as *preassessment activities*. An objective test or quiz is often used as a preassessment activity for instruction that focuses on producing a change in a learner's knowledge. For instruction focusing on a change in skill, a learner may be asked to perform tasks that relate to the skill. For instruction focusing on a change in attitude, the learner may be asked to complete a questionnaire or short essay. A role-play scenario can also provide insight into a learner's attitude.

When developing preassessment activities, keep in mind that the purpose is to gather data about a learner's *current* abilities, which will allow decisions to be made about how instruction might be altered. In addition to gathering data about a learner's ability, preassessment activities can be useful as a way to gain learner attention at the start of instruction. A preassessment activity can be used to focus a learner on the instruction by providing an overview of what outcome the learner is expected to attain.

During Instruction

Evaluation during instruction provides data that indicate how a learner is progressing. Numerous assessment activities can be used during instruction. Many of them can be completed quickly and without much advance preparation.

One such assessment activity that can be extremely effective is observation. The instructor can observe a learner as he or she participates in the instruction. The instructor can then modify the instruction on the basis of what is observed. He or she can also take notes about the learner, which can then be analyzed after instruction. This technique is useful if the instruction continues for multiple sessions. However, effectively taking notes in some instructional environments may be difficult, if not impossible. Observing and taking notes on multiple learners during instruction is also challenging.

Other assessment activities such as a quick write or a random call can be used throughout instruction to provide data on how a learner is progressing. A *quick write* involves having a learner write a response to either a question the instructor has asked or to the major ideas he or she has learned to that point in the instruction. A *random call* is conducted by selecting several learners at random to respond to a question about the content or to demonstrate a skill. Some learners may not react favorably to being asked to share what they have learned with a group of learners. Thus, a supportive environment is necessary if this type of assessment activity is to work effectively.

Postinstruction

Postinstruction evaluation can be considered summative evaluation because it occurs after instruction. The goal of postinstruction learner evaluation is to determine how successful a learner was. What level of achievement did the learner attain? Did the instruction produce a change in learner knowledge, skill, or attitude? Was the learner able to meet the instructional objectives?

A common assessment technique used during postinstruction evaluation to determine a change in knowledge is a paper-and-pencil test: an objective or a constructed-response test. A change in skill is determined with a performance assessment in which both the process and the product are evaluated. Determining a change in attitude is most difficult and is typically accomplished by using assessment techniques such as observations, self-reporting inventories, and surveys and questionnaires, which focus on a learner's words and behaviors.

Determination of the Success of Learner Evaluations

A successful learner evaluation provides sufficient data to help the individuals involved in the instructional intervention (e.g., instructor, instructional designer) make decisions about what took place and what should subsequently be done. Generally, what is being established by looking at the data is whether a learner was able to meet the instructional objectives, and to what degree.

Much of the learner evaluation, after it has been developed, is out of the instructional designer's hands. The instructor plays a crucial role in executing the assessment activities and then making decisions based on the data collected. An instructional designer should be available and willing to help an instructor look at the data and make recommendations based on the data. If a learner evaluation indicates that a learner was not able to meet instructional goals and objectives, the instructor, possibly with the help of the instructional designer, will attempt to determine why. Finding out why will help establish what appropriate next steps need to take place for a learner. It could indicate that the learner needs remediation or that the instructional materials need to be improved.

If adequate data were not collected during the learner evaluation to allow for the learner to be properly evaluated, the learner evaluation should be examined. Such an examination could indicate that the assessment techniques used to gather data were inappropriate. Most likely this situation would result if the instructional objectives were not properly matched with the proper type of assessment technique (e.g., an objective test was used to evaluate a change in a learner's attitude). If the instruction were to be used again, the learner evaluation would need to be redone. Another possible issue with the learner evaluation could be how it was implemented. If the assessment techniques were not implemented properly, inadequate data may have been collected. Individuals responsible for implementing the learner evaluation may need training.

Instructional Designer's Role

The role of an instructional designer is to help create and execute a plan of action to design, develop, and implement an efficient and effective learner evaluation. Such an evaluation provides appropriate data that help determine the success level an individual has achieved as a result of instruction. This plan of action should include the following elements:

- Analyze the instructional goals and objectives; determine the intended learning outcomes.
- On the basis of the instructional objectives and learning outcomes, determine the appropriate type of learner evaluation needed.
- Design and develop the appropriate assessment techniques that will be used to gather data about the learner.
- Assist, as necessary, in the implementation of the assessment techniques, which can include analyzing the data, determining whether the learners have been successful, and deciding what steps need to take place on the basis of the results of the data analysis.

SUMMARY

Evaluation is a process for determining the success of an individual, a product, or a process. An instructional designer will use three main types of evaluation: learner, formative, and summative. Each is used at different times in the instructional design process to gather data. The gathered data are analyzed to determine the level of success that has been achieved. Various decisions can be made on the basis of the success level. A common decision an instructional designer makes (often in consultation with an instructor, a subject matter expert, or a client—or possibly all three) is whether to make changes to the instruction that was developed. Properly designed and implemented evaluations allow instructional designers to create effective and efficient interventions.

Learner evaluation is often considered the most critical type of evaluation. It is used to determine the success level a learner has achieved by participating in instruction. The success level is based on the extent to which a learner can meet the instructional goals and objectives. The results can be compared against a set of standards (criterion referenced) or with those of other learners (norm referenced). A criterion-referenced learner evaluation is used to determine learner competence. A norm-referenced learner evaluation is used to compare and rank learners. Most learner evaluations an instructional designer helps develop are criterion referenced.

Assessment techniques, which are part of a learner evaluation, are typically implemented at three times: before instruction, during instruction, and after instruction. The data collected during these three times provide different information about the learner. Prior to instruction, data are gathered to determine what a learner may or may not know about the instructional objectives. Data gathered during instruction help determine how a learner is progressing. Data gathered after instruction help determine what a learner achieved.

Development of a learner evaluation starts by examining the instructional goals and objectives and determining the expected outcome—a change in knowledge, skill, or attitude. The expected outcome will influence the type of learner evaluation that will be developed. Assessment techniques are then developed and implemented to determine whether the expected outcome occurred.

A properly designed learner evaluation will provide appropriate data that will allow an instructor to determine whether a learner was successful. If a learner was not successful (i.e., did not meet the learning objectives and the intended outcome), decisions must be made about what needs to be done. An instructional designer will often work with an instructor to determine the appropriate next steps, such as learner remediation or a change in the instructional materials.

CONNECTING PROCESS TO PRACTICE

1. Compare and contrast criterion-referenced and norm-referenced learner evaluations.
2. Describe the process you would go through to develop a learner evaluation for an instructional design project on which you are working. List the steps and describe what you would do during each step.
3. When is it most appropriate to use:

   - an objective test?
   - a constructed-response test?
   - a performance assessment?

4. The instruction you have helped design has the following instructional objectives:

- The nurse will be able to explain the difference between the natural rhythmicity of the heart and breathing.
- The nurse will be able to explain why the control of breathing must involve both automatic and conscious aspects.
- The nurse will be able to list the muscles involved in both normal and hard (labored) breathing.
- The nurse will be able to name three chemical factors that influence respiration.
- The nurse will be able to assess a patient's breathing to determine whether any significant breathing problems exist.
- The nurse will be able to articulate to his or her supervisor the assessment of the patient.
- The nurse will be able to help a patient control his or her breathing through the use of proper breathing techniques.

What types of learner evaluations would you develop to determine whether a learner was successful?

5. Why are validity and reliability, as they relate to learner evaluation, important concepts for an instructional designer to understand?

RECOMMENDED READINGS

Aiken, L. (1995). *Rating scales and checklists.* New York: Wiley.

Aiken, L. (1997). *Questionnaires and inventories: Surveying opinions and assessing personality.* New York: Wiley.

Carmines, E. G., & Zeller, R. A. (1991). *Reliability and validity assessment.* Newbury Park, CA: Sage.

Hopkins, K. D. (1998). *Educational and psychological measurement and evaluation.* Boston: Allyn & Bacon.

Morrison, G., Ross, S., & Kemp, J. (2004). *Designing effective instruction.* Hoboken, NJ: Wiley.

Worthen, B., Sanders, J., & Fitzpatrick, J. (1997). *Program evaluation: Alternative approaches and practical guidelines.* New York: Longman.

REFERENCES

Carmines, E. G., & Zeller, R. A. (1991). *Reliability and validity assessment*. Newbury Park, CA: Sage.

Herman, J. L., & Winters, L. (1994). Portfolio research: A slim collection. *Educational Leadership, 52,* 48–55.

Hopkins, K. D. (1998). *Educational and psychological measurement and evaluation*. Boston: Allyn & Bacon.

Millman, J., & Greene, J. (1989). The specification and development of tests of achievement and ability. In R. L. Linn (Ed.), *Educational measurement* (3rd ed., pp. 335–366). New York: Macmillan.

Morrison, G., Ross, S., & Kemp, J. (2004). *Designing effective instruction*. Hoboken, NJ: Wiley.

Novak, J. R., Herman, J. L., & Gearhart, M. (1996). Establishing validity for performance-based assessments: An illustration for collections of student writing. *Journal of Educational Research, 89*(4), 220–233.

Worthen, B., Sanders, J., & Fitzpatrick, J. (1997). *Program evaluation: Alternative approaches and practical guidelines*. New York: Longman.

Chapter 12

DETERMINING THE SUCCESS OF THE INSTRUCTIONAL DESIGN PRODUCT AND PROCESS

Key Terms

Formative evaluation
(page 238)

Group processing
(page 255)

Program evaluators
(page 248)

Summative evaluation
(page 248)

Usability testing
(page 246)

We have several methods of evaluating the success of instruction. One of the primary methods is an evaluation form used for all classroom instruction. We also use a similar form for online training. In addition, we evaluate the success of the instruction by collecting data before the instruction and comparing the performance results after the instruction has been implemented. For example, if the problem statement is that consistent training is leading to increased tool downtime and increased costs, we collect that data at the beginning of the instructional design method. Once the instructional plan has been implemented, we watch the costs and tool downtime issues to see whether they improve. If so, we can associate our training with that event, if no other variables exist.

—Jona Titus,
Senior Training Specialist,
Intel Corporation,
Hillsboro, OR

Guiding Questions

- What information can formative and summative evaluations provide to help the instructional designer improve the instructional design process?
- Why is including various types of evaluation in the instructional design process important?
- How can the success of formative and summative evaluations be judged?
- How can an instructional designer use evaluation to improve the design team's effectiveness?

Chapter Overview

Evaluation is a crucial part of instructional design. As we discussed in Chapter 11, evaluation is a process that allows data to be gathered that help determine someone's level of success or the worth of something. In instructional design, a major purpose of evaluation is to help determine how successful a learner has been as a result of participating in instruction. This type of evaluation is called *learner evaluation*. Although learner evaluation is extremely important, two other evaluation types—formative and summative—are also critical. These two types of evaluation concentrate on the instructional design process and the instruction developed as a result of the process. The focus of this chapter is on defining formative and summative evaluations, describing specific instructional design experts' approaches to such evaluation, and explaining how formative and summative evaluations can be designed and implemented.

Formative and Summative Evaluation

A common misconception many beginning instructional designers have is that evaluation of learners takes place only at the conclusion of instruction. Although evaluation is conducted to test the learners, it should also take place at various stages of the instructional design process through the use of formative and summative evaluations (Table 12.1). Knowing when and how to use various evaluation types helps instructional designers develop instructional interventions that are efficient and effective.

Formative Evaluation

Formative evaluation is used throughout the instructional design process to gather data that can be used to provide feedback on the process. It is especially useful during the early stages of the instructional design process. The feedback allows an instructional designer to make improvements to the instruction before it is completely developed, which helps ensure that high-quality instruction is created. In addition to helping improve the instruction, data gathered through a formative evaluation can be shared with a client to indicate how the project is progressing. Periodic communication with your client on the progress of the project helps ensure that project goals and expectations will be met.

TABLE 12.1

Differences Between Formative and Summative Evaluation

Criterion	Formative Evaluation	Summative Evaluation
Purpose	To determine value or quality	To determine value or quality
Use	To improve a program or instruction	To make decisions about the future or adoption of instruction
Audience	Program administrators and staff	Program administrators and potential consumer or funding agency
Evaluators	Primarily internal evaluators, supported by external evaluators	External evaluators, supported by internal evaluators in unique cases
Major characteristics	Provides feedback so program personnel can improve the instruction	Provides information to enable program personnel to decide whether to continue the instruction or whether consumers should adopt it
Design constraints	What information is needed? When?	What evidence is needed for major decisions?
Purpose of data collection	Diagnostic	Judgmental
Measures	Sometimes informal	Valid and reliable
Frequency of data collection	Frequent	Infrequent
Sample size	Generally small	Usually large
Questions asked	What is working?	What results occur?
	What needs to be improved?	With whom?
	How can it be improved?	Under what conditions?
		With what training?
		At what cost?

Source: Adapted from *Program Evaluation: Alternative Approaches and Practical Guidelines,* (p. 17), by B. Worthen, J. Sanders, and J. Fitzpatrick. Published by Allyn and Bacon, Boston, MA. Copyright © 1997 by Pearson Education. Adapted with permission of the publisher.

Approaches to Formative Evaluation. Instructional design experts take a variety of approaches to formative evaluation. Despite their differences, these approaches all have the goal of helping improve the instruction that is being developed. Let us begin by looking at three approaches to formative evaluation.

Smith and Ragan's Approach. Smith and Ragan (1999) wrote that formative evaluation is conducted to "determine the weakness in the instruction so that revisions can be made to make them [*sic*] more effective and efficient." This determination helps the instructional designer know "whether the instructional materials are 'there' yet, or whether she needs to continue the design process" (p. 388). The stages Smith and Ragan advocated for formative evaluation are design reviews, expert reviews, learner validation, and ongoing evaluation.

The first stage, design reviews, is completed before the development of instruction. Expert reviews, stage 2, typically occur after the instruction is completed but before it is used with learners. The final two stages involve use of the actual instruction with learners who represent the intended learners.

In stage 1, *design reviews* are conducted after various phases of the instructional design process—such as the needs, task, goals and objective, and learner analyses—are complete. Design reviews help verify the accuracy of information at each stage of the instructional design process before instruction is developed. Smith and Ragan (1999) advocated revisiting the data gathered during these instructional design phases to determine how accurate they are.

In the second stage, *expert reviews* are conducted to gather information about the instruction to determine whether the instruction is accurate and current. Various experts, such as content experts, instructional design experts, pedagogical experts, and experts on the learners, can provide various perspectives on the instruction. The instruction provided for expert reviews is typically at the draft stage. Smith and Ragan (1999) suggested that expert reviewer comments should be divided into three categories: revisions that need to be made immediately, suggested revisions that require additional data that can be gathered during the final two stages of the formative evaluation, and suggested revisions that should be ignored.

Learner validation, stage 3, includes three levels: one-on-one evaluation, small-group evaluation, and field trials. These three levels are identical to those promoted by Dick, Carey, and Carey (2001).

The final stage, *ongoing evaluation*, includes gathering data on the long-term effectiveness of instruction. Smith and Ragan (1999) stated that if instruction is meant to be used multiple times, provisions need to be made in a formative evaluation plan to collect effectiveness data. These data, which are similar to data collected during a field trial, provide feedback on what revisions need to be made to instruction on the basis of its actual use and whether the revisions made have been effective.

Morrison, Ross, and Kemp's Approach. Morrison, Ross, and Kemp (2004) advocated a basic model for formative evaluation based on the work of Gooler (1980). Gooler's approach includes the following eight steps:

1. Purpose
2. Audience
3. Issues
4. Resources
5. Evidence
6. Data-gathering techniques
7. Analysis
8. Reporting

This approach has three main phases: planning, conducting, and reporting. Phase 1 includes steps 1 through 5, phase 2 includes steps 6 and 7, and phase 3 is the eighth and final step, reporting the results.

Phase 1 involves determining the evaluation purpose, the primary audience to which the results will be disseminated, the issues that need to be addressed, the resources needed to address the issues, and the types of evidence that will be acceptable to address these issues. Working closely with the client during phase 1 is extremely important in order to clearly articulate and manage expectations.

The first step, determining the purpose or purposes of the evaluation, is done in consultation with the client. The two most common purposes are to improve the instruction being developed and to satisfy the administrative requirements of the client for whom you are working. Many corporations and institutions require evaluations to be conducted. Most state agencies are required to include an evaluation component to help ensure that project goals are being met and to report how monies have been spent.

The audience of the evaluation (step 2) is important to determine because it will dictate the types of information that need to be collected and reported. The client will be able to help define the intended audience. Conducting an evaluation for multiple audiences should be avoided because satisfying varying needs within a single report will be difficult. The best approach is to try to narrow the audience as much as possible.

After determining the purposes of the evaluation and the intended audience, the instructional designer must determine the issues that need to be addressed (step 3). The issues are generally stated as questions that need to be answered. For example, in the case of an interactive, instructional kiosk, the issues could be as follows:

- Are learners able to successfully use the kiosk after completing the instruction?
- What elements of the kiosk do learners find most understandable and least understandable?

In the case of Web-based instruction, these could be the issues:

- What is the average time spent on the summary exercises?
- Do the learners find the Web-based self-instructional materials helpful in learning the content?

After questions are developed on the basis of the evaluation issues, the resources needed to answer the questions should be identified (step 4). People, artifacts, and equipment are common types of resources often needed to address evaluation issues. Securing all these resources may be difficult. If so, the instructional designer must communicate this difficulty to his or her client. Issues may need to be adjusted if the necessary resources cannot be secured. The final step (step 5) in phase 1 is to identify the types of evidence that are needed to satisfy the evaluation issues.

Phase 2, conducting the evaluation, involves determining the data-collecting techniques that will be used (step 6), gathering the data, and analyzing the data (step 7). Morrison et al. (2004) stated that when you are determining the data-collecting techniques to be used, "two key, and often opposing, factors need to be weighed: precise measurement versus feasible or practical measurement" (p. 313).[1] For example, during the planning stage of a formative evaluation of a training program for nurses, the instructional designer determined that hospital patients would evaluate specific skills of all participants. However, because of logistical impracticalities (e.g., the amount of time required), the nurses' skills were tested on other nurses in the training program. An instructional designer must often choose between what is ideal and what is practical when gathering data.

The various data-collecting techniques that can be used are the same as those presented in Chapter 11. They include observations, questionnaires, interviews, paper-and-pencil tests, and performance tests. Using a variety of

[1]Reprinted from Morrison, Ross, and Kemp, *Designing Effective Instruction*, 4th ed. 2004. Reprinted with permission by John Wiley & Sons.

techniques to gather multiple sources of data is highly recommended to help triangulate the findings.

Analyzing the data, step 7, should reflect the purpose of a formative evaluation: to provide usable and useful information that helps the instructional designer improve instruction. Complex statistical analyses are typically not required. Morrison et al. (2004) recommended the following typical analysis procedures:

- Frequency distributions
- Frequency graphs or histograms
- Descriptive statistics, such as percentages, means, and medians
- Listing of actual comments made by respondents (p. 313)[2]

The final phase, step 8, is reporting the results of the evaluation to the primary audience. Typically, an evaluation report is tailored to a specific audience and is formatted as follows:

1. *Executive summary:* An abstract that outlines the major findings, conclusions, and recommendations
2. *Evaluation purpose*
   - Evaluation issues, stated as questions
   - Description of the instruction being evaluated
3. *Methodology used*
   - Participants
   - Instruments used to gather data
4. *Results*
   - Analysis
   - Findings
5. *Conclusions and recommendations*

In addition to a written report, an oral report of the project is often requested. The oral report can be conducted either one on one with the client or more formally to a larger group. You should remember that the purpose of the evaluation is to provide recommendations based on the data collected. When disseminating a final report, you should be certain to highlight the conclusions and recommendations.

[2]Reprinted from Morrison, Ross, and Kemp, *Designing Effective Instruction,* 4th ed. 2004. Reprinted with permission by John Wiley & Sons.

Dick, Carey, and Carey's Approach. Dick and colleagues (2001) wrote, "The emphasis in formative evaluation is on the collection and analysis of data and the revision of instruction" (p. 285). They provided three basic phases of formative evaluation: one on one, or clinical; small group; and field trial. Note that the type of formative evaluation Dick et al. advocated is designed to work specifically with self-instructional materials. Nevertheless, elements of their approach can be used with other types of instruction and materials.

During phase 1, the instructional designer works with individual learners to gather data that are used to revise the instruction. The purpose of this phase is to remove obvious errors and omissions in the instruction, to gauge initial learner performance, and to determine learner reactions to the content. Dick et al. (2001) suggested that the instructional designer work with at least three learners (with varying abilities, attitudes, or experiences) who represent the target population for the instruction. However, he or she should work with only one learner at a time. The instructional designer should be actively involved during this phase.

After selecting the learners who will participate in the one-on-one evaluation, the designer should take the following steps:

1. Explain to the learner that you would like his or her reactions to new instructional materials that have been developed.
2. Give a pretest on the content.
3. Encourage him or her to talk about the materials as he or she goes through the instruction and to be candid about what he or she likes and does not like, what makes sense, and what does not make sense.
4. Give a posttest; discuss the results with the learner by asking him or her to explain his or her responses.
5. Note the time the learner took to complete the instruction.

Phase 2 has two primary purposes: to determine how effective the changes are that were made as a result of phase 1 and to determine whether learners can go through the instruction without the instructor's assistance. For this phase, eight or more learners should be selected who are a representative sample of the entire intended group of learners. After selection of the learners who will participate in the small-group evaluation, the six steps to this phase are as follows:

1. Explain to the group of learners that you would like reactions to new instructional materials that have been developed; you want them to work through the material on their own as best they can.
2. Conduct the instruction as it is intended to be used in its final form; give a pretest if that is part of the instruction.

3. Observe what is taking place without involvement unless the learners are unable to continue the instruction; make note of any difficulties learners have in completing the instruction.

4. Conduct a posttest once the instruction is finished.

5. Administer an attitude questionnaire.

6. Debrief the group of learners.

The final phase, the field trial evaluation, is intended to help determine the effectiveness of the changes made during the small-group evaluation and whether the instruction can be used in its intended environment. A representative group of 30 learners should be used for this phase. The environment chosen for the field trial evaluation should be similar to the environment for which the instruction is being developed.

The steps in this phase are similar to those for the small-group evaluation. The major difference is that an instructor, not the instructional designer, should administer the instruction. The role of the instructional designer is to observe and take notes on what occurs. The outcome of a field trial evaluation is determination of the learners' attitudes toward the instruction as well as the learners' achievement.

In addition to advocating these three phases, Dick et al. (2001) advised that the instruction should be given to subject matter experts or instructional experts who can note whether it is accurate and current. This information, along with the data gathered during the three phases, should provide the instructional designer with enough information to make necessary revisions to the instruction being developed.

Rapid Prototyping and Usability Testing. In addition to the three approaches we described in the previous section, two related approaches to formative evaluation are important for instructional designers to understand and have as part of their instructional design skill repertoire: rapid prototyping and usability testing. Both are often overlooked as formative evaluation approaches because they are traditionally thought of as "product processes" rather than formative evaluation processes. However, built into each approach is formative evaluation, which allows the instructional designer to determine how well the instructional intervention is being designed.

As we discuss in Chapter 1, the essential idea behind rapid prototyping is to arrive at a final product through the creation of a series of prototypes. Each prototype is evaluated by a combination of experts and end users, and each successive prototype is more like the final product: That is, the "fidelity" of the prototypes increases with each new one until a working product is achieved. A rapid prototyping approach requires that the design environment allow for the relatively quick and easy creation of instructional materials (Tripp & Bichelmeyer, 1990).

With rapid prototyping, each member of the design/development team is considered a "co-inquirer" (Rathburn, Saito, & Goodrum, 1997) and, in a social process of design and development, everyone offers feedback and criticism to one another. Each time a new version of the product is tested, the team can critically reflect on what the final product should look like. The analysis of learners' needs and the content of the final product depend in part on the knowledge gained by actually building and trying out a prototype (Tripp & Bichelmeyer, 1990).

Usability testing is a concept originally borrowed from engineering that has gained popularity among software developers, multimedia producers, and instructional designers. Usability testing is a type of formative evaluation that consists of evaluating the product by observing it in action with potential end users. Typically in a usability test, evaluators observe one or more users interacting with the product under controlled conditions. The users interact with the product for a specified amount of time, having been asked to complete a set of tasks determined in advance by the evaluation team. The tasks are based on the goals and objectives the product is designed to meet. The results of a usability test inform the production team of the problems inherent in the design (e.g., the graphic for a button is not well understood, or the instructions are worded in a confusing manner). Observation of the end users in action also suggests ways to effectively eliminate the problems.

PROFESSIONALS IN PRACTICE

Usability in an IT Shop: The Home Depot

Usability testing has become an integral part of the software development life cycle at The Home Depot. The Home Depot information technology (IT) department works on dozens of projects every year, most of which have a user interface component that requires periodic input from end users. Required at several stages throughout the development process, usability testing primarily takes the form of qualitative data collection based on observations of users interacting with an application in the usability lab. We are fortunate to have a permanent in-house usability lab and internal resources to support testing and usability analysis work. The usability team works with various project teams to plan and conduct usability tests of applications during design, late in development, and during testing.

By putting an application in front of users at these various stages, particularly during design, we have a better chance of providing a high-quality product and a positive user experience, which translates into everything from increased productivity to higher sales and better associate retention rates.

Usability testing for internal applications is unique in several ways from usability for the Web, for example. Most of the applications The Home Depot deploys are for internal use, meaning that we have a well-defined and available user group to draw from when usability testing is conducted. Users are a more homogeneous group than the general population, and we have a better understanding of them. The environment, hardware, software, and network speed are predefined.

We use a relatively informal process in our usability cycles, in order to conform to aggressive development time lines and to provide rapid feedback to project teams. A usability strategy and protocol are formulated in hours or days, users are brought in as soon as schedules allow, and an analysis document is produced immediately. Usability problems are listed in order of importance, and solutions are suggested. For a small or midsize application, a single usability cycle can be completed in a few days. For larger and more complex applications, or for applications that are in late stages of development and are database driven, more time is required for technical setup. However, even these tests, once scheduled, are completed in days.

Because we are all part of the same organization, usability is more of a collaborative process that evolves as the IT department evolves, and as we do more and more testing, our understanding deepens with regard to our organization and the IT systems that support it. One critical issue that the usability team stresses is that each application can't be tested in isolation; how it works in relation to other applications a particular user group would use must be considered. Given the dozens of applications that are built, updated, or changed every year, an overall picture of usability and user interface design must be maintained.

—Lisa Hansen,
Usability Lead,
The Home Depot,
Atlanta, GA

Design and Implementation of a Formative Evaluation. Seasoned instructional designers understand the importance of formative evaluation in helping create efficient and effective instruction. Because of this understanding, they consistently include plans for formative evaluation when beginning instructional design projects. The approach to formative evaluation an instructional designer will take is dictated by the scope of the project. Conducting a complete formative evaluation by using one of the three approaches described in this chapter may not be feasible for every project. A less robust formative evaluation may need to be developed and carried out for smaller instructional design projects. However, no matter the scale of the project, some type of formative evaluation must be carried out.

Summative Evaluation

As part of the instructional design process, **summative evaluation** takes place after an instructional intervention has been implemented. The major goal of a summative evaluation is to gather data that allow for the effectiveness of the intervention to be determined. Did the instruction bring about the desired changes? Were the client's goals met? Summative evaluations help answer these two major questions.

The results of a summative evaluation are described in a formal report outlining the impact of the instructional intervention. This report typically includes who participated in the instructional intervention, what activities impacted them, and what changes occurred from their participation. The evaluation report also often includes the costs and benefits of implementation, descriptions of the conditions necessary to continue the program or reproduce it, and recommendations on whether the instructional intervention should be modified, discontinued, or continued as is.

Approaches to Summative Evaluation. For the beginning instructional designer, summative evaluation can be a daunting task. It is a complex process that requires a great deal of skill and experience to carry out successfully. Evaluation experts whose sole professional activity is to conduct summative evaluations are typically referred to as **program evaluators.** A program evaluator uses various approaches to conduct a summative evaluation. In *Program Evaluation: Alternative Approaches and Practical Guidelines,* Worthen, Sanders, and Fitzpatrick (1997) described six such approaches. Describing the intricacies of these approaches and how to become a program evaluator is beyond the scope of this book. If you want to learn more about summative evaluation than is presented in this chapter, you can start by reading their book and by taking a course on program evaluation. The knowledge and skills gained as a result will certainly help you as an instructional designer.

We focus our discussion of summative evaluation on four approaches that instructional design experts have advocated. The purpose is to introduce how summative evaluation is approached in instructional design; it is not to make you an expert.

Kirkpatrick's Four Levels of Evaluation. One of the most cited approaches to summative evaluation in instructional design is Kirkpatrick's four levels of evaluation. Kirkpatrick (1994) developed this model to evaluate the effectiveness of training programs—specifically training programs in industry. The four levels of his model are as follows: (1) reactions, (2) learning, (3) transfer, and (4) results. According to Kirkpatrick, evaluation should always begin with level 1, then progress through the remaining levels as time and the budget allow. However, to truly evaluate the effectiveness of a training program, you should use all four levels.

Each of Kirkpatrick's levels requires more time and rigor than the previous level did. Data collected from each level serve as a base for the next level and the evaluation that takes place at that level. As each level is conducted, more precise measures of the effectiveness of the training program are gathered.

Level 1, reactions, is designed to provide data on how participants reacted to the training. Did participants enjoy the training? Was the training relevant to the participants? Kirkpatrick (1994) indicated that all training programs should at least include this minimum level of evaluation in order to provide data that will help improve the training. A typical method used to gather data at this level is an attitude survey, in which participants indicate how satisfied they were with the training. If students indicate negative feelings toward the training, typically little to no learning occurred (however, positive reactions do not necessarily indicate that learning took place).

Level 2, learning, is conducted to determine whether participants' skills, knowledge, or attitudes changed as a result of the training. Determining this factor is much more laborious than level 1 because it requires gathering data at multiple times. Typically, pre- and posttests are used to measure these changes.

Level 3, transfer, attempts to answer the question of whether participants are using the newly acquired skills, knowledge, or attitudes in their real-world environments. In other words, have participants transferred what they learned in the training into their everyday environment? Such transference is often considered the truest measure of the effectiveness of a training program. Evaluating at this level is complicated because determining when a participant will display what he or she learned is difficult. Therefore, decisions will need to be made about when, how often, and how long the evaluation will take place in order to determine whether transference has occurred.

The final level, level 4, results, attempts to evaluate the effectiveness of the training program in business measures, such as increased sales, improved product quality, fewer on-the-job accidents, and so forth. Evaluation at this level must be long term so that trends that take place can be determined. Data that help support the effectiveness of training at this level are often gathered through methods such as interviews with managers, focus-group meetings with customers, and posttraining surveys.

Smith and Ragan's Approach. Smith and Ragan (1999) wrote,

> Within the context of instructional design, the purpose of summative evaluation is to collect, analyze, and summarize data to present to decision makers in the client organization so that they can make a judgment regarding the effectiveness, and perhaps appeal and efficiency, of the instruction. (p. 352)

The judgment that is being made is whether the instruction should continue to be used. The specific question being asked is "Does the instruction adequately solve the 'problem' that was identified in the needs assessment and that resulted in the development of the instructional materials?" (p. 353).

Smith and Ragan (1999) provided an eight-step process for conducting a summative evaluation:

1. *Determine the goals of the evaluation.* Identify the questions that should be answered. To do so, be sure to consult with the client. Typically, you will develop more questions than can be answered during the evaluation. You and the client must agree on the exact questions that are feasible to answer given the available resources.
2. *Select indicators of success.* Where will data be gathered? What needs to be looked at in order to answer the evaluation questions? Again, in consultation with the client, you need to address and agree on these issues.
3. *Select the orientation of the evaluation.* Will the evaluation be objective or subjective? An *objective orientation* focuses on answering the evaluation questions on the basis of data collected through quantitative methods (e.g., questionnaires, paper-and-pencil tests,

performance tests). The advantage of this orientation is that results are generally replicable. A *subjective orientation* is based on the perspective of the individual conducting the evaluation. Qualitative methods (e.g., interviews and observations) are used to gather data that describe the impact of the instructional intervention. The advantage of this orientation is that a rich description is provided that describes the impact the instructional intervention has had. The downside to this orientation is that the results can be influenced by the evaluator's biases. Most summative evaluations do not strictly follow one orientation or the other; typically, a combination is used.

4. *Select the design of the evaluation.* Determine how the data will be collected, when it will be collected, and under what conditions.

5. *Design or select the evaluation measures.* Determine the measures to use to evaluate the effectiveness of the instructional intervention. Learning transfer, learning outcomes, attitudes, level of implementation, and costs are all measures that can be used.

6. *Collect the data.*

7. *Analyze the data.*

8. *Report the results.* A summative evaluation report should include the following sections: summary, background information, description of the evaluation study, results, and conclusion and recommendations. The background information will come from the analyses conducted early in the instructional design process (e.g., needs, learner). The description of the evaluation study includes the purpose of the evaluation, the evaluation design, and the outcome measures. The results should include a discussion on how well the outcomes were met.

Morrison, Ross, and Kemp's Approach. The approach Morrison et al. (2004) took is similar in many ways to the approach Smith and Ragan (1999) described. Morrison et al. (2004) wrote, "A summative evaluation permits a designer or instructor to reach unbiased objective answers to evaluation questions concerning expected program outcomes and then to decide whether the program is achieving those outcomes" (p. 320).[3] A summative evaluation can help examine the following issues:

- Effectiveness of learner or trainee learning
- Efficiency of learner or trainee learning

[3]Reprinted from Morrison, Ross, and Kemp, *Designing Effective Instruction*, 4th ed. 2004. Reprinted with permission by John Wiley & Sons.

- Cost of program development and continuing expenses in relation to effectiveness and efficiency
- Attitudes and reactions to the program by learners, instructors, and staff
- Long-term benefits of the instructional program (p. 320)

These issues fall within three major areas: program effectiveness, program efficiency, and program costs. In this context, a *program* is the instructional intervention that has been designed and implemented. Program effectiveness is the major issue addressed in a summative evaluation. It helps answer the question "How successful have learners been in meeting the learning objectives?" Specifically, what is being determined is whether change has taken place with the learners. For example, are employees able to do their jobs more efficiently and effectively after participating in an instructional intervention?

Morrison et al. (2004) listed the seven major steps of a summative evaluation process as follows:

1. *Specify program objectives.* Revisit the instructional goals and objectives of the instructional intervention that was developed.
2. *Determine the evaluation design for each objective.* How will data be collected that will help determine whether the learning goals and objectives have been met? Determine what types of data are needed.
3. *Develop data-collection instruments and procedures for each objective.* Appropriate data-collection instruments and procedures are discussed in Chapter 11. Pretests, posttests, questionnaires, and observations are all examples of data-collection instruments or procedures.
4. *Carry out the evaluation.* Data should be collected from the beginning stages of the project. Doing so will ensure that the necessary data are collected—especially data on costs and time involvement. Data collection may need to be scheduled.
5. *Analyze the results from each instrument.*
6. *Interpret the results.*
7. *Disseminate the results and conclusions.* Develop a summative evaluation report (refer to Smith and Ragan's approach to summative evaluation to see how an evaluation report can be formatted). Individual discussions and group presentations are often useful (and required by the client) to disseminate evaluation findings.

Dick, Carey, and Carey's Approach.   The approach Dick et al. (2001) advocated differs significantly from the two preceding approaches. Despite the differences, the fundamental goal is the same: to determine the effectiveness of the instructional intervention.

Dick et al. (2001) defined summative evaluation as "the design of evaluation studies and the collection of data to verify the effectiveness of instructional materials with target learners" (p. 350). Its major purpose is to help the decision makers determine whether currently used instructional materials should continue to be used or whether new instructional materials need to be adopted that have the potential to meet the instructional needs of an organization.

Dick et al. (2001) stated that a summative evaluation has two main phases: an expert judgment and a field trial. The purpose of the expert judgment phase is to determine whether instruction that is currently being used or instruction that is being considered for use has the potential to meet the instructional needs of an organization. The purpose of the field trial phase is to document the effectiveness of "promising instruction" given to learners from the intended target group in the actual setting. A series of steps take place during each phase that help achieve these purposes.

Design and Implementation of a Summative Evaluation.

In an ideal situation, the instructional designer would be directly involved in designing the summative evaluation but would not be responsible for conducting it. The evaluation would be conducted by an evaluator outside the organization that contracted the instructional design project. Having the instructional designer responsible for designing and conducting the summative evaluation is often seen as a conflict of interest because the instructional designer is biased and has a tremendous stake in the success of the project. Although an instructional designer can be unbiased, such a situation only complicates the evaluation.

As we mentioned, conducting a successful summative evaluation is complex and requires a great deal of skill and experience. We advise that, if possible, beginning instructional designers not take on the role of primary evaluator for a summative evaluation. In reality, however, as an instructional designer you will sometimes be required to conduct a summative evaluation. If this is the case, be sure to plan for a summative evaluation at the beginning of the instructional design project. Discuss with the client what the expectations are for the summative evaluation, especially the summative evaluation goals. Although they may change once the summative evaluation is formally

PROFESSIONALS IN PRACTICE

Was the Training Successful?

Generally, the success or failure of a person to install and use our system after spending 5 days in class is a good indicator of whether or not the instruction was successful. To throw a little twist into things, we have a session called "Break–Fix" on the fourth day, in which one student deliberately "breaks" some software or hardware component in another student's system (either by introducing a configuration error or by doing something as simple as unplugging a telephone from its jack, for example). The "victim" must then determine what the problem is. This type of problem solving is a great way to measure whether a concept has been retained because it doesn't allow a person to react to a problem by rote response.

Because of the constant evolution of software, we must conduct formative evaluation in every class to ensure that the course content is valid. We rely on support engineers, software developers, and the students themselves to do this. Often, we use addendums to books, paper handouts, or other alterations to adapt to changing software. The simple question "Are our facts accurate today?" drives this process.

Measuring the success of online learning materials is different. Formative evaluation is much more difficult because of the lag between production time and SME [subject matter expert] input. Consequently, we rely on written test scores and student feedback (using a survey and e-mail feedback). We use summative evaluation when we have the luxury of time to revise course content according to SME input.

—Erik Novak,
Distance Learning Course Developer,
Interactive Intelligence, Inc.,
Indianapolis, IN

developed, the goals will help you know what the client's expectations are for the project. In addition, early planning will allow data to be gathered in the formative evaluation that can be used in the summative evaluation.

The evaluation goals will dictate the remaining steps of the summative evaluation. A process, such as that advocated by Smith and Ragan (1999), can be used as a guiding model for a beginning instructional designer.

Continual and consistent communication with the client is a key element in determining the success an instructional designer will have in conducting a summative evaluation.

Group Processing: Evaluating the Instructional Design Team

Rarely does an instructional designer work alone. Most projects require instructional designers to work in teams that often comprise individuals with various roles such as subject matter expert, programmer, graphic artist, content editor, Web developer, and media developer. In addition to working with these individuals on a team, instructional designers are often called on to be the project manager and manage the team. Being the project manager requires the instructional designer to be able to manage all aspects of the instructional design process—including how the team works together.

Although project management is formally dealt with in Chapter 4, one aspect of project management that we focus on in this section deals with evaluating how well a team is working together. One technique that can be used is group processing. **Group processing** can be considered a type of formative evaluation. It refers to group members' reflections on their work and on interactions with team members. These reflections help the team focus on improving the group's working relationship to ensure that the team effectively meets project goals. Group processing allows team members to voice concerns, share successes, and provide feedback that will help the team complete projects successfully.

Johnson, Johnson, and Holubec (1998) have written much about group processing. Although their work focuses on teams in a classroom environment, what they have written is appropriate for instructional design teams. We have often used group processing in our instructional design projects. Doing so has allowed us to form positive working relationships within our teams. According to Johnson et al., group processing helps do the following:

- Improve the quality of how the team approaches tasks
- Increase individual accountability of team members by focusing attention on the tasks a team member must complete
- Learn from one another by spending time discussing the tasks individuals are completing
- Eliminate problems that may be occurring

During group processing, team members can share information. Four parts of processing should be included: feedback, reflection, goal improvement, and celebration. Team members should be given feedback about how well they are completing their tasks and how well the team is working together. They should then have time to *reflect* on this feedback. If how the team is working together needs improvement, the team should discuss ways to improve and devise a plan of action. In addition, the team members should help one another and the team as a whole to set goals for improving their work quality. Finally, the team should celebrate the team members' hard work and the team's success (Johnson, et al., 1998).

SUMMARY

Sustained and varied evaluation is a crucial element of the instructional design process. Evaluation provides information that allows decisions to be made about learners, instruction, and the instructional design process. Formative, summative, and learner evaluations are three types of evaluation that instructional designers commonly use.

Formative evaluation is used throughout the instructional design process to gather data that can be used to provide feedback on how the process is progressing. Typically, formative evaluation is used to provide feedback on the instruction being developed. Feedback obtained during a formative evaluation can help the instructional designer make changes to the instruction that increase its efficiency and effectiveness. Formative evaluation should be built into an instructional design project from the beginning stages.

Although instructional design experts conduct formative evaluation for a common reason, the approaches they take are different. We described three approaches to formative evaluation. Dick et al. advocated three basic phases of formative evaluation: one-on-one, or clinical; small-group; and field trial. Smith and Ragan provided a four-step approach to formative evaluation that includes design reviews, expert reviews, learner validation, and ongoing evaluation. Morrison et al. recommended Gooler's eight-step process: purpose, audience, issues, resources, evidence, data-gathering techniques, analysis, and reporting.

Summative evaluation takes place after an instructional intervention is implemented. The major goal of a summative evaluation is to gather data that allow the effectiveness of the intervention to be determined. Two main questions need to be answered: Did the instruction bring about the desired changes? Were the client's goals met?

Having the instructional designer conduct a summative evaluation on a project he or she has worked on is often considered a conflict of interest. If possible, the instructional designer should not be the primary evaluator. He or she should act in a supporting role by helping design the evaluation and provide necessary data. Reality dictates, however, that instructional designers are sometimes asked to conduct summative evaluations on projects on which they have worked. To ensure the success of a summative evaluation, the instructional designer should meet with the client early in the project to discuss expectations of the evaluation, especially the evaluation goals. A process such as that advocated by Smith and Ragan is a good model for a beginning instructional designer to use.

One additional type of formative evaluation, group processing, should be included as part of the instructional design process. Group processing allows instructional design team members to regularly reflect on and communicate how well the team is working to meet project goals. It consists of four areas: feedback, reflection, goal improvement, and celebration. Group processing helps build healthy and productive instructional design teams.

CONNECTING PROCESS TO PRACTICE

1. How would you describe to your client the differences among learner, formative, and summative evaluations?
2. In each type of evaluation, what decisions are being made?
3. Your client asks you to justify why you have suggested multiple evaluations throughout the instructional design process. What do you tell your client?
4. A large law firm (approximately 50 employees) has contracted you to design its intranet. The firm would like the following initial functionalities built into the intranet: client billing, document uploading and retrieval, and a calendar of firm events (e.g., court and deposition dates and times, scheduled vacations). As part of the contract, you have been asked to train the paralegals and legal secretaries working at the firm. What types of evaluations do you include in your plan? What do you anticipate using, and how do you communicate this information to your client?

5. You are the lead instructional designer on a project that has a team of six people. Why should you include group processing as part of this instructional design project? Describe how you would incorporate group processing.

RECOMMENDED READINGS

Flagg, B. N. (1990). *Formative evaluation for educational technologies.* Hillsdale, NJ: Erlbaum.

Kirkpatrick, D. L. (1994). *Evaluating training programs: The four levels.* San Francisco: Berrett-Koehler.

Rathburn, G. A., Saito, R. S., & Goodrum, D. A. (1997). Reconceiving ISD: Three perspectives on rapid prototyping as a paradigm shift. In *Proceedings of Selected Research and Development Presentations at the 1997 National Convention of the Association for Educational Communications and Technology* (pp. 291–296). Washington, DC: Association for Educational Communications and Technology.

Tripp, S. D., & Bichelmeyer, B. (1990). Rapid prototyping: An alternative instructional design strategy. *Educational Technology Research and Development, 38*(1), 31–44.

Worthen, B., Sanders, J., & Fitzpatrick, J. (1997). *Program evaluation: Alternative approaches and practical guidelines.* New York: Longman.

REFERENCES

Dick, W., Carey, L., & Carey, J. (2001). *The systematic design of instruction.* New York: Longman.

Gooler, D. D. (1980). Formative evaluation strategies for major instructional development projects. *Journal of Instructional Development, 3,* 7–11.

Johnson, D., Johnson, R., & Holubec, E. (1998). *Cooperation in the classroom.* Boston: Allyn & Bacon.

Kirkpatrick, D. L. (1994). *Evaluating training programs: The four levels.* San Francisco: Berrett-Koehler.

Morrison, G., Ross, S., & Kemp, J. (2004). *Designing effective instruction.* Hoboken, NJ: Wiley.

Rathburn, G. A., Saito, R. S., & Goodrum, D. A. (1997). Reconceiving ISD: Three perspectives on rapid prototyping as a paradigm shift. In *Proceedings of Selected Research and Development Presentations at the 1997 National Convention of the Association for Educational Communications and Technology* (pp. 291–296). Washington, DC: Association for Educational Communications and Technology.

Smith, P., & Ragan, T. (1999). *Instructional design.* Hoboken, NJ: Wiley.

Tripp, S. D., & Bichelmeyer, B. (1990). Rapid prototyping: An alternative instructional design strategy. *Educational Technology Research and Development, 38*(1), 31–44.

Worthen, B., Sanders, J., & Fitzpatrick, J. (1997). *Program evaluation: Alternative approaches and practical guidelines.* New York: Longman.

Index

"ABCD" approach, 146–147
Achievement, evaluating, 204–235
Active participation, 183
ADDIE. *See also* Models
　　defined, 8, 11
　　as prescriptive model, 11–12
　　process, 11
　　process illustration, 13
Advanced organizers, 198
Affective domain, 54
Albion, P. R., 184
Albright, M., 169
Alessi, S. M., 17, 74, 79
Almog, J., 34
Analogies, 190–192
Analysis of the learning task.
　　See Task analysis
Analyzing tasks, 108
Anderson, L. M., 52
Andrew, Kara, 29, 45, 65
Anecdotal records, 223–224, 227
Anglin, G. J., 195
Animations, 195
Appelman, R., 19
Art directors, 65
Ashcraft, M. H., 50
Assessment
　　defined, 206
　　learning styles, 128
　　needs, 89, 93–97
　　performance, 94, 220
Assessment-centered environments,
　　180
Asynchronous distance education, 168
Attitude change evaluation. *See also*
　　Evaluations
　　anecdotal records, 227
　　attitude examples, 226–227
　　interviews, 228
　　learner evaluation and, 228–229

observations, 227
self-reporting inventories, 228
surveys/questionnaires, 227
Average learners, 134

Bainer, D. L., 179
Banathy, B., 14
Behaviorism
　　assumptions, 49
　　defined, 36
　　foundational work, 36
　　in learning, 47–50
　　role of learner, 49–50
　　what is learned, 50
Bell, A. W., 122
Berliner, D. C., 5, 34, 39
Bichelmeyer, B., 22, 23, 246
Binet, Alfred, 4
Bishop, M. J., 195
Blackburn, S., 34, 35
Bleiberg, J., 32
Bloom, B. S., 52, 53, 54, 151
Bloom taxonomy
　　defined, 151
　　domains, 151
　　Gagne hierarchy of intellectual skills
　　　versus, 152
　　headings, 151
Boring, E. G., 32
Brandt, R. S., 36, 37, 48, 50
Bransford, J. D., 122, 180, 181
Brooks, J. G., 51
Brown, Abbie, 76, 131, 136, 148, 166,
　　186, 192
Brown, A. H., 123, 151, 161
Brown, A. L., 122, 180
Bruner, J., 37, 51, 165, 166
Burton, J. K., 47, 50
Butler, C., 38
Butler, K. A., 128

Cagiltay, Kursat, 19, 153
Calhoun, E., 187
Callahan, R. C., 123, 151, 161
Cangelosi, J., 52, 54, 55
Captive audiences, 124
Carey, J. O., 10, 110, 129, 146, 240
Carey, L., 10, 110, 129, 146, 240
Carmines, E. G., 210
Carrigan, D., 74
Cates, W. M., 195
Challenged learners, 134
Changing differences, 131
Changing similarities, 131
Chaos theory, 15
Chieuw, J., 18, 19
Classical conditioning model. *See also*
    Conditioning models
    defined, 36, 48
    operant conditioning comparison, 49
Classification
    analogies, metaphors, similes,
        190–192
    chart illustration, 190
    graphic organizers, 190, 191
    scattergrams, 190, 191
Classroom teaching, 167–168
Clients, 66
Cocking, R. R., 122, 180
Cognition
    defined, 30
    thinking and, 31
Cognitive abilities, 32
Cognitive domain. *See also* Learning
    domains
    Bloom, Engelhart, Frost, Hill, and
        Krathwohl, 53
    bottom level, 53–54
    defined, 53
    highest level, 54
    levels, 53
Cognitive functions
    executive abilities, 32
    memory, 31
    mental power, 31–32
    metacognition, 32
    special abilities, 32

Cognitivism
    defined, 36
    foundations, 37
    in learning, 50–51
    role of learner, 50–51
    set-in-place algorithms, 50
    what is learned, 50
Collins, A. M., 50
Collinson, D., 33
Comenius, John Amos, 5
Communication
    in formative evaluation, 101
    in production management, 76–77
    strategies, 76–77
    teamwork and, 78
Community-centered environments, 181
Conditioning models
    classical, 48, 49
    operant, 48–49
Conflict resolution, 76–77, 81
Consensus, teamwork and, 78–79
Constructed-response tests, 219–220
Constructivism
    defined, 37, 51
    educational sequence and, 19
    in learning, 51–52
    learning conditions, 51–52
    underlying principle, 51
Content analysis. *See* Task analysis
Contracts
    individualized learning, 197
    production, 80–81
Cooperative learning, 196
Cowboy syndrome, 77
CPM charts, 70
Criterion referenced evaluations, 211
Critical incident method, 109–110
Critique sessions, 197
Cruickshank, D. R., 179, 183
Cues, 198
Cunningham, K. L., 195
Curriculum
    defined, 160
    hidden, 170
    scope, 161
Curry, C., 132

Dale, E., 164, 165, 172, 173
Dale cone of experience
    defined, 164
    enactive experiences, 165
    iconic experiences, 165
    illustrated, 165
    instructional designer use, 166
    symbolic experiences, 165–166
Deductive reasoning, 197
Delphi method, 94
Dempsey, J., 12
Describing tasks, 108
Design reviews, 240
Desired change. *See also* Needs analysis
    determination, 98–99
    implementation location, 99
    party requesting, 99
Dewey, J., 6, 30, 37, 51
Diagnostic teaching, 122
Dick, Carey, and Carey approaches
    formative evaluation, 243–245
    goal setting, 146, 240
    learning analysis, 129
    summative evaluation, 253
Dick, W., 10, 110, 117, 129, 137,
    146, 148, 154, 243, 244, 245,
    253, 256
Differences. *See also* Similarities
    changing, 131
    identifying, 189–190
    stable, 130
Directed learning environments. *See also*
    Learning environments
    comparison, 182
    defined, 181
    instructional goals, 182
    instructional objectives, 183
Direct teaching, 183
Direct testing, 221
Discrepancy-based needs assessment
    model, 97
Distance education. *See also*
    Instructional delivery
    asynchronous, 168
    defined, 161
    instruction delivery, 169

LMS, 169
    synchronous, 168
Dowden, B., 39
Driscoll, M. P., 32, 33, 47, 48, 51
Drop-dead dates, 68, 69
Dual coding, 194
Dunning, G., 74

Eclectic approach, 21
Eclecticism, 39
Educational innovations, 188
Educational psychology, 5
Effort, reinforcing, 193
Eisner, E. W., 52
Ellis, A. K., 128, 188, 196
Enabling objectives, 147
Enactive experiences, 165
Engelhart, M. D., 53, 151
Entry competencies, 127
Epistemology, 34
Essay items, 219–220
Evaluations
    achievement, 204–235
    attitude change, 226–229
    criterion referenced, 211
    defined, 207
    development, 210–229
    field trial, 245
    formative, 100–101, 116, 209,
        238–248
    goals, 208–209
    implementation of, 229–231
    instruction, 230
    instructional designer role, 231–232
    instructional design team, 255–256
    learner, 208–233
    learner objectives, 212–229
    norm referenced, 211
    ongoing, 240
    postinstruction, 230–231
    practical exam, 205
    preinstruction, 229–230
    purpose, 207
    reliability, 210–211
    reports, 243
    skill, 220–225

Evaluations (*continued*)
  success determination, 231
  summative, 100, 110, 116, 209,
    248–255
  use example, 207–208
  validity, 210
  written exam, 205
Events of instruction
  defined, 162, 172
  generative, 164
  goals, 178
  nine, 163
  order, 164
  as reciprocal process, 164
  supplantive, 164
Executive abilities, 32
Expert reviews
  defined, 79
  in formative evaluation, 240
Extrinsic motivation, 125

Feedback
  in formative evaluation, 238
  group processing, 256
  immediate, 169–170
  as instructional strategy, 196–197
  providing, 196–197
Field trial evaluation, 245, 253
Fieser, J., 39
Finegan, A., 18
Fischer, B., 168
Fitzpatrick, J., 207, 248
Flanagan, J. C., 109
Flavell, J. H., 32
Formative evaluation. *See also*
  Summative evaluation
  analysis procedures, 243
  approaches, 239–245
  audience, 241
  conducting, 242–243
  defined, 238
  design/implementation, 248
  Dick, Carey, and Carey approach,
    243–245
  emphasis, 243
  feedback, 238
  field trial, 245

learner evaluation versus, 209
learner selection, 244
Morrison, Ross, and Kemp approach,
  241–243
in needs analysis, 100–101
purpose, 241
rapid prototyping, 245–246
reporting, 243
Smith and Ragan approach, 240
summary, 256
summative evaluation versus, 239
in task analysis, 116
usability testing, 246
use, 238
Frost, E. J., 53, 151
Functional analysis system technique
  (FAST) charts, 149

Gagne, R., 152, 163
Gagne hierarchy of intellectual skills
  defined, 151–152
  illustrated, 152
Games
  defined, 186
  as instructional activity, 186
  instructional purposes support,
    185–186
Gantt, Henry Laurence, 70
Gantt charts, 70
Gardner, H., 127
Gearhart, M., 224
General systems theory
  concepts/principles, 14
  defined, 4
  goal, 15
  influence, 15, 16
  unified field theory search and, 15
Gifted and talented learners, 134
GLAD (guided language acquisition and
  development) strategies, 159
Glare, P. G., 160
Gleick, J., 15
Goal analysis procedure, 110
Goals
  "ABCD" approach, 146–147
  articulation, 154, 155
  articulation importance, 152

defined, 147
development, 145
Dick, Carey, and Carey approaches,
    146
evaluation, 208–209
examples, 145
instructional, 144–145
instructional event, 178
Mager approach, 146
missing, 155
Morrison, Ross, and Kemp approach,
    147
objectives versus, 144–145
as organizing topics, 144
perception, 147–148
setting, 147–149
setting success evaluation, 153–154
state standards, 159
summative evaluation, 250, 254
translating, into objectives, 149–152
working backwards to, 148–149
Goals analysis, 94–95
Goodrum, D. A., 22, 246
Gooler, D. D., 256
Graduate Record Examinations (GRE),
    211
Graphic artists, 65
Graphic organizers, 91, 190, 195
Gredler, M., 185
Green, T., 76, 117, 208
Greene, J., 213
Greeno, J. G., 50
Gronlund, N. E., 53
Group processing
    benefits, 255
    defined, 255
    feedback, 256
    information sharing, 256
    summary, 257

Hall, G. Stanley, 4
Hannafin, M., 181, 182, 184
Hannum, W. H., 106, 107
Hansen, Lisa, 247
Harder, R. J., 123, 151, 161
Harrow, A. J., 54
Hawking, Stephen, 144

Heinich, R., 5, 127, 137, 146, 154,
    164, 185, 186
Heinrich, Molenda, Russell, and
    Smaldino approach, 127–128
Herman, J. L., 224
Hernstein, R. J., 32
Hidden curriculum, 170
Hierarchy of needs
    defined, 123
    illustrated, 124
    learner needs according to, 123–124
Highsmith, J. A., 18
Hill, W. F., 47
Hill, W. H., 53
Hlynka, D., 16, 17
Hoban, C. F. Jr., 16
Holubec, E., 255
Homework, assigning, 194
Hopkins, K. D., 214, 228
Howard, J., 132
Human needs, 123–124
Human performance technology
    (HPT), 99, 170–171
Hypotheses, generating/testing, 197

Iconic experiences, 165
Idealism, 32
Illustrations, 195
Immediate feedback. *See also* Feedback
    categories comparison, 170
    students, 169
    students and instructor, 169
Indirect teaching, 183
Inductive reasoning, 197
Innovation model, 98
Instruction
    creating, 141–156
    development of, 178–180
    effective, 171–172
    events of, 162–164
    just-in-time, 193
    organizing, 158–175
    scope and sequence, 160–162
Instructional activities
    based on proven effective practices,
        189–198
    choosing, 172

Instructional activities (*continued*)
decisions, 186–187
hypotheses-generating, 197
in noneducational situations, 170–171
Instructional analysis, 110
Instructional delivery
categories, 169–170
categories comparison, 170
classroom teaching, 167–168
distance education, 168–169
immediate feedback (students), 169
immediate feedback (students and
instructor), 169
methods, 167–169, 173
programmed instruction, 168
Instructional design. *See also* Goals;
Objectives
"big picture," 8
discipline, 7, 16
eclecticism and postmodern
approaches, 17–23
four-part definition, 7
historian view, 4
learning types and, 52
as "linking science," 7, 9, 24
models, 9–13
nontraditional approaches, 16–23
philosophy, 18
pitfall, avoiding, 178–180
premise, 8
process, 7
professional practice, 13–23
as reality, 7
scholasticism influence, 33
success determination, 236–259
three-step process, 8
traditional approaches, 14–16
Instructional designers
activity recommendation, 178
evaluating, 255–256
job, 8, 88
learner evaluation role, 231–232
needs analysis process, 89
systems approach limitations, 20–21
in task analysis, 107
views on thinking, 38

Instructional games
defined, 185
support purposes, 185–186
Instructional media production
management, 60–83
Instructional simulations, 185
Instructional strategies
categories, 189
classification, 190–192
cooperative learning, 196
generating/testing hypotheses, 197
homework and practice, 194
nonlinguistic representations, 194–195
note taking summary, 192–193
objectives and feedback, 196–197
questions, cues, and advance
organizers, 198
reinforcing effort and providing
recognition, 193–194
similarities/differences identification,
189–190
Instructional systems design
as behavioristic approach, 16
complexity, 19
criticism, 17
defined, 16
use of, 16
Instruments, 206–207
Interface designers, 65
Interpretivism, 35
Interviews, 228
Intrinsic motivation, 125
Inventory tasks, 108

James, William, 4, 39
Jenlink, P. M., 14
Job aids
availability, 172
defined, 171
Johnson, D., 255, 256
Johnson, R., 255
Jonassen, D. H., 18, 106, 107, 108
Jonassen, Hannum, and Tessmer
approach, 108
Joyce, B., 187
Just-in-time teaching, 193

Kemp, J. E., 10, 89, 93, 94, 106, 133, 145, 209, 213, 241
Kinesthetic representation, 195
King, J. W., 18
Kirkpatrick, D. L., 249
Klein, J., 106
Knowledge-centered environments, 180
Krathwohl, D. R., 52, 53, 54, 151

Lancaster, Joseph, 167
Land, S., 181
Learner ability chart
    illustrated, 134
    learner profile comparison, 134–135
Learner analysis
    approaches, 125–133
    Dick, Carey, and Carey approach, 129
    example use, 121
    Heinich, Molenda, Russell, and
        Smaldino approach, 127–128
    human needs and, 123–124
    Mager approach, 125–127
    member check, 136
    Morrison, Ross, and Kemp approach,
        133
    procedure, 133–135
    quantifiable aspects, 123
    recommended practices, 123
    Smith and Ragan approach, 129–131
    success evaluation, 136
    summary, 137
    target audience, 126, 127–128
    use examples, 130, 131
Learner-centered environments, 122, 180
Learners
    achievement evaluation, 204–235
    average, 134
    challenged, 134
    characteristics data, charting, 133–134
    current abilities, 229
    educator perception, 183
    as "empty vessels," 122
    gifted and talented, 134
    motivation, 125
    prior knowledge use, 51
    profile, 134–135

role in behaviorism approach, 49–50
role in cognitivism approach,
    50–51
selection, 244–245
typical, fictitious profile, 134
unconventional, 133
validation, 240
Learning
    approaches, 47–51
    behaviorism in, 47–50
    change with experience, 47
    classical conditioning model, 48, 49
    cognitivism in, 50–51
    as complex process, 48
    constructivism in, 51–52
    continuum of experiences, 164–167
    cooperative, 196
    defined, 56–57
    enactive experiences, 165
    experiences, 164–167, 173
    goals, 111
    iconic experiences, 165
    online, 64
    operant conditioning model, 48–49
    problem-based, 184–185
    symbolic experiences, 165–166
    types, 52–55
    what is learned, 50
Learning domains
    affective, 54
    cognitive, 53–54
    defined, 52
    idea behind, 52
    learning objectives and, 53, 55–56
    psychomotor, 54–55
Learning environments
    assessment-centered, 180
    community-centered, 181
    creating, 176–201
    defined, 180
    directed, 181–182
    knowledge-centered, 180
    learner-centered, 122, 180
    open-ended, 182–183
    perspectives, 180–181
    types of, 180–181

Learning management system (LMS), 169
Learning objectives. *See also* Objectives
   defined, 56
   developing, 56
   learning domains and, 53, 55–56
Learning styles
   assessment, 128
   categories, 128
   defined, 127–128
Lee, D., 10, 22
Lepper, M. R., 125
Lesson plans
   defined, 161
   example, 163, 179
Likert-type scale, 227
Locke, J., 34

Mager, Robert, 56, 90, 92, 101, 125,
   126, 137, 146, 147, 154
Mager approaches
   goal setting, 146
   performance analysis, 90–92
Mager leaner analysis
   important elements, 126
   procedure, 125
   target audience data, 126
   target audience questionnaires and,
     126–127
Magliaro, S. G., 47
Maier, David, 10
Malone, T. W., 125
Margulies, S., 168
Marzano, R. J., 51, 53, 188, 189, 194,
   196, 197, 198
Masia, B. B., 54
Maslow, A. H., 123
Matching items, 217–218
Mayer, Richard, 195
Measurement, 206
Media-production triangle, 67
Member checks, 136
Memory, 31
Mental power
   in cognitive domain, 31–32
   defined, 31
Meta-analyses, 187, 188–189

Metacognition, 32
Metaphors, 190–192
Metaphysics, 34
Metcalf, K. K., 179
Milestones. *See also* Production calendar
   date agreement, 69
   defined, 68
   dependencies and, 69–70
   working backwards to establish, 70
Miller Nelson, Laurie, 78
Millman, J., 213
Mission creep, 80
Models
   ADDIE, 11–13
   defined, 9
   Kemp, Morrison and Ross plan,
     10–11, 12
   systems approach (Dick & Carey),
     10, 11
Modern age, 16
Molenda, M., 5, 12, 127, 146, 164, 185
Moore, D. M., 47
Morrison, G. R., 10, 11, 89, 93, 94,
   101, 106, 107, 108, 109, 117, 133,
   137, 145, 147, 154, 209, 213, 241,
   242, 243, 251, 252, 256
Morrison, Ross, and Kemp approaches
   formative evaluation, 241–243
   goal setting, 147
   learner analysis, 133
   summative evaluation, 251–252
Morrison, Ross, and Kemp three
   techniques
   critical incident method, 109–110
   defined, 108
   procedural analysis, 109
   topic analysis, 108–109
Morrison needs assessment approach,
   93–95
Mosenfelder, D., 168
Motivation, 125
Multiple-choice items. *See also* Objective
   tests
   examples, 216–217
   guidelines, 216
   use, 215–216

Navigation layout. *See also* Storyboards
  defined, 74
  illustrated, 75
Needs analysis
  approaches, 90–98
  defined, 88
  desired change determination, 98–99
  desired change implementation
    location, 99
  formative evaluation, 100–101
  goal analysis method, 94–95
  instructional designer use, 89
  intervention, 100
  Mager performance analysis, 90–92
  need for, 89
  needs assessment approach, 93–95
  overview, 88–90
  party requesting desired change, 99
  procedure, 98–100
  process, 89
  property conducted, 100
  questions, 89–90
  Rossett five-step approach, 95–97
  Smith and Ragan three needs
    assessment models, 97–98
  success evaluation, 100–101
  summative evaluation, 100
Needs assessment
  compilation phase, 94
  data analysis phase, 94
  data collection phase, 93
  defined, 93
  discrepancy-based model, 97
  functions, 93
  planning phase, 93
  role, 89
  in stages, 96–97
Nelson, W., 106
Nichols, A., 33
Nixon, E. K., 10, 22
Nonlinguistic representations, 194–195
Norm referenced evaluations, 211
Note taking, 192–193
Novak, Erik, 64, 87, 116, 130, 150,
    177, 205, 254
Novak, J. R., 224

Objectives. *See also* Goals
  Bloom taxonomy, 151
  change in attitude, 226–229
  change in knowledge, 213–220
  change in skill, 220–225
  development, 145
  enabling, 147
  examples, 145
  goals versus, 144–145
  instructional, 144–145
  instructional outcomes and, 212–213
  in learner evaluations, 212–229
  learning, 53, 55–56
  performance, 146
  setting, 196–197
  setting success evaluation, 153–154
  state standards, 159
  subordinate, 145
  terminal, 147
  translating goals into, 149–152
  well-stated, 150
Objective tests
  constructed-response, 219–220
  development/implementation
    guidelines, 214–215
  development plan, 213–215
  essay items, 219–220
  items, 215–219
  matching items, 217–218
  multiple-choice items, 215–217
  questions, 213
  short-answer items, 218–219
  true-false items, 215
O'Brien, D., 122
Observations, 223, 227
Oliver, K., 181
Ongoing evaluation, 240
Online learning, 64
Open-ended learning environments. *See*
    also Learning environments
  comparison, 182
  defined, 182
  instructional goals, 182
  learner support components,
    184–185
Operant conditioning, 36

Operant conditioning model. *See also*
  Conditioning models
  classical conditioning comparison, 49
  defined, 48
  response, 48–49
Organization
  instruction, 158–175
  levels, 162
  structures, 162
Orlich, D. C., 123, 151, 161
Ormrod, J. E., 32, 36, 46, 47, 48, 49,
  52, 56

Paper trail maintenance, 77
Passive reception, 183
Pavio, A., 194
Pavlov, I., 36
Peerless, Jody, 159
Peer review, 79
Performance analysis. *See also* Needs
  analysis
  completion time, 92
  defined, 90
  flowchart, 91
  steps, 90–92
Performance assessment, 94, 220
Performance objectives, generating,
  146
Performance ratings
  examples, 222
  focus, 221
  process, 222–223
  scale development, 222
  techniques, 222
Performance technology approach, 146
Perkins, D. N., 36, 37, 48, 50
PERT charts, 70
Pickering, D. J., 188
Planning and costing, 63
Pollock, J. E., 188
Portfolios
  defined, 224
  examples, 224
  focus, 224
  process, 225
Positivism, 35

Posner, George, 162
Postinstruction evaluations, 230–231
Postmodern approach
  computing tool proliferation and, 20
  core tenets, 19–20
  defined, 17
  example, 21–23
  factors, 17–19
  as postpositivism, 19
Postmodernism, 37
Postproduction. *See also* Production
  defined, 62
  process, 63
Practice, 194
Pragmatism, 39
Preassessment activities, 229
Preinstruction evaluations, 229–230
Prensky, M., 153
Preproduction. *See also* Production
  defined, 62
  process, 62–63
  production calendar, 67–70
Prescriptions, 178
Problem-based learning (PBL), 184
Problem-finding, problem-solving
  model, 97
Procedural analysis, 109
Product evaluation
  expert review, 79
  iterative, 79
  peer review, 79
  usability testing, 80
Production
  calendars, 67–70
  charting, 70
  communication, 76–77
  conflict resolution, 76–77
  management, 66–76
  media, triangle, 67
  phases, 62–63, 81
  planning items, 80–81
  process, 62–63
  product evaluation, 79–80
  prototyping, 74
  storyboards, 71–74
  style guides, 71

Production calendar
   defined, 67
   drop-dead dates, 68, 69
   establishment, 67
   illustrated, 68
   milestones, 68–70
Production managers, 63, 64
Production teams
   art director, 65
   clients and priorities, 66
   cowboy syndrome, 77
   effective, 77
   graphic artist, 65
   interface designer, 65
   manager, 63, 64
   organization of, 63–66
   programmer, 65
   roles, 65, 78
   SME, 64
   sound designer, 65
   successful teamwork, 78–79
   talent, 63, 65
   video director, 65
   video editor, 65
   writer, 64
Program evaluators, 248
Program of study, 161
Programmed instruction, 168
Programmers, 65
Prototypes
   examples, 22
   fidelity, 74
   intermediate, 22
   mini, 76
   number of, 74
   in rapid prototyping, 21–22
   storyboards as, 74
   successive, 23
Prototyping
   defined, 74
   rapid, 21–23, 74
Psychomotor domain. *See also* Learning
   domains
   Simpson, 55
   taxonomies, 54–55
   as voluntary muscle capabilities, 55

Questionnaires, 87, 126–127, 227
Questions
   instructional strategy, 198
   needs analysis, 89–90
   objective test, 213
Quick write, 230

Ragan, T. J., 7, 97, 98, 101, 110, 111,
   117, 129, 130, 137, 150, 162, 164,
   240, 250, 251, 254, 257
Random call, 230
Rapid prototyping
   defined, 21, 74
   disadvantage, 23
   example prototypes, 22
   formative evaluation approach,
      245–246
   intermediate prototypes, 22
   as new instructional design view, 22–23
   prototypes, 21–22
   theatrical production, 23
   warning, 23
Rathburn, G. A., 22, 246
Reason, 32
Recognition
   providing, 193
   rewards and symbols, 194
Reigeluth, C. M., 5, 17
Reiser, R., 12
Reliability, 210–211
Reports
   formative evaluation, 243
   needs analysis, 94
   summative evaluation, 251
Research, for instructional practices,
   186–189
Resnick, L. B., 50
Respect, 76
Richey, R. C., 106
Ross, S. M., 10, 89, 93, 94, 106, 133,
   145, 209, 213, 241
Rossett, A., 89, 95, 101
Rossett five-step approach. *See also*
   Needs analysis
   defined, 95
   information factors, 95

Rossett five-step approach (*continued*)
  initiators and purposes, 96
  steps, 95–97
Rubrics, 225–226
Russell, J. D., 5, 127, 146, 164, 185

Saettler, P., 4, 33, 167, 168
Saito, R. S., 22, 246
Sanders, J., 207, 248
Scaffolding, 185
Scattergrams, 190, 191
Scholastic Aptitude Test (SAT), 6
Scholasticism, 33
Schriver, K. A., 21
Schwandt, T., 35
Scope and sequence of instruction
  curriculum, 160, 161
  development, 161
  for instructional events, 161
  organization levels, 162
  organization structures, 162
  possibilities, 160
  program of study, 161
Seddon, G. M., 53
Seffah, A., 135
Selecting tasks, 108
Self-deception, 228
Self-reporting inventories, 228
Semantic problems, 229
Sequencing tasks, 108
Set-in-place algorithms, 50
Shiu, C., 122
Short-answer items, 218–219
Shuell, T. J., 50
Similarities. *See also* Differences
  changing, 131
  identifying, 189–190
  stable, 129–130
Similes, 190–192
Simonson, M., 169
Simpson, E., 54, 55
Simulations, 185
Skill-and-drill programs, 168
Skill evaluation
  direct testing, 221
  guidelines, 220

observations/anecdotal records,
  223–224
performance ratings, 221–223
portfolios, 224–225
Skinner, B. F., 36, 49
Smaldino, S. E., 5, 127, 146, 164, 169,
  185
Smith, P. L., 7, 97, 98, 101, 110, 111,
  117, 129, 130, 137, 150, 162, 164,
  240, 250, 251, 254, 257
Smith and Ragan approaches
  formative evaluation, 240
  summative evaluation, 250–251
Smith and Ragan learning analysis
  approach
  changing differences, 131
  changing similarities, 131
  defined, 129
  stable differences, 130
  stable similarities, 129–130
Snellbecker, G., 6
Social-desirability responses, 228
Solomon, D. L., 17, 19
Sorell, T., 34
Sound, 195
Sound designers, 65
Specificity, 77
Stable differences, 130
Stable similarities, 129–130
Sternberg, R. J., 32, 37
Storyboards. *See also* Production
  completion, 68
  defined, 71
  as early prototypes, 74
  examples, 72–73
  illustrated, 72–73
  multimedia, 74
  navigation layout, 74, 75
Style guides, 71
Subject matter analysis. *See* Task analysis
Subject matter experts (SMEs)
  defined, 65
  in goal setting, 146
  interview/questionnaire, 87
  in task analysis, 107, 112
Subordinate skills analysis, 110, 146

Summarizing, 192–193
Summative evaluation. *See also*
    Formative evaluation
    approaches to, 248–253
    defined, 248, 253
    design, selecting, 251
    design/implementation, 253–255
    Dick, Carey, and Carey approach,
        253
    expert judgment, 253
    field trial, 253
    formative evaluation versus, 239
    goals, 250, 254
    Kirkpatrick four levels of evaluation,
        249–250
    learner evaluation versus, 209
    measures, 251
    Morrison, Ross, and Kemp approach,
        251–252
    in needs analysis, 110
    orientation, selecting, 250–251
    phases, 253
    program evaluators, 248
    results, 248, 251
    Smith and Ragan approach, 250–251
    successful, conducting, 253–254
    success indicators, 250
    summary, 256–257
    in task analysis, 116
Surveys, 227
Syllabus, 161
Symbolic experiences, 165–166
Synchronous distance education, 168
Systems approach model. *See also* Models
    defined, 10
    illustrated, 11
Systems theory. *See* General systems
    theory

Talent, 63, 65
Target audience. *See also* Learner analysis
    actors and, 127
    general characteristics, 127
    information on, 126
    learning styles, 127–128
    specific entry competencies, 127

Task analysis
    approaches, 107–111
    conducting, 104–119
    defined, 106
    Dick, Carey, and Carey approach, 110
    effectiveness, evaluating, 116
    example use, 116, 117
    formative evaluation, 116
    influencing factors, 112–115
    instructional designer determination
        in, 107
    Jonassen, Hannum, and Tessmer
        approach, 108
    Morrison, Ross, and Kemp three
        techniques, 108–110
    problems solved by, 107
    procedure, 111–115
    SMEs in, 107, 112
    Smith and Ragan approach,
        110–111
    steps, 111
    summary, 117–118
    summative evaluation, 116
Task analysis documents
    defined, 112
    flowchart format, 115
    outline format, 113–114
Tasks
    analyzing, 108
    describing, 108
    inventorying, 108
    performance, 87
    selecting, 108
    sequencing, 108
Teaching. *See also* Instruction
    direct, 183
    indirect, 183
    just-in-time, 193
    pitfall, 178–180
Teamwork. *See also* Production teams
    benefits/drawbacks, 78
    communication and, 78
    consensus and, 78–79
    successful, 78
Terminal objectives, 147
Tessmer, M., 106, 107

Tests
    constructed-response, 219–220
    development/implementation
        guidelines, 214–215
    development plan, 213–215
    essay items, 219–220
    items, 215–219
    matching items, 217–218
    multiple-choice items, 215–217
    questions, 213
    short-answer items, 218–219
    true-false items, 215
Theatrical production, 23
Thinking
    cognition and, 31
    defined, 30
    historical perspective, 32–34
    instructional designers' views, 38
    modern views, 34–38
Thornburg, D. D., 149
Thorndike, Edward, 4
Titus, Jona, 3, 61, 105, 121,
    143, 237
Topic analysis, 108–109
Training review groups (TRGs), 61
Trevisan, M. S., 123, 151, 161
Tripp, S. D., 22, 23, 246
Trollip, S. R., 17, 74, 79
True-false items, 215

Unconventional learners, 133
Unified field theory, 15

Units, 161
Universal design for education
    defined, 132, 133
    instructional opportunities, 132
    movement, 132
Unstructured interviews, 228
Usability testing
    defined, 80, 246
    elements, 80
    example, 246–247
    as formative evaluation, 246
    for internal applications, 247
User-centered design, 135–136

Vaez, H., 195
Validity, 210
Video directors, 65
Video editors, 65

Walberg, H. J., 196
Weil, M., 187
Willing volunteers, 124
Winn, W., 51
Winters, L., 224
Woolfolk, A., 32, 48, 51
Worthen, B., 207, 248
Writers, 64

Zatz, D., 76
Zeller, R. A., 210
Zook, K., 152
Zvacek, S., 169